BEING
URBAN

BEING URBAN

URBAN

A Social
Psychological
View
of City
Life

DAVID A. KARP / Boston College

GREGORY P. STONE / University of Minnesota

WILLIAM C. YOELS / Indiana University Northwest

D. C. HEATH AND COMPANY
Lexington, Massachusetts   Toronto

International Standard Book Number: 0-669-95703-8

Library of Congress Catalog Card Number: 76–12940

Preface

The growth of cities and the urbanization of social life have long stood at the center of social science inquiry. Urban housing, city politics, intergroup relations in the city, urban class and stratification patterns, the economic structure of city life, urban demographic trends, and the nature of urban communities are among the most frequent areas of scientists' investigations. Indeed, so much has been written on the city in recent years that it is virtually impossible for even the urban specialist to keep abreast of the literature. Curiously, however, despite this extraordinary volume of research, little systematic effort has been expended in detailing the social psychology of city life; in thinking about how persons experience and give meaning to their lives as urbanites. Even a quick evaluation of textbooks in the area reveals that a discussion of the social psychology of city life is either absent altogether or passed over rather hastily.

In *Being Urban* we have not tried to cover the full range of issues and topics found in most urban sociology textbooks. Rather, we have three somewhat more modest goals to meet here. First, we want to pose some of the social psychological questions typically neglected in most treatments of the urban scene. Second, we want to illustrate how our answers to these questions lead us to reevaluate certain traditional, longstanding images of the city. In this respect we view ours as a work of revision. We do not seek to disprove or reject traditional and current sociological understanding of the urban place. We wish, instead, to indicate how these understandings may be incomplete or partial. Finally, the authors share a common theoretical orientation that gives impetus and unity to this enterprise. We wish to show throughout this work the value of "symbolic interaction theory" for analyzing the meaning of being urban. Because of the critical importance of this perspective to what follows, we must say a few words about it here.

The perspective of symbolic interaction is based on the uncomplicated idea that the social world is composed of acting, thinking, defining, reacting, interpreting human beings in interaction with one another. Persons are not merely puppets pushed around by forces over which they have no control. As symbolic interactionists we hold a picture of social life in which persons are the architects of their worlds. Reality is, then, socially constructed and to understand human behavior we must inquire into those processes through which persons do construct and transform their social worlds. Following Herbert Blumer's discussion (1969: 2), there are three central premises underlying the theory of symbolic interaction:

1. Human beings act toward things or situations on the basis of the meaning that the things or situations have for them.
2. The meaning of things is derived from or arises out of the interaction that one has with his or her fellows.
3. These meanings are handled or modified through an interpretive process used by persons in dealing with the objects or situations that they encounter.

For those who accept the validity of these premises, the major concern of any social psychological treatment is to establish the relationship between the meanings persons attach to their environments and the consequences of these "definitions of the situation" for their behavior.

Having made our general intentions clear, we want to explain how they are to be fulfilled. We have organized the book's chapters such that the beginning urban sociology student will become progressively acquainted with the major theoretical traditions basic to an urban social psychology. Simultaneously, we indicate in each chapter how these traditional views may be critiqued and extended. In this respect we will not be offering any further explanations of symbolic interaction theory, rather we will be exercising that theory. Moreover, the reader will find that we have organized the chapters so that they are substantively and theoretically cumulative—each chapter logically builds on the previous chapter.

In Chapters 1 and 2 we examine the effects the Industrial Revolution exerted on the origins and development of urban sociology. In these chapters we look at the recurrent themes and concerns essential to a social psychological view of city life. Themes, such as alienation, freedom, and social integration, are discussed with the focus on their differing treatments in the works of classical European and early American sociologists. We have been selective in reviewing only the ideas of those who have had a definitive influence on the development of urban sociology.

In Chapter 1 we analyze how the transformation of European social life during the nineteenth century is reflected in Sir Henry Maine's distinction between societies founded on status relations and those founded on contract relations; in Tönnies' distinction between *Gemeinschaft* and *Gesellschaft;* and in Durkheim's distinction between mechanical and organic solidarity. The overall image presented in these theoretical writings on the modern urban structure is an abidingly negative one. The theoretical conceptions of the city described in this chapter were influential guiding forces in the empirical investigations of urban sociologists at the University of Chicago in the 1920's and 30's.

Chapter 2 demonstrates how the theoretical conceptions of urban life formulated by the thinkers discussed in Chapter 1 were carried over and expanded in the works of early American sociologists, where an essentially negative image of the city is reaffirmed. The observations made by Robert Park and his students by and large supported the idea that the city destroyed the communal bonds characteristic of nonurban life.

Chapters 1 and 2, taken together, outline the major themes inherited by more contemporary sociologists. In the following two chapters we provide evidence that communal ties do exist in large cities. We want to show how the works of more recent writers necessitate a new paradigm for the study of urban social relations.

Chapter 3 illustrates how persons faced with the city's impersonal rationality will seek out alternatives in the environment to provide them a source of personalization, identity, and community involvement. The literature discussed in this chapter leads us to the notion of "symbolic" urban communities. The thrust of the work of the writers discussed here is that community is not dead in the city. It took several years to realize this because our former conceptions of community stood as obstacles to our seeing the transformations in social life that have gone on in urban settings. The rediscovery of community depended, in part, on sociologists' ability to forge new tools for looking at the urban world. We find these tools in the work of the sociologists mentioned. The rediscovery of community provides us with the platform necessary for our argument in Chapter 4 where we show that a clear social organization exists in even the most anonymous public sectors of large cities.

The guiding question for Chapter 4 is: In what ways are persons relating or failing to relate to one another in "anonymous" public settings? It would appear in most urban public settings that persons do not at all interact with one another. Persons seem to avoid each other, to close themselves off from communication with each other. We argue in this chapter that ordered everyday life demands a high degree of cooperation among persons. We elaborate on a paradox of public urban interaction whereby persons must systematically take each other into account in order to avoid unwanted encounters. We develop a mini–max hypothesis of urban life in an attempt to capture the complexity of urbanites' daily encounters. Urbanites seek to minimize involvement and to maximize social order. We try to show how urban persons are required to strike a balance between involvement and indifference, intimacy and anonymity; how they collectively work to maintain a kind of public privacy.

In Chapters 1 through 4, then, we largely explore the nature of interactions among individuals in the urban milieu. A focus, however, solely on individuals as a means of understanding the quality of city experience is incomplete. In the following chapters, therefore, we consider the interrelationships between urban social groups and the effects of large institutional arrangements.

Chapter 5 examines the issue of urban tolerance. We introduce here the notion of "controlled contact" as the process by which urbanites are able to both interact with and remain aloof from those whose life styles may differ radically from their own. We describe the manner in which the spatial segregation of diverse urban groups contributes to the development of urban tolerance. We conclude this chapter with a discussion of the relationship between power, politics, and tolerance in the urban setting, illustrating our argument by presenting a case study of the "breakdown of tolerance."

Having raised the issue of power and politics, we then turn our attention in Chapter 6 to an examination of social stratification in the city. Here we suggest interactionist alternatives to the dominant conception of social stratification in contemporary sociology—a conception heavily influenced by the work of W. Lloyd Warner and his colleagues. We conclude this chapter with an examination of the processes affecting community power arrangements.

All endings should reflect and account for their beginnings as well as provide the basis for new beginnings. If the literature dealt with and the theoretical perspective offered in this book raise questions for the reader, then our earlier chapters will have succeeded. One such question must center around the future of city life. A task in the final chapter is to examine the changing nature of the contemporary city. In particular we examine, in Chapter 7, documented demographic trends. Our concern is not with these trends per se, but rather with the examination of these trends within the framework of a broader social psychological perspective. We conclude with a treatment of the relationship between the changing demography of the city and the changing meanings of city life.

ACKNOWLEDGMENTS

We would like to thank a number of persons whose help and encouragement have been instrumental in the completion of this book. We are grateful for the support offered by Ron Farrell, Mark LaGory, Paul Meadows, Russ Ward, Patricia Manning, and John Williamson.

Our colleagues and wives, Darleen Karp, Gladys Stone, and Bren Yoels have influenced our thinking through their critical—and sometimes painfully critical—responses to our work. Wendell Bell and W. Clark Roof reviewed the manuscript in detail and their comments were most helpful.

Alice Close and Shirley Urban patiently and with great skill typed several drafts of the manuscript. They also read our work with discerning eyes and alerted us to a number of points requiring clarification.

Contents

Part One

Issues and Perspectives in Urban Sociology

Classical Conceptions
of Urban Life

The development of sociology as a discipline, as Nisbet (1966) has demonstrated, arose out of the social and ideological upheavals brought about by the French and Industrial Revolutions. Indeed, sociology from its earliest beginnings was simultaneously a response to, and critique of, the emergence of a new urban industrial order in nineteenth-century Western Europe. The rapid development of urban industrial centers throughout the nineteenth century precipitated a still ongoing conversation about the nature of the "social bond." Fore-

3

most in the minds of individuals writing about society during the nineteenth century is the contrast between forms of social life seen as rooted in a small, agrarian order and the kinds of social relations viewed as characterizing an urban industrial order.

What kinds of social developments, in particular, were nineteenth-century social theorists responding to in their writings? Nisbet (1966: 24) has noted five "Themes of Industrialism" that were especially influential in the thinking of the early, or "classical," sociologists: "the condition of labor, the transformation of property, the industrial city, technology, and the factory system."

While Nisbet lists the industrial city as a specific theme in the above listing, for our purposes in *Being Urban* it is important to note that, in one way or another, all five of the above themes interlap, so to speak, and have their common center and locus in the development of the industrial city.

Concomitant with the emergence of an industrial city is the development of new social categories, such as the working class (or "proletariat" in Marx's sense), which coalesces in the city and forms the mass base for the manpower "needs" of the developing factory system. The social heterogeneity and apparent formlessness of this social class occasioned great concern among the classical sociologists. The explosive potential of this class, which was no longer bound by the traditions of the former feudal society nor tied into the larger society through property ownership, made the classical sociologists apprehensive about the "fragility" of the social bond in the cities. Marx, himself, as Nisbet notes, was ambivalent about the development of the working class. On the one hand, he saw its uprooting from its previous rural condition as a necessary catalyst for the eventual transformation of the capitalist system. At the same time, however, he voiced concern over the living and working conditions that confronted members of the working class.

The emergence of new forms of property such as industrial and finance capital also focused the attention of the classical sociologists on the urban industrial order. Previously, the ownership of land, transmitted from one generation to the next, insured the continued dominance of certain elites in West European society. With the development of these new forms of property, however, an emerging middle class, concentrated in the cities, was accumulating wealth at a rapid rate; as *nouveau-riche,* they were attempting to buy their way into the sacred preserves of the traditional landed gentry. The cities became the arenas within which this status struggle took its most dramatic form. In the United States, as Hofstadter (1955) has demonstrated, the period after the Civil War witnessed the "robber-barons'" full-scale assault on the status prerogatives of the traditional elites who traced their lineage and land-owning heritage back to the earliest Colonial times.

The development of technology and the emergence of the factory as a socially organized system of labor were instrumental in attracting newcomers of varied social origins to the cities. Much of this migration was a result of policies (in England, for example) whereby local peasants were prevented from farming through the enactment of "enclosure acts." As a result, they were forced off the land and had to seek a livelihood in the urban factories. The most dramatic effect, however, of technology on the social life of the masses was its role in separating work from the household situation. As Peter Laslett has noted in his impressive study, *The World We Have Lost: England Before the Industrial Age:*

> The factory won its victory by outproducing the working family, taking away the market for the products of hand-labour and cutting prices to the point where the craftsman had either to starve or take a job under factory discipline himself. (1971: 18)

It is also important to note Laslett's statement:

> In the vague and difficult verbiage of our own generation, we can say that the removal of the economic functions from the patriarchal family at the point of industrialization created a mass society. It turned the people who worked into a mass of undifferentiated equals, working in a factory or scattered between the factories and mines, bereft forever of the feeling that work was a family affair, done within the family. (1971: 19)

As our brief discussion indicates, a profound shift in the basis of social organization attended the growth of cities in Western civilization during the nineteenth century, with far-reaching consequences for institutional and personal life. Probably the most important advances in sociological theory have originated from the many different attempts made by social scientists and social philosophers alike to explain this fundamental transformation in the nature of the social bond. While we may speak here of a "fundamental transformation," we must simultaneously recognize that the nature of a social bond between persons is continuously in a state of transformation. Our society, for example, has moved beyond what might be called the epoch of urban industrialization into one characterized by Rostow (1960) as an "age of high mass-consumption." With this in mind, let us now examine some of the specific classical conceptions of the city offered by sociologists writing in the nineteenth and early twentieth centuries.

A FRAME OF REFERENCE:
THE CITY AND BEING URBAN

With the end in view of providing a theoretical reference for this book, this section deals with some major contributions that classical sociologists have made to the study of urbanism and being urban. Our objectives here are twofold: (1) to demonstrate how three major theories of social organization have proposed similar, but not identical, conceptual schemes in terms of which more specialized theories of urban life have been constructed; and (2) to show how sociological interpretations of urbanism in terms of these schemata have resulted in a neglect of the place of *interpersonal* relations in urban social organization.

The review of these contributions is necessarily selective. Any thorough survey of all the attempts that have been made in sociological theory and research to describe and to explain the effects upon social relationships flowing from the rise of cities would encompass the entire history of sociological theory. Five criteria have guided the selection of sociologists discussed in Chapters 1 and 2: (1) relevance for the sociological interpretation of being urban; (2) recognized prominence in the field of social organization; (3) social-psychological relevance; (4) the historical and logical interrelatedness of their contributions; and (5) their diversity of national background.

SIR HENRY SUMNER MAINE:
STATUS AND CONTRACT

Maine, an Englishman writing in the latter part of the nineteenth century, continued a discussion that had begun earlier in the works of the Scottish moral philosophers, in whose writings sociology is said to have its origins as a science. The Scottish moralists were primarily concerned with the kinds of social relations that characterized early community life (see Bryson, 1945: 171). In this sense, they provided later social theorists with a reference point from which changes in the nature of the social bond could be investigated.

Like the Scottish moralists, Maine was most concerned in his researches with depicting and ascertaining the origins of the early village-community and its institutions.[1] In his book *Ancient Law*, Maine also made the additional contribution of providing a framework within which an analysis of the changing basis of social solidarity could proceed.

Maine began his analysis with an inquiry into the origins of codified law (that is, law that had been formulated in a written code), and he concluded that two distinct periods in legal development preceded the emergence of written legal codes. He called the first of these periods the age of "heroic kingship," since, in the ordinary sense of the word, there was no "law" present. During this period the actions of every person were controlled largely by the personal whims and wishes of patriarchal despots. According to Maine, the later development of legal precepts had their origin during this period in the judgments (called Themistes) of these despots, who founded such judgments at times upon custom or usage, and at other times upon personal whim or caprice. In effect, law at this stage is largely a result of the pronouncements of the "heroic" leader.

The period of heroic kingship was transformed as a result of the development of an oligarchy—a small group of persons who collectively seized power from the heroic kings. Such a phenomenon ushered in the period of "customary law," that is, law based primarily upon custom and tradition. Customary law was known only to a privileged minority who exercised a monopoly over the secrets of the "law." The knowledge of these unwritten laws was the exclusive possession of a select group, whose power allowed them to monopolize the definitions of what was not law.

According to Maine (1870: 15), the monopoly of the oligarchy was not dissolved until the discovery and diffusion of writing paved the way for the written specification of law. Once literacy develops in a population, the monopolistic control of secrets about the law is weakened, since individuals are now in a more favorable position both to communicate with others and to question the decisions of governing elites.

---

[1] For the stages in the development and refinement of this problem, see Washburne (1950: 41–77).

Maine did not conceive of law as some transcendent, self-evolving agency. The changes in law as it progressed from the pronouncements of heroic kings to a written code were viewed as responses to changes in the more fundamental conditions of life. For Maine, the fundamental conditions of life were rooted in the social relations of people, which were transformed as the family's importance in determining one's life chances gave way to the place of individual responsibility. That is to say, as the role of the family decreased in importance over time, there was a simultaneous enlargement of opportunities for personal choice and decision-making. Such opportunities, for example, developed in the areas of marital choice, freedom of physical movement, and occupational preference.

Since earliest human settlements were tribal clans—a social organization based on blood lines—the large-scale population growth of the clans was problematic. Through the development of a "legal fiction," however, it became possible to incorporate nonclan members into the group. Such a process of "adoption" greatly facilitated the incorporation of conquered peoples and the continued growth of the clan. In his treatment of this issue, Maine provided a beautiful example of "functional analysis"—that is, of the functions of law (or legal fictions) in society.[2]

In examining the view that the origin of society is to be found in a social contract, that is, an unwritten agreement about the nature of social relationships arrived at by freely consenting individuals, Maine noted:

> Society in *primitive times* was not what it is assumed (by the social contract theorists) to be at present, a collection of *individuals*. In fact, and in view of the man who composed it, it was an *aggregation of families*. The contrast may be most forcibly expressed by saying that the unit of ancient society was the Family, of a modern society the Individual. (Italics ours.) (1870: 126)

The transformation of society's basic units was not accomplished suddenly and all at once. A new principle of community organization gradually replaced that of kinship. People now became related through

---

[2] This work obviously anticipated the "functionalist school" of sociology and social anthropology peopled by such writers as Durkheim, Malinowski, Radcliffe-Brown, and, more recently, Robert K. Merton and Talcott Parsons. The influence upon Durkheim was direct. See Sir Henry Sumner Maine (1870: 21–43) and especially p. 26.

their physical proximity to one another rather than through common lineage. The family, however, persisted as a "fictitious" (in Maine's sense of the word) source of authority. In other words, the role of legal fictions in facilitating social change assumed prominence, since it permitted the family circle to escape its earlier household limits and distribute itself over territory. By "legal fictions" Maine was referring to the phenomenon whereby nonblood members of the original family had been incorporated, through a process of adoption, into the family unit and treated as if they were legally in fact members of the original family. Thus, the notion of "legal fiction."

Once the principle of local geographic residence was established as a basis of community organization, the way was paved, according to Maine, for the dissolution of the family and the emergence of the individual as the fundamental unit of society. And this meant, of course, an unqualified change in the nature of social relations. No longer were the relations of individuals defined by family origin and position (that is, status); they now arose out of mutual agreement (that is, contract). Hence, we can see clearly how Maine conceived of the major change in the social bond as being the process whereby *contract* replaced *status* as the fundamental condition of human association. Maine asserted that this trend was not only universal but also irreversible in Western culture, for "whatever its pace, the change has not been subject to reaction or recoil" (1870: 169).

The remainder of Maine's *Ancient Law* is devoted to an application of the principles sketched above to the study of property, contract, and crime; those considerations are not relevant here. What would seem to be relevant is the fact that the general propositions formulated by Maine were explicitly recognized and taken into account by sociologists in their later attempts to understand and explain essentially the same kind of change in social relations. These later attempts are indicative of a continuing concern evidenced by social theorists with this issue. In the writings of Ferdinand Tönnies and Emile Durkheim, we see a treatment of the historical change in social relations that was clearly influenced by Maine's distinction between *status* and *contract*. We turn first to a treatment of Tönnies' [3] distinction between *Gemeinschaft* and *Gesellschaft*.

---

[3] For a critique of Tönnies that takes us up to at least the twentieth century, see a free translation of Herman Schmalenbach, "The Sociological Category of Communion," by Kaspar D. Naegele and Gregory P. Stone. Pp. 331–47. In Talcott Parsons et al. (eds.), *Theories of Society.* New York: Free Press, 1961.

FERDINAND TÖNNIES:
GEMEINSCHAFT AND GESELLSCHAFT

In his attempt to describe and explain theoretically the changing modes of social relationships that accompanied the emergence of capitalism in Western civilization, Ferdinand Tönnies, as noted, owed much to the work of Sir Henry Sumner Maine; and, like Maine, he was influenced by the works of Thomas Hobbes, a seventeenth-century English social contract theorist. Unlike Maine, however, Tönnies, in his formulation of *Gesellschaft,* accepted many of the notions put forth by Hobbes concerning the inherent conflict between the individual and society.[4]

It is misleading, however, to draw too close a parallel between the contributions of Maine and Tönnies. Tönnies' *Gemeinschaft and Gesellschaft,*[5] first published in 1887, seems to differ from Maine's *Ancient Law* in at least three important respects. First, although Tönnies did apply his concepts to the analysis of social change, he was primarily concerned with distinguishing types of social relationships that had no necessary empirical historical reference. The terms *Gemeinschaft* and *Gesellschaft* were intended to be applied in either contemporary or historical analysis. They were thus formulated independently of the characteristics of any particular society, past or present. This is what is meant by saying that they had no necessary empirical historical reference. Second, Tönnies' methodology contrasted sharply with that employed by Maine, whose concepts *status* and *contract* were designed to refer explicitly to historical situations that had actually occurred. Tönnies, on the other hand, formulated his concepts in terms of "ideal types"; that is, as notions allowing for the comparison of particular kinds of social relations, even though such relations might not exist in a pure form. Third, Tönnies resorted to a psychological level of analysis, that is, the level of individual motivation, in his explanation of sociological events. In this regard Maine was more accurately the "sociologist" of the two, seeking, as he did, to explain institutional change in terms of institutional agencies rather than of individual motivation.

If it can be said that Maine was more the sociologist, it should also be said that he was the more naïve a theorist. By focusing primarily on

---

[4] Maine and Hobbes were nót, of course, the only influences upon the social thought of Tönnies; nor were they necessarily the major influences. Salomon (1945), for example, has specifically stressed the influence of Marx.

[5] This, the best known of Tönnies' works, has been translated and supplemented by Charles F. Loomis as *Fundamental Concepts of Sociology* (1940). All references are to this translation. It is conventional, when discussing Tönnies' theoretical system, to leave the terms *Gemeinschaft* and *Gesellschaft* untranslated.

the operation of large institutional arrangements, Maine tended to lose sight of the importance of individuals' relations with one another. Tönnies' alternative emphasis on the psychological level, however, also gives rise to problems. "Human will" was for Tönnies the fundamental basis of social relations, and the resultant blurring of analytical distinctions between individual and social phenomena accounts in large part for the difficulty that he has apparently had in communicating his theory.

"Human wills stand in manifold relations to one another. . . . This study will consider as its subject of investigation only the relationships of mutual affirmation" (Tönnies, 1940: 37). These two introductory sentences state the central unit of inquiry and delimit the scope of Tönnies' major work, *Gemeinschaft und Gesellschaft*. Significant here is the fact that Tönnies focuses his inquiry *only* on relations of *mutual affirmation,* that is, on relationships based on a shared liking or respect. He did not consider *conflict relationships* in his analysis. The principal objective of this study was the description and explanation of the ways that human wills enter into relationships of mutual affirmation.

To realize this objective, Tönnies constructed a continuum along which all concrete relationships of mutual affirmation could be placed as they approximated one or another of two theoretically distinct (but not necessarily opposed) concepts. He defined *Gemeinschaft* as the kind of traditional community that existed before the French and Industrial Revolutions—one in which persons were bound together by shared values and sacred traditions. In the *Gemeinschaft* social solidarity stemmed from members' common identity and kinship. In contrast, industrialization and the rise of urban centers marked the transition to a *Gesellschaft* type of society, with its heterogeneity of values and traditions. In such a situation, according to Tönnies, individual differences operate to reduce social solidarity, and individualism becomes the paramount value at the expense of communal cohesiveness.

The construction of *Gemeinschaft* as ideal type proceeded from "the assumption of perfect unity of human wills as an original or natural condition which is preserved in spite of actual separation" (1940: 99).[6]

---

[6] Just as the primary group derives from, and in turn conditions, those primary ideals that constituted human nature, so is *Gemeinschaft* characterized as a *natural* relationship. See Cooley (1902: 23–31). Wirth (1926: 419–20) has noted the parallel between Tönnies' *Gemeinschaft* and Cooley's primary group: "The community (*Gemeinshaft*), as Tönnies sees it, has a great deal in common with the primary group of Cooley, for it includes all those relationships which are familiar and intimate, spontaneous, direct, and exclusive (although apparently Tönnies is unfamiliar with Cooley's work and his concepts have a different setting from those of the American sociologist)."

Tönnies cited the relationships of the mother to her child, the sexual union of a man and his wife, the bond that unites brothers and sisters in a family circle, and, less exactly, the relationship of the father, in the capacity of an educative and authoritative model, to his children. Other kinds of relationships approaching the type included kinships; the neighborhood (where the "proximity of habitation (is) supported by well defined habits of reunion and sacred custom") (1940: 49); friendship; and authority in the sense of dignity based on courage,[7] age, or wisdom.

All such relationships are premised upon, and foster consensus in, the sense of a "reciprocal, binding sentiment . . . [which constitutes] . . . the peculiar will of a *Gemeinschaft*" (1940: 53). And this consensus is reinforced among the members of a *Gemeinschaft* by their "intimate knowledge of each other in so far as this is conditioned and advanced by direct interest of one being in the life of the other, and readiness to take part in his joy and sorrow" (1940: 54).

Tönnies expressed the logic of *Gemeinschaft* in terms of three metaphorical "laws":

> (1) Relatives and married couples love each other or easily adjust themselves to each other. They speak together and think along similar lines. Likewise do neighbors and friends. (2) Between people who love each other there is understanding and consensus. (3) Those who love and understand each other remain and dwell together and organize their common life. (1940: 55)

Gemeinschaft, then, is an ideal construct that abstracts the essence of the organization of the common life among people who share a sympathetic consensus and physical proximity. Moreover, although this condition is most closely approximated in the home or the household, it persists under the impact of such patently disruptive factors as the emergence of town and country distinctions, the manor, and the village.

In contrast to *Gemeinschaft* relationships—in which human beings are essentially united despite the presence of apparently divisive influences—*Gesellschaft* relationships are entered into by individuals who are "essentially separated in spite of all uniting factors" (1940: 74). It is in this sense that *Gesellschaft* must always be seen as an artificial, "mechanical," rationally contrived structure of human relationships.

---

[7] This phrase seems more accurately to render Tönnies' meaning than does the translated "authority based on power or force." See Tönnies (1940: 47–53) and especially pp. 47 and 51.

For when *Gesellschaft* associations are removed—when the artificial structure is destroyed—a residue remains where "everybody is by himself and isolated, and there exists a condition of tension against all others" (1940: 74). *Gesellschaft,* for Tönnies, is an elaborate superstructure of human relationships precariously erected upon an incipient Hobbesian war of all against all. He notes that in the *Gesellschaft* "the relation of all to all may therefore be conceived as potential hostility or latent war" (1940: 88).

In his formulation of *Gesellschaft,* Tönnies was heavily influenced by his antipathy to the social contours of his own contemporary Germany. Having observed the social consequences of the growth of capitalism and industry in late nineteenth-century Germany, Tönnies was inclined toward an idealization of the past rather than toward Marx's "future heaven." Thus he yearned for a return to the loving sentimentality of the *Gemeinschaft.*

The associations of *Gesellschaft* are typically contracted in commodity exchange and sealed by promises and "conventions" that are as likely breached as they are fulfilled. For Tönnies, then, the development of *Gesellschaft* is part and parcel of the growth of commerce or trade. As commerce and trade become further elaborated, *Gesellschaft* becomes more pervasive. The crucial agent in the furtherance of *Gesellschaft* is the merchant; and, for Tönnies, *Gesellschaft* is literally the instrument of the merchant or capitalist. They are the natural masters of a *Gesellschaft* that is called into being for the pursuit of their aims.

It is the essence of *Gesellschaft* that no social relationship has value in and of itself. Tönnies' depiction of life in the *Gesellschaft* is strikingly similar to Marx's portrayal of life under the beginning stages of industrial capitalism. Tönnies, like Marx, sees this as a situation in which people relate to one another only through a *cash nexus.* Here is "alienation" in its most dramatic form—people measuring each other's and, even more important, their own worth, by the yardstick of monetary value. This image of urban life became a standard ingredient in the classical conception of urban relations. The notion that no social relation has value in and of itself, that "money is desired by no one for the sake of keeping it, but by everyone with a view to getting rid of it" (1940: 81), was later portrayed by Simmel as the ultimate essence of interpersonal relations in the city. Relationships in *Gesellschaft,* then, are characterized by an inherent instability. It is a loosely coordinated structure held together by the interests of discrete individuals—individuals working for their *own* interests.

Viewed historically, the demands upon the merchant who commands the *Gesellschaft* are altered with the rise of industry. Early in the development of *Gesellschaft*, the merchant rules by virtue of his control over the disposition of commodities in commerce. Yet he must consolidate this rule by dominating labor and the retailing of manufactured goods as the production of these goods passes through the phases of "(1) simple cooperation, (2) manufacture, (3) industry based on machinery (real 'large scale' industry)" (1940: 102). When the merchant class dominates the commodity market, the labor market, and the retail market, *Gesellschaft* may be said to have realized itself historically.

A little reflection upon the assumptions underlying the conceptualization of *Gesellschaft*, as depicted above, suggests that they are essentially analogous to the assumptions of such classical economic thinkers as Adam Smith and David Ricardo. These assumptions have been enumerated by Mayo (1945: 40):

1. Natural society consists of a horde of unorganized individuals.
2. Every individual acts in a manner calculated to secure his self-preservation or self-interest.
3. Every individual thinks logically, to the best of his ability, in the service of his aim.

It is clear, then, that if you presume that society is built on a horde of individuals working rationally in their own self-interests, you must explain the social organization of society as a consequence of self-interest or the exercise of individual volitions. Tönnies made this premise explicit in a proposition: *Gesellschaft* associations were "willed" into being by concrete individuals capable of perceiving that such relationships would benefit their own (individual) interests.

In pursuing his analysis Tönnies devoted the bulk of his volume to the elaboration and description of two contrasting forms of human will. "Natural will," the basis of *Gemeinschaft*, is conceived by Tönnies as an innate, unified motivating force that directly determines personal activity. "Rational will," the basis of *Gesellschaft*, on the other hand, emerges from experience and is produced out of conscious deliberation.

It is important to note that while in Tönnies' terms "natural will" (or passion) and "rational will" (or reason) can be distinguished analytically, they are always intertwined empirically. Thus, no passion can ever occur without reason, by which the passion finds its expression and vice versa. The implication of this point is far-reaching because it clarifies why the terms *Gemeinschaft* and *Gesellschaft* are not unreservedly antithetical as are Maine's notions of status and contract—terms that are viewed as entailing two different types of relationship. In short, there is a tendency, rooted in individual will, for every *Gemeinschaft* to become a *Gesellschaft* and (what has been largely neglected by urban sociologists who have based their theories in part upon these distinctions) for every *Gesellschaft* to become a *Gemeinschaft*.

This crucial insight for urban sociology unfortunately gets obscured in the work of later theorists, for example, Louis Wirth, who presents us with a notion of urban life's becoming more and more impersonal, more rational, more calculating. But Wirth misses the point—central to symbolic interaction we might add—that people do not live in their immediate environment; rather, they live in their *interpretations* of their environments. Thus, as the city becomes more impersonal, it is at this point that we may expect people to transform the city symbolically, injecting into it some sentiment, some passionate sources of life, thereby recasting the symbolic environment of the city. Had Tönnies carried out some systematic observations deriving from the implications of his own theorizing, he might have found that even a supposed cradle of impersonality—the urban marketplace of sellers and buyers —may itself be buffeted by the comforting cushion of intimate and friendly relations.

Tönnies' emphasis on the priority of individual volitions affirmed his belief in the necessity of building sociological concepts upon a psychological base. In reviewing Emile Durkheim's book *The Rules of Sociological Method* in 1898, he took issue with Durkheim's notion that the study of individual behavior could only be understood through the investigation of the individual's membership in social groups. Although this marked one of the chief differences between the theoretical systems of Tönnies and Durkheim, it was not the only difference. Earlier in 1889 Durkheim had, in reviewing the 1887 edition of *Gemeinschaft and Gesellschaft,* rejected Tönnies' notion that present-day industrial society is a mechanical and artificial structure as opposed to the organic and natural structure of earlier society. Contemporary society, Durkheim held, is clearly as "organic" and "natural" as life was before the Industrial Revolution.[8] This thesis was documented

---

8 These reviews are discussed by Loomis in his introduction to the Tönnies translation (1940: xviii).

four years later, in 1893, when Durkheim published his well-known *De la division du travail social.*[9]

EMILE DURKHEIM: MECHANICAL AND
ORGANIC SOLIDARITY

Like Tönnies, Durkheim was disturbed about the drift of contemporary civilization; he was particularly concerned with the issue of occupational specialization. During the period in which Durkheim wrote about the division of labor—the late nineteenth century and early twentieth century—there was an intense intellectual argument that particularly emphasized the negative consequences of occupational specialization. The question that Durkheim raised in regard to this issue centered on whether there was any moral function in specialization. Contemporaries of his, such as Tönnies, argued that specialization contributed to the disintegration of the larger social order. Durkheim's response was that that which is moral contributes to both the solidarity and healthy continuity of society. For him, the division of labor did have this function. Durkheim developed the further argument that this was the most important method by which people were linked to one another in complex societies. To test his argument, societies in which the division of labor had not progressed so extensively were sought out for comparison with industrialized societies. He looked for relatively small isolated communities—such as the Australian aborigines—as testing grounds for this theorizing. Durkheim's selection of such communities derived from his assertion that all societies have some division of labor—such as sex, age, family status kinds of divisions—but in small communities the division of labor differs from that found in complex societies.

According to Durkheim, Western civilization was caught up in an irreversible historical trend from an aggregate of undifferentiated, homogenous "social segments" to a unity of heterogeneous, functionally interrelated "social organs." Theoretically, the social segment is composed of mentally and morally homogenous people whose beliefs, opinions, and manners are similar. These similar sentiments are representations (or, rather, re-presentations) of society's collective life. They

---

[9] This has been translated by George Simpson (1947) as *The Division of Labor in Society.* All references are to the Simpson translation.

represent those forms of behavior that have been repeated to the extent of becoming habitual. Taken together, such collective representations comprise the collective conscience[10] of the segment; that is, "the totality of beliefs and sentiments common to average citizens" (1947: 79) Because it is a commonality of beliefs and sentiments, and because it may be perceived in a special sense as external to, and constraining, individual conduct and thought, the collective *conscience* is referred to as a *thing, sui generis.* We call attention once more to the fact that Tönnies, in his review of Durkheim noted earlier, took issue with this conceptualization of social life.

Much debate has ensued among sociologists about whether Durkheim was saying that society is really a thing. In our view, all he is saying is that we should look upon society as a social object that can be examined. By saying that this collective *conscience* is external to, and constraining of, the conduct and thought of society's members, Durkheim means that no *particular person* is responsible for that commonality of beliefs.

Ordinarily, no single person can master the entire range of beliefs and sentiments that make up the collective consciousness or *conscience.* No specific individual reading this book, for example, is responsible for the English language. Perhaps someone may introduce a word or so in our lifetime, but our individual contribution will still be minimal. In this sense language is *external* to any given individual member of society. Sports may serve as another instance. With reference to football, for example, no living football player is responsible for the rules of the game; such rules are external to any individual player.

In effect, then, when Durkheim says that society is real, he is not saying that it is something physically outside of us that commands individual behavior. Rather, he is saying that it is more than any one person is responsible for and that it severely limits alternative forms of behavior. Through this collective *conscience,* then, the behavior of society's members is brought into line. Through the diffused constraining power of the collective *conscience,* solidarity is insured in the social segment, and the activity of its members is brought automatically into rapport. Solidarity, conditioned in this manner is termed "mechanical solidarity." In other words, "mechanical solidarity prevails where in-

---

10 The term *conscience* is left untranslated. Parsons et al. (1949: 309, footnote 3) have indicated the wisdom of this by pointing out that it means both "consciousness" and "conscience" in single contexts as it is employed by Durkheim.

dividual differences are minimized and the members of society are much alike in their devotion to the common weal" (Coser, 1971: 131).

Given such a view of mechanical solidarity, the question now arises as to how Durkheim was able to detect the operation of mechanical solidarity. Like his predecessor, Maine, Durkheim turns to the operation of law for the investigation of this issue. In Durkheim's (1947: 68) view, "law reproduces the principal forms of social solidarity" and represents the entire institutional basis of a society.

When the sanctions attached to the legal rules of a society are repressive in nature, that is, demanding retaliation and punishment, they reflect the presence of mechanical solidarity. In its most unqualified form, the collective conscience is represented by an impersonal force violently and passionately embraced by the society's members. Consequently, offenses against it evoke an immediate and direct response. Such offenses must be repressed, for, symbolically, they threaten and violate the integrity of the society as a whole. Punishment of offenders, in these instances, not only guarantees conformity to social rules, but—more important—also serves as an occasion for reinforcing the sentiments that make up the violated collective *conscience*.

Durkheim is here making a very important observation. In effect, he is saying that without the existence of sinners you cannot have a church, because the very existence of sin provides the opportunity for believers to reaffirm the faith that has been offended by the sinner. The worst thing that can happen to a church, therefore, is to eliminate sin from the world completely and to propagate the faith to society completely!

The test of mechanical solidarity is to be found in the sanctions exerted when the rules of society are violated. In a sense, then, to the extent that a common morality exists in a particular society, the society comes to depend upon its deviants for the maintenance of social "boundaries." Kai Erikson, in his provocative book *Wayward Puritans,* showed how such an insight clarifies the nature of the witch-hunts in Colonial America. With reference to deviance, Erikson notes:

> Like an article of common law, boundaries remain a meaningful point of reference only so long as they are repeatedly tested by persons on the fringes of the group and repeatedly defended by persons chosen to represent the group's inner morality. Each time the community moves to censor some act of deviation, then, and convenes a formal ceremony to deal with the responsible offender, it sharpens the authority of the violated norm and restates where the boundaries of the group are located. (1966: 13)

In contrasting the notion of repressive law with the kinds of law that characterize present-day advanced industrial societies, what is strikingly apparent is the paucity of offenses in such societies that are construed as offenses against society in general. What has happened is that there has been a transformation in the character of offenses so that punishment is no longer repressive in many cases; rather, it has become more restitutive in character (that is, offenders are expected to repay society for their transgression). Civil litigations offer examples of restitutive law in action. The civil suit does not often imply a crime against society—a moral offense—and, accordingly, the defendant in such cases is seldom subject to general social censure. Instead, one is asked to make amends to the party or parties injured.

What kinds of offenses, Durkheim asks, culminate in civil suits? Usually, he observes, they are either of two types: offenses against rights or breaches of (usually contracted) obligations. Adherence to the rules built up to guarantee the inviolability of rights, however, has little positive influence upon the formation of solidary associations between people. Obedience to the law requires merely that the members of society abstain from infringing upon the privileges of one another. The solidarity that results is of a negative character. It takes the form of persons' *not doing* certain things to one another. But, as Durkheim (1947: 120) notes, this "negative solidarity is possible only where there exists some other (solidarity) of a positive nature." The positive force making for social solidarity in this regard is manifested by a whole series of legal forms, such as domestic law, contract law, commercial law, procedural law, administrative law, and constitutional law, which, taken together, can be called "cooperative law," since such laws specify obligations that members of various social circles have toward one another.

Contracted relationships best exemplify the form, but not the basis, of solidary association in societies distinguished by an extensive division of labor. "In effect, the contract is *par excellence,* the juridical expression of cooperation" (Durkheim, 1947: 123). Here obligations are established and their fulfillment guaranteed so that individuals with different interests may be brought together in complementary relationships. Contrary to Tönnies, Durkheim did not perceive contracts as discrete associations of otherwise unrelated persons who came together momentarily for the sake of a contract and then disbanded the relationship after the contract's fulfillment. Contracts can be built only upon implicit *social* foundations. As Durkheim (1947: 114) notes: "Every contract thus supposes that behind the parties implicated in it there is society very ready to intervene in order to gain respect for the engagements which have been made."

Any time one enters into a contract, much of the arrangement is taken for granted in spite of all the small print. What this means is that this body of beliefs (this mechanical solidarity) never completely disappears, even in advanced industrial societies. Such beliefs must persist to a certain extent so that contracts can be enforced. With reference to these implicit beliefs, for example, we can examine the instance of cashing a check in present-day society. The physical appearance of the person who applies for getting a check cashed is critical to the success of the venture. People make assumptions, based on the appearances of others (see Stone, 1962, on this issue), which are anchored in the belief systems of society. In effect, then, elements of mechanical solidarity can still be found in societies organized in terms of an extensive division of labor.

Cooperative law is not charged with the sentiment and passion of repressive law, nor is it diffused so that it is incorporated into the conscience of every member of society. Nevertheless, its solidarity-building role is apparent. For cooperative laws "fix the manner in which the different functions of society ought to concur in diverse combinations of circumstances." (1947: 128). The society held together by the concurrence of functions in this way is termed "organically solidary."

In sum, Durkheim isolated two contrasting types of social solidarity —the one mechanical, the other organic. "The first binds the individual directly to society without any intermediary. In the second, he depends upon society, because he depends upon the parts of which it is composed" (1947: 129). Placing the two types in historical perspective, Durkheim (1947: 144) agreed with Maine that "the place of penal law ... was ... as great as the societies were ancient." There could be no doubt that repressive law was gradually replaced by restitutive law as societies advanced sociohistorically. "The further back one goes in social history, the greater the homogeneity ... the further one approaches to the highest social types, the greater the development of the division of labor" (1947: 138). Societies, insofar as they advance at all, advance from a condition of mechanical solidarity to a condition of organic solidarity, and the progressive preponderance of the division of labor is the prime impetus for such an advance.

Accordingly, the next problem to which Durkheim turned in his inquiry was the explanation of the development of organic solidarity through the growth of the division of labor. Proceeding deductively, he singled out three interrelated factors related to the increase of organic solidarity in society: (1) dynamic density, that is, the rate of communication between societal members;[11] (2) material density, that is, "the number of individuals that are to be in contact per unit of space" (1947: 257); and (3) volume, that is, the geographical space defining the physical boundaries of a particular society.

In Durkheim's view, the growth in any one of the above factors was dependent upon the simultaneous growth in the other two. In short, it must be emphasized that the conditions for the division of labor are multiple and interrelated. Nor are volume, material density, and dynamic density[12] sufficient to account for the growth of the division of labor. They alone cannot explain the dynamic of that process. For Durkheim, the division of labor is, ultimately, a further reflection of a response to the sheer biological struggle for existence and competition for control of scarce resources.[13]

The significance of the collective *conscience* for the establishment of social solidarity in society is progressively weakened with the emergence of organic solidarity as a new organizing principle. As Durkheim (1947: 172) notes: "This is not to say, however, that the common conscience is threatened with total disappearance.... There is even a place where it is strengthened and made precise: that is the way in which it regards the individual. As all the other beliefs and all the other practices take on a character less and less religious, the individual becomes the object of a sort of religion." In effect, then, Durkheim is suggesting that as traditional forms of religion decline, the belief in the worth of the individual gradually develops into a religion itself.

It may be, as Durkheim argued, that in complex societies individuation is buttressed by a cult. When we look at the city, however, it is not a case of *individuals* set apart under conditions of urbanism, but rather a separation of *social groups or social circles*. Such a phenomenon, we may argue, makes for greater freedom than the cult of individualism implies, for here we have a multiplicity of different selves that we can realize in a number of varying social circles.

---

11 Durkheim drastically underestimated technological developments in communication as effecting the moral density of society, but, after all, he was writing at the turn of the nineteenth century.

12 Throughout his entire career, Durkheim was concerned with this question of the importance of moral or dynamic density, which we choose to call the rate of communication, or the rate of symbolic interaction. On this point see Stone and Farberman (1970: 100–11).

13 In another work (1938: 92–93), Durkheim recognized the implicit inadequacy of explaining the division of labor by biological factors.

With the transformation of the division of labor, new sentiments are introduced into other areas of social life. Durkheim recognized the proliferation of contractual relationships in contemporary society; but, as has already been mentioned, he denied that the contract functioned as a basis of social solidarity. Noncontractual elements underlying and regulating the formation of contracts must develop simultaneously. "In sum, a contract is not sufficient unto itself, but is possible only thanks to a regulation of the contract which is originally social" (1947: 215). Any society, in any condition of solidarity, is, at bottom, a moral order.

> Men cannot live together without acknowledging and consequently making mutual sacrifices, without tying themselves to one another with strong durable bonds. Every society is a moral society. (1947: 228)

Having demonstrated the social function, or the moral value, of the division of labor, Durkheim turned to an examination of the effectiveness with which the function was performed in modern life. Asserting that the full moral value of the division of labor was not realized in contemporary society, he conceptualized that fact in terms of three distinct types of the division of labor which were "dysfunctional" in that they prevented the division of labor from performing its solidarity-building role. First, the interdependent parts of society cannot be efficiently coordinated when the division of labor is anomic. *Anomie* (social normlessness) results from economic crises such as inflation, depression, strikes, boycotts, or any crisis that does not contribute either to the adequate formulation of moral values or to the achievement of social ends. Second, if the division of labor is based on a compulsory caste or class system, it "sometimes gives rise to anxiety and pain instead of producing solidarity . . . because the distribution of functions on which it rests does not respond, or rather no longer responds to the distribution of natural talents" (1947: 228). Finally, the division of labor may assume a character so that "functions are distributed in such a way that they do not offer sufficient material for individual activity" (1947: 389). Thus, it is possible for us to become so finely specialized that there is not enough work to be done to give meaning to individual activity. There may be no meaning forthcoming from the effort that one is involved in. In camping groups, for example, there is an optimum number for a canoe trip because there is only so much work to be done—portaging, getting food, gathering wood, and so on; otherwise, some people would worry when they were not "working" and the others were. Here is a case in which the functions are distributed in such a way that they do not offer sufficient material for everyone to be occupied.

It is to such "abnormal" forms of the division of labor, rather than to the division of labor itself, Durkheim concludes, that we must look for the source of the moral "inadequacies" of our age.

CONCLUSION

Small wonder that all these—an Englishman intent on critiquing the method of the social-contract theorists, a German concerned with the changing character of human wills in industrial society, and a Frenchman concerned with the moral value of occupational specialization—should have addressed like questions and consulted the same authorities, as well as one another, in quest of solutions. That men of diverse national origins and unlike interests inquired into the varied roots of human association is demonstration enough of the problem's salience. Furthermore, the problem is still the central problem of sociology. Sociological thought continues to converge around the following questions: What is the nature of the social bond? And how has the basis of the social bond been historically transformed?

The persistent devotion of social scientists to the question raised by Maine, Tönnies, and Durkheim emphasizes the strategic place that such inquiries still assume in the extension and refinement of sociological knowledge. To cite only a few well-known names: Becker (1932: 138–54) has made extensive analyses of the contrast between sacred and secular societies; Redfield (1947: 293–308) has collated those features of the "folk society" that ideally set it off and distinguish it from "urban civilization"; and Wirth (1948) has consistently stressed the necessity for maintaining a clear analytical distinction between "society" built upon the consensus and understanding of its members and "community" integrated by the interdependence of population aggregates. The theoretical contexts proposed by Maine, Tönnies, and Durkheim continue to be refined as the study of social organization is extended and given precision by contemporary sociologists. Yet (at least in the case of Tönnies and Durkheim) the distinctions between *Gemeinschaft* and *Gesellschaft,* and between mechanical solidarity and organic solidarity, were more than devices for the conceptual delimitation of contexts within which human association could be investigated.

The social types were related to one another as the basic terms of theoretical propositions. Neither Tönnies nor Durkheim, as we have shown, was content to rest his inquiry with the demonstration that all human existence ranged between polar types of social organization. Both perceived the interdependence of the typical elements in concrete reality.

The impact of Maine's distinctions between the familial and territorial bases of social relations, on the one hand, and between status and contract, on the other, upon Tönnies' theoretical system is clear.[14] As a matter of fact, the notion of contract is central to Tönnies' construction of *Gesellschaft* as a pure type. Similarly, but in a less detailed way, Maine's thinking influenced Durkheim's study of the division of labor, and it is not unlikely that Durkheim was affected in that work by Tönnies' writings more than a perusal of the citations and references would indicate.[15] Accordingly, the conceptual schemes developed by these three men do have many similarities, although each is clearly distinguishable from the other. Probably more than anything else, the dependence of these scholars upon one another has contributed to the superficial and erroneous equation of the different schemata by many sociologists in their effort to organize and to contrast in a theoretically significant way the empirical characteristics of rural and urban life. This lumping together of heterogeneous concepts from diverse theoretical schemes for the sake of classification rather than analysis has had a definitive influence upon the character of urban sociology.

REFERENCES

Becker, Howard. "Processes of Secularization: An Ideal Typical Analysis with Special Reference to Personality Change as Affected by Population Movements." *The Sociological Review,* 24 (April–July 1932): 138–54.

Bryson, Gladys. *Man and Society.* Princeton, N.J.: Princeton University Press, 1945.

Cooley, Charles H. *Social Organization.* New York: Charles Scribner's Sons, 1902.

---

[14] Tönnies quoted Maine frequently and often at considerable length. See Tönnies (1940).

[15] Although Durkheim never made explicit reference to Tönnies in his principal works, Sorokin (1928: 491) has noted: "One cannot help thinking that Durkheim intentionally gave to his social types names which were opposite those given by Tönnies."

Coser, Louis. *Masters of Sociological Thought.* New York: Harcourt, Brace and Jovanovich, 1971.

Durkheim, Emile. *The Division of Labor in Society.* Translated by George Simpson. Glencoe, Ill.: The Free Press, 1947.

Durkheim, Emile. *The Rules of Sociological Method.* Edited by George R. G. Catlin. Translated by Sarah A. Solovay and John H. Mueller. Chicago: University of Chicago Press, 1938.

Erikson, Kai T. *Wayward Puritans: A Study in the Sociology of Deviance.* New York: John Wiley and Sons, 1966.

Gerth, Hans, and C. Wright Mills. *From Max Weber: Essays in Sociology.* New York: Oxford University Press, Galaxy Book, 1958.

Hofstadter, Richard. *The Age of Reform.* New York: Alfred A. Knopf, 1955.

Laslett, Peter. *The World We Have Lost: England Before the Industrial Age.* New York: Charles Scribner's Sons, 1971.

Maine, Sir Henry Sumner. *Ancient Law.* London: John Murray, 1870.

Maine, Sir Henry Sumner. *Village-Communities in the East and West.* New York: Henry Holt and Co., 1889.

Mayo, Elton. *The Social Problems of an Industrial Civilization.* Cambridge, Mass.: Harvard University Press, 1945.

Mills, C. Wright. *White Collar.* New York: Oxford University Press, 1951.

Nisbet, Robert. *The Sociological Tradition.* New York: Basic Books, 1966.

Parsons, Talcott. *The Structure of Social Action.* Glencoe, Ill.: The Free Press, 1949.

Redfield, Robert. "The Folk Society." *American Journal of Sociology,* 3 (January 1947): 293–308.

Rostow, W. W. *The Stages of Economic Growth.* Cambridge, England: Cambridge University Press, 1960.

Salomon, Albert. "German Sociology." Pp. 586–614 in Georges Gurvitch and Wilbert E. Moore (eds.), *Twentieth Century Sociology.* New York: The Philosophical Library, 1945.

Schmalenbach, Herman. "The Sociological Concept of Communion." Translated by Kasper D. Naegele and Gregory P. Stone. Pp. 331–47 in Talcott Parsons et al. (eds.), *Theories of Society.* New York: Free Press, 1961.

Sorokin, Pitirim. *Contemporary Sociological Theory.* New York: Harper and Brothers, 1928.

Stone, Gregory P. "Appearance and the Self." Pp. 86–118 in Arnold Rose (ed.), *Human Behavior and Social Processes.* Boston: Houghton Mifflin, 1962.

Stone, Gregory P. and Harvey A. Farberman. "Was Durkheim Moving Towards Symbolic Interaction?" Pp. 100–11 in Stone and Farberman (eds.), *Social Psychology Through Symbolic Interaction.* Waltham, Mass.: Ginn-Blaisdell, 1970.

Tönnies, Ferdinand. *Fundamental Concepts of Sociology.* Translated and supplemented by Charles F. Loomis. New York: American Book Co., 1940.

Washburne, Chandler. "The Origin, Essence, and Development of Sir Henry Sumner Maine's Theory of the Original Village Community. Unpublished Master's thesis, Michigan State University, 1950.

Weber, Max. *The Theory of Social and Economic Organization.* Translated by A. M. Henderson and Talcott Parsons. New York: Oxford University Press, 1947.

Wirth, Louis. "The Sociology of Ferdinand Tönnies." *American Journal of Sociology* 32 (November 1926): 412–22.

Wirth, Louis. "World Community, World Society, and World Government: An Attempt at a Clarification of Terms." Pp. 9–20 in Quincy Wright (ed.), *World Community*. Chicago: University of Chicago Press, 1948.

2

Classical Observations
of the City

In the preceding chapter we dealt at length with the general contours of the theoretical schemes on urban industrial society put forth by the classical sociologists. In this chapter we shall examine the manner in which those conceptual schemata influenced the kinds of *observations* of urban life made by an ensuing generation of sociologists.

THE CITY AND THE SOCIOLOGIST

Tönnies (1940: 265) had spoken of "the city . . . where the general conditions of *Gesellschaft* prevail," and Durkheim (1947: 258) submitted the proposition that "as long as the social organization is essentially segmental, the city does not exist." When they have made use of the conceptual apparatus of Durkheim or Tönnies, urban sociologists have paid little heed to the qualifications contained in such remarks; and they have characterized the city, *often absolutely,* in terms of *Gesellschaft* and organic solidarity. In this regard, they seem not to have recognized that the value of a concept is never realized solely from its application as a classificatory device. A concept is valuable to the extent that it facilitates the discrimination of empirical events so that the relationships among them may be better perceived and more adequately explained. Sociologists have used the terminology of Maine, Tönnies, and Durkheim to differentiate the character of urban living from that of rural existence and to detect the social consequences of urbanization. Interest in this regard has been mobilized around the investigation of the historical impact of contract upon status, *Gesellschaft* upon *Gemeinschaft,* and organic solidarity upon mechanical solidarity. The place of status in contract, *Gemeinschaft* in *Gesellschaft,* or the social segment in the solidary society has been slighted and often unperceived. More often than not the status, *Gemeinschaft*-like, or segmental elements that have been perceived as occurring in the context of urbanism have been described as rural survivals or remnants left over from some earlier form of social organization. As a consequence, urban sociologists have been preoccupied with the disorganizing, alienating, and so-called individualizing influences of urbanism. Certain disruptive results of the rise of cities have been completely studied, but *social life* in the city was never adequately explored until the middle 1940s. Urban sociologists had not systematically taken into account in their researches either Tönnies' proposition that every *Gesellschaft* tends to become a *Gemeinschaft* or Durkheim's axiom that every society is a moral order.

GEORG SIMMEL: THE METROPOLIS AND
MENTAL LIFE

Simmel's writings on the city may be viewed as a transitional link between the conceptual schemata provided by nineteenth-century sociologists and the observations of urban life made by a later generation of sociologists located at the University of Chicago in the early part of the twentieth century. Like Durkheim and Tönnies, the German sociologist Georg Simmel also recognized the study of the historical transfiguration of social solidarity in Western civilization as a legitimate problem. Simmel's discussion of the metropolis and what might be termed the urban personality type (1950: 409–24) centered on the question of "how the personality accommodates itself in the adjustments to external forces" (1950: 409) (in this case, forces exerted by the metropolitan environment). Such a question is obviously a significant one for a social psychology of urban life.

Simmel isolated several distinctive features of the metropolis that elicit from the metropolitan person a unique pattern of responses not found among the inhabitants of small towns. Primarily the large city can be seen as a setting for contrasting physical and social stimuli so numerous and diverse that any single individual exposed to them cannot possibly respond to them all; nor can one escape a vague subliminal awareness of their presence. Consequently, the first difference that one might detect between the resident of the metropolis and the resident of the small town is the heightened awareness and greater critical acumen of the former as over and against the depressed awareness and greater naïveté of the latter. "The urban man reacts with his head instead of his heart" (1950: 410). This may be attributed to the fact that he must select out from an ubiquitous shower of highly varied stimuli the ones appropriate for his response. That the metropolis is characteristically the seat of a money economy gives added impetus to the development in the urban person of a detached rationalistic view of the world. "Money economy and the dominance of the intellect are intrinsically connected" (1950: 411). Moreover, in the city, time is an all-important coordinator of human activity. Without a meticulous devotion to punctuality on the part of most of the metropolis' inhabitants, the metropolis would become a bedlam. The very necessity of arranging a schedule for transportation to and from one's place of work, for example, heightens the significance of punctuality for the urban dweller. The interlocking activities of varied businesses in the urban area also reinforce a respect for punctuality, so as to maximize operating efficiency.

Insofar as the intense stimulation of the metropolis and the prominence of its money economy promote the intellectuality of the urban person, they also cultivate in one a characteristically blasé reaction to events. The incessant bombardment of incompatible stimuli upon individuals ultimately exhausts their mental energies and renders them incapable of response to every new occurrence. In the same fashion the blasé response is evinced by the money economy. "The essence of the blasé attitude consists in the blunting of discrimination . . . and . . . money with all its colorlessness and indifference becomes the common denominator of all values; irreparably it hollows out the core of things, their individuality, their specific value, and their incomparability" (1950: 414).

On almost every day of his life, the metropolitan person is somehow involved in the exchange of dollars and cents. Perpetually reminded of the purchasability of things, one makes a habit of evaluation. Inevitably this habit mediates one's estimation of others and, reflexively, one's estimate of his own worth. Dwarfed by an awesome and overpowering milieu, the urbanite, in the struggle to maintain his self-esteem, devaluates the objects and persons that surround him. In its most controlled state, this mechanism is expressed as a typical reserve that sets the individual apart from the objects and persons challenging his ideal self-image. Often "the inner aspect of this reserve is not only indifference but . . . a slight aversion, a mutual strangeness and repulsion which will break into hatred and fight at the moment of closer contact" (1950: 415–16). Those processes that pit persons against persons in the city and disrupt the collective life are a *sine qua non* of urban existence.

Here again we are presented with the notion that underneath the social order of the city lies the hostility of each person against every other. Simmel, like Tönnies, is here echoing a kind of Hobbesian motif. For Simmel, this "chip-on-the-shoulder" demeanor of the city dweller is one guarantee of the great personal freedom that abounds in metropolitan life. But personal freedom in Simmel's view is more basically a product of a "universal tendency" underlying the rise of the metropolis and the development of all social groupings. Any group is originally "a relatively small circle firmly closed against neighboring, strange, or in some way antagonistic circles" (1950: 416). In it the self-expression of its numbers is circumscribed by dogma and petty prejudice. As the group extends itself over territory and increases its size and importance, its structural rigidity and negative orientation to other groups is considerably weakened. Consequently, the demands that it makes upon its members are weakened, and personal freedom is enhanced "so that today metropolitan man is 'free' in a spiritualized and refined sense in contrast to the pettiness and prejudices which hem in the small town man" (1950: 418). One must occasionally pay a price for this increment of freedom in the currency of an overpowering sense of loneliness and deprivation. "It is obviously only the obverse of this freedom if, under certain circumstances, one nowhere feels as lonely and lost as in the metropolitan crowd" (1950: 418).[1]

The freedom of the urban person cannot, however, be viewed only in this negative sense—as the absence of social control. One's breadth of vision and areas of interest are both extended and objectified in the city. "The most significant characteristic of the metropolis is [its] functional extension beyond its physical boundaries. And this efficacy reacts in turn and gives weight, importance, and responsibility to metropolitan life" (1950: 419). The overflow of metropolitan institutions carries the spirit of the inhabitants with it into an awareness of a larger world and a sense of involvement with impersonal history.

In effect, then, cities are inevitably providing functions that affect people and institutions lying outside the political boundaries of the city. We might argue here that it is primarily this phenomenon that has heightened urban growth and exacerbated urban problems. Since so many of our cities' political boundaries are based on rivers and other geographical demarcation points, the spilling over of city functions makes the earlier physical boundaries of the city increasingly archaic. The financial plight of the cities is thereby intensified as a result of a structurally generated inability to raise the necessary revenue to provide for an increasing series of additional functions.

At the base of the functional expansion of the metropolis is the division of labor. With the proliferation of occupations that Durkheim noted in the division of labor, the inhabitants of the city are looked upon more in terms of what they *do* rather than who they *are*. It follows that opportunities for close social contact with others are greatly lessened. This limitation, taken together with the imposing dimensions of the city's "objective culture," stimulates in metropolitan people considerable anxiety about their self-importance *vis-à-vis* the importance of events around them. "This results in the individual's summoning the utmost in uniqueness and particularization, in order to preserve his most personal core. He has to exaggerate this personal element in order to remain audible even to himself" (1950: 722). The historical significance of this state of affairs becomes apparent in a larger context:

---

1 Note here the idea of the "lonely crowd" later developed by Riesman (1950).

> In this situation the cry for liberty and equality arose, the belief in the individual's full freedom of movement in all social and intellectual relationships. Freedom would at once permit the noble substance common to all to come to the fore, a substance which nature had deposited in every man and which society and history had only deformed. Besides this eighteenth century ideal of liberalism, in the nineteenth century, through Goethe and Romanticism, on the one hand, and the economic division of labor, on the other hand, another ideal arose; individuals liberated from historical bonds now wished to distinguish themselves from one another. The carrier of man's values is no longer the "general human being" in every individual, but rather man's qualitative uniqueness and irreplaceability. The external and internal history of our times takes its course with the struggle and in the changing entanglements of those two ways of defining the individual's role in the whole of society. It is the function of the metropolis to provide the arena for this struggle and its reconciliation. (1950: 423)

With this characterization of urban "freedom," Simmel evidences an ambivalence about city life that is later continued by the classical observers of the city such as Park and Wirth. In one sense Simmel portrays the city as the source of personal freedom. At the same time, however, the city is seen as the basis of a larger kind of "social disorganization." These two conflicting themes continually reappear in the writings of the sociologists who established urban sociology as a particular area of study. It should also be noted that a view of urban life as "disorganized" was also reinforced in the writings of American sociologists concerned about social problems in early twentieth-century America. As C. Wright Mills (1943) noted in his probing essay on "The Professional Ideology of Social Pathologists," such sociologists often traced the "pathology" of contemporary life to predominately urban "causes." For Simmel, the ideological function of the city is the provision of a setting within which the tension between equality and freedom can be resolved.[2]

As Simmel conceived it, then, urbanism has the cardinal effect of promoting the intellectuality and individuality of those who are exposed to it. Emotional reserve and the blasé attitude that distinguish the conduct of urban people are to be understood as the principal adaptive mechanisms of individual life in the metropolis. Their im-

---

[2] The incompatibility of freedom and equality is discussed in another of Simmel's essays. See Simmel (1950: 58–89).

portance lies in making an intellectual and individualistic life psychologically possible. These propositions and the inferences drawn from them concerning the nature of urban groups and social structures have left an indelible stamp on the character of urban sociology in America. Further, they provide a kind of connecting link between the observations of Maine, Tönnies, and Durkheim about the character of social organization and current observations about the social psychology of the city dweller. Fruitful as such propositions may be, they are inadequate for a detailed treatment of the social psychology of urban life.

We take issue with Simmel's notion that urban life can be described in terms of individualization. This is not to deny that the chances for individual autonomy are obviously enhanced in the urban environment. As Simmel argues, emotional reserve psychologically sustained by a powerful charge of negative emotion may be an efficient way of preserving individual autonomy, once it is secured. At least two questions, though, are suggested by those observations. First, does the increase of potential individual autonomy mean that urban life is increasingly individualized (as most sociologists have inferred); that is, that human beings must more and more look to their own individual selves for resources capable of facilitating their daily lives? Second, is latent hostility a *sufficient* means of sustaining emotional reserve? The questions are interrelated, and the answer seems to be negative in both instances.

People are first and foremost social animals. It is only—as Charles Horton Cooley, an early twentieth-century social psychologist, and others before him recognized long ago—through one's relationships with others that one's individuality can in any way be realized. There are essentially two reasons for this. First, the self (which includes the idea of individuality) is a reflexive phenomenon. That is to say, persons come to view themselves as they believe that others view them; they look at themselves from the point of view of others. Second—and this was also recognized by Cooley—self-expression premises *intimate* social association. Simmel observed the first point in his essay when he indicated the devaluation of the other as a means of heightening one's self-esteem. Although he singled out only the technique of devaluation, there is its opposite: one can so devaluate himself that others will respond by bolstering one's self-esteem. Here is the power of depression. We suppose, too, that there is a positive aspect to this that is often neglected. One can attempt to fulfill, beyond the demands of adequacy, the expectations that others have of one in the effort to secure one's sense of dignity and moral worth. The second point that we have

raised, namely that self-expression presumes intimate association, constitutes a basic premise of contemporary "neo-Freudian" psychiatric
theory. The absence of satisfactory primary relationships with *significant* others has negative consequences for one's conception of self,[3]
and the *significance* of others transcends one's relationship to parents
and siblings. This should not be taken to mean that the identification
of the self with social groupings *assures* the expression of individuality.
When this qualification is properly understood, it would seem that the
basis of the difference between cities and towns, and between large,
complex environments and small, relatively closed, social circles becomes clearer insofar as such differences are manifested social-
psychologically. In the small town, one may easily lose his individuality *in his relationship with others,* whereas in the large city one
establishes his individuality *through his social relationship with others.*

It is not, therefore, that life in the city has become individualized in
any usual sense of that word. One cannot depend upon oneself alone
as one lives from day to day, and this is especially true if one lives in a
large city. Sociologists have recognized this in their studies of gangs
(Thrasher, 1926), the taxi dance hall (Cressey, 1932), and commer-
cialized vice (Landesco, 1929). However, one of the points of this book
is that the isolation of individuals in the city is offset by the purposive
establishment of commercial ventures such as massage parlors, lonely
hearts clubs, and the like. Other institutions such as shopping and
sport provide both intended and unintended settings within which
fairly intimate associations may be formed between presumable
strangers.[4] It is such relationships that prevent the individual from
becoming "lost" in the city and offer a platform from which one can
express one's individuality. Instead of the individualization of urban
life, then, we might well speak of the "socialization" of urban life in
the specific meaning of that word, that is, the collectively shared aspect
of urban existence. The observation was never put this way in any of

---

3 See Harry Stack Sullivan (1949: 98–121).
4 This does not presuppose the equal distribution of such opportunities throughout
the city. In areas of transition, retail establishments are oriented to a transient
clientele, and it is in such areas that the sense of personal loss or anomie is aggravated. In this respect, however, it should be pointed out that such areas are
peopled by recent immigrants to the city and not by indigenous urbanites. Moreover, the sense of anomie that Simmel describes as the obverse of freedom, if left
unallayed, calls forth psychological responses that reduce the opportunity for self-
expression. On the latter point, consult Erich Fromm (1941), especially pp. 136–206.

the studies referred to earlier, and we believe that it marks an important point on which our treatment of urban life differs from previous accounts.

Similarly, it is difficult to understand how emotional reserve can be maintained over any great length of time merely because it is fortified with "latent hostility." The hypothesis does not pass the test of introspection. For instance, we have experienced neighbors who trespassed upon those areas of our personal life that we have "reserved" as our own (or, better, our family's). They have penetrated our shell of reserve to the extent that we have become all too clearly aware of the antagonism beneath it. Sometimes the antagonism has been expressed or, at best, all too thinly disguised; sometimes the reserve prevailed and the antagonism was suppressed. What can account for the difference? Although we cannot be certain of all the reasons, we are sure of this much: when we had entered into an intimate social relationship with someone close to the presumptuous neighbor, let us say a husband or good friend, we suppressed the hostility; when we were not linked closely to the social circle of the neighbor, the hostility was not as effectively controlled. Thus, it appears that close social relationships may be as important for the *maintenance* of emotional reserve as they probably are for the *assertion* of individuality.

Such a line of argument is not entirely fair to Simmel, since it is directed partly at inferences suggested by his essay and partly at the actual propositions he submitted. Also, Simmel was fond of uncovering the apparently profound opposites in social life only to demonstrate their superficiality later on (as in his discussion of reserve and suppressed hostility), and often his enthusiasm in discovery supplanted his power of balanced judgment. Wolff has quoted one of Simmel's listeners:

> Simmel took "his students down an oblique pit into the mine. . . . Just about the time when . . . one felt he had reached a conclusion, he had a way of raising his right arm and, with three fingers of his hand, turning the imaginary object so as to exhibit still another facet." (1950: xvii)

Finally, in further defense of Simmel's seminal contributions, we should note that he devoted a great deal of intellectual effort to precisely the area of investigation that we have accused him of avoiding, viz., the function of membership in small groups or closed circles.[5] His essay on the metropolis, which has been forced to withstand the burden of our attack, does not begin to represent his sociological endeavors.

It was these other works—those in the area of formal sociology—that were first introduced to sociologists in this country largely through the efforts of Albion W. Small.[6] Later, Robert E. Park and Ernest W. Burgess (1921) made additional essays and fragments of essays available to American sociologists. But it was not until the mid 1920s that an attempt was made to give a comprehensive view of Simmel's theoretical system to interested Americans. In that period Nicholas J. Spykman (1925, 1926) attempted to weave Simmel's social psychology of metropolitan life into a "philosophy" of the city.

NICHOLAS J. SPYKMAN: A SOCIAL PHILOSOPHY OF THE CITY

Spykman's brief sketch of what was presumably to become at some later time a comprehensive sociological view of the city is essentially a polemical document, that is, "an illustration of sociological determinism ... offered as one of many possible alternatives to the economic determinism so prevalent in modern thought" (1925: 55). European and American culture is, for Spykman (who took his cue from Spengler), a city culture and, to that extent, "will a sociological interpretation of the city be a sociological interpretation of the whole of that Euro-American culture" (1926: 58).

According to Spykman, certain characteristics of the city appear to differentiate it from other structures as a unique phenomenon. The city, first of all, is peopled by multitudes. It is large. Second, from the point of view of the urban person, social contacts are enormously multiplied; and the most frequent social contacts that one makes are "based neither on a sharing of common values nor on a cooperation for a common purpose. They are formal in the most complete sense of

---

[5] See, for example, Simmel (1950: 105–17), "The Quantitative Determination of Group Divisions and of Certain Groups"; Simmel (1950: 118–44), "The Isolated Individual and the Dyad"; Simmel (1950: 145–69), "The Triad"; Simmel (1950: 307–76), "The Secret and the Secret Society"; Simmel (1950: 379–95), "Faithfulness and Gratitude."

[6] Small's translations of Simmel's essays in the early volumes of the *American Journal of Sociology* are listed in Simmel (1950: lviii–lix).

the term in that they are empty of content" (1926: 58). Spykman is suggesting here that most city contacts are patterned and ritualized. Third, people are brought together in the city not as members of communities but as members of interest groups or associations. This does not mean that primary groups are absent from the metropolitan milieu. Rather, and fourth, the nature of the primary group is altered, since, in the city, one rationally selects the primary groups in which one participates. "It is characteristic of the city environment that its primary group life, not excepting the family . . . [is based on] rational, purposive living in terms of individual interests, rather than the unconscious dissolution of the individuality in the life of the group, which is characteristic of small communities" (1926: 57). Fifth, the city is highly complex—"a social universe with a plurality of social standards and relative values" (1926: 58).

A summation of these characteristics is offered as a description of the city in sociological and psychological terms:

> The social behavior pattern of city life is characterized from the formal social point of view, that is, from the point of view of structure, by a numerical preponderance of large over small circles; secondary over primary groupings; associations over communities; transitory over permanent contacts. The social behavior pattern of the city is characterized from the formal individual point of view, that is, from the point of view of behavior process, by a numerical preponderance of unrestrained over restrained; individualistic over conformative; rational over emotional; formal, objective over personal, intimate; self-assertive over self-effacing behavior. (1926: 59)

Without questioning, for example, how the behavior process can be both unrestrained and rational, Spykman submitted that this aggregation of traits is a pattern—a kind of sociological mold—that leaves its impression upon every area of urban life. To demonstrate his point, he examines briefly the morality, politics, economics, art, and philosophy of the city.

In the city common morality is supplanted by unique, often ad hoc moral decisions, which in the extreme are reflected in the high incidence of urban crime. Since the urban milieu requires the self-assertion of its inhabitants, egoism takes its place as the prevailing rationale of the moral life. Like Simmel, Spykman recognized that equality and liberty had their historical roots in the rise of cities and stimulated the democratization of urban politics. The consequences for social control are presumably obvious, since democracy "means the substitution of restraint by laws of one's own making for restraint by autocratic decree" (1926: 61), or custom.[7] In urban culture, the role of law is no longer conservative, but constructive, as the increased emphasis upon political reform indicates. Moreover, "this belief in the possibilities of reconstruction by legislation is itself an expression of the unqualified faith in reason" (1926: 61).

Just as freedom, equality, and reason condition the political life of the city, they are also (with the apparent exception of equality) highly developed in the economy. Freedom of contract and competition are the cornerstones of the modern economy. The counterpart of freedom is individualism, and its growth is stimulated by the pervasive division of labor characteristic of urban life. In the money economy, consumers are forced constantly to calculate the value of goods in terms of the price. Their critical abilities are therefore, according to Spykman, recurrently sharpened, and their power of abstract reasoning is heightened. According to Spykman, intellectual life is also influenced by these same tendencies. Works of art, for example, have become abstracted aesthetic forms without objective meaning. They represent the self-expression of the artist unqualified by formal restraints. "Music without themes, novels without plots, verse without rhyme, and language without grammar—such is modern art" (1926: 63).

Although Spykman's sketch was admittedly an outline of a larger work in process, his absolutist assertions about city life have the principal effect of suggesting exceptions. His discussion of political affairs is devoid of reference to the political machine, which played such an important role in the governmental organization of urban life. One thinks also of the problem of political apathy so widespread in American cities.[8] This hardly reflects "the unqualified faith in reason" underlying political behavior. Nor does free competition, or competition at all, seem precisely to typify the operation of modern business.[9] In art can one think of the music of Roy Harris, Hindemith, or Stravinsky

---

[7] Spykman did not perceive the tension between unqualified liberty and equality as did Simmel.

[8] For example, in the Minneapolis mayoralty election on November 6, 1973, while 254,501 persons were registered to vote, only 127,178 actually showed up to vote—a total of 49.9 percent. In the St. Paul mayoralty election on April 30, 1974, 162,814 persons were registered to vote; only 65,318, or 40.2 percent actually voted. We discuss this issue in more detail in Chapter 6.

[9] Ably documented in Berle and Means (1933). With reference to small business, C. Wright Mills (1946) has discussed how the small entrepreneur has come to feel that competition is fine as long as *he* does not have to compete. For some recent critiques of the American economy, see Phillip Bronner et al. (1974).

without thematic imagery? Are Kafka's novels, or even those of Joyce, devoid of plot? Is there no rhyme in Auden? Can one distinguish "primitive" from contemporary plastic art in terms of the relatively more abstract quality of the latter? These are, of course, rhetorical questions which can only be answered negatively. It is for these reasons —the unrepresentativeness of his empirical observations—that Spykman presents, at best, a distorted picture of the city.

Moreover, in his discussion of primary groups in the metropolitan environment, Spykman seemed to be on the verge of extending Simmel's observations by pointing out new targets for sociological research. But his initial considerations were never followed through. He noted the altered nature of primary association in the city without inquiring into its functional significance. Indeed, he did not perceive its significance at all. Like most other urban sociologists, the frequency and visibility of secondary, formal, empty, social contacts impressed Spykman as relevant for the interpretation of urban life. Though such contacts obviously distinguish (at least in part) life in the city from life in the small town, an adequate understanding of city life would require more data than one can gather merely by observing the jostlings of anonymous individuals in crowded centers of urban dominance. Even in these situations, however, as our discussion in the following chapters will indicate, these "anonymous" individuals are devoting a great deal of attention to taking account of the activities of other strangers.

Spykman was not the only sociologist in this country who, under the direct influence of Georg Simmel, endeavored to set down his reflections concerning life in the city. Far more influential in this regard was Robert E. Park, a student of Georg Simmel, who had inherited his teacher's interest in the problems of modern urban society. And, as we shall see, Park's interest in urban society practically excluded the study of intimate association except as it characterized the interrelationships of the members of segregated groupings and adolescent gangs. Yet he did apprehend the importance of the altered primary group in urban social organization and offered propositions to explain its function.

ROBERT E. PARK: THE CITY—A SPACIAL PATTERN AND A MORAL ORDER

It can probably be said that Park had Simmel's gift of trenchant insight without his ability to present observations systematically. Consequently, it is difficult, if not impossible, to provide a precise and integrated résumé of Park's ideas about the city and, at the same time, to do justice to their scope and depth. Nor shall we review the entire range of his contributions in this chapter. Instead, we shall focus on those aspects of his writings that are of the greatest relevance for the development of a social psychology of city life. Park viewed the city as the central phenomenon of modern life; this theme recurs in all his writings. For our purposes in *Being Urban,* we shall examine in detail two of Park's (1925, 1926) better-known essays in which he exclusively addressed himself to problems of urban sociology.

Both essays proceed from the elementary observation that the city, or for that matter, any human community, is occupied by human beings who are distributed over, and confined within, a territory. In this sense, the city has a spacial aspect that the discipline of human ecology is peculiarly fitted to study. "All things ... which tend to bring about at once a greater mobility and a greater concentration of the urban population ... are primary factors in the ecological organization of the city" (1925: 2). More specifically, the subject matter of an ecological investigation of the city is constituted by the number, position, and mobility of city dwellers. And ecological investigation derives from the assumption that these elements are useful indices of such social events as the rates of crime, divorce, and mental illness. In addition, these units are quite amenable to measurement and, hence, lend themselves to quantitative description of social phenomena that are otherwise difficult to treat with statistical precision. For Park, an examination of the modern city's spacial features facilitates the determination of its sociology.

Since in Park's view the city is a product of natural forces rather than of preconceived design, its periphery never coincides with legislated boundaries. The outer limits of the modern city, as we noted in our treatment of Simmel, are constantly changing and are extended outward in a piecemeal fashion along established routes of transportation as land is privately acquired and developed. However, the bounds of the city are only the most general features of the spacial pattern that shapes its physical organization. "Everywhere the community tends to conform to some pattern, and this pattern invariably turns out to be a constellation of typical urban areas, all of which can be geographically located and spacially defined" (1926: 11). The area that first comes into focus is the city center.

As opposed to the ancient city which grew up around a fortress, the growth of the modern city represents the elaboration of a market. It is in the urban marketplace, the city's business center, that the concentration and mobility of the population is intensified. Here, each day, large masses of people are emptied by a complex transportation system to earn the money that they spend or to spend the money that they earn. At night they are transported out of the city center and are deposited in the various areas radiating out of, toward, and beyond the metropolitan periphery. The great density and mobility of the daytime population in the business center is expressed by the incredible height of buildings and the concentration of transportation terminals in the vicinity. Both these factors—density and mobility—capture the essence of the modern city. In fact, because of this, "the business center . . . is the city *par excellence*" (1926: 10). In emphasizing the importance of business-related activities, Park is here echoing a theme (as we noted in our treatment of the classical sociologist) that played a central role in the view of city life taken by urban sociologists.

According to Park, the growth of the city's business center is always viewed by the investor with an eye to profit, and characteristically there is much speculation in the land immediately surrounding the center. Underlying the acquisition of this land is the expectation that its value will automatically and inevitably increase as the business center is extended. As a result, the investors must hold on to their land only so long as they can make the greatest margin of profit. The maintenance and upkeep of this land does not affect the speculator's chances for realizing a profit on his investment. Consequently, the land surrounding the city center is in a state of physical deterioration. In brief, the business center of any modern city is always surrounded by a slum.

But the business center and the slum are only two of many distinctive areas that make up the spacial pattern of the city. The city is organized territorially as a constellation of diverse natural areas, and "natural areas are the habitats of natural groups" (1926: 11). These natural areas may be examined in terms of the extent to which they approach or depart from the typical characteristics of neighborhoods "where proximity and neighborly contact are the basis for the simplest and most elementary forms of association" (1925: 7). Urban neighborhoods manage to retain their identity over time only occasionally and, even then, with the greatest difficulty. The increasing proliferation of transportation and communication facilities in the city stimulates population mobility, and, thus, tends "to break up the tensions, interest, and sentiments which give neighborhoods their individual character" (1925: 8). Often, stabilizing influences strong enough to isolate neighborhoods from the rest of the city and its disruptive forces are exerted by race, language, and belief. Yet, such culturally isolated colonies as the ghetto, the black belt, or "little Sicily" cannot maintain a perpetual hold on their inhabitants. Processes of selection recruit the intelligent, specially skilled, and ambitious residents of the culturally segregated areas and deposit them in other less isolated places. As a consequence of the birth, persistence, and dissolution of neighborhoods and other natural areas, the growth of the city may be conceived as a kind of social metabolism. Like food being incorporated and digested in the body, persons here are assimilated to, and eliminated from, the independent organs comprising the urban physical pattern.

For Park, the principal selective mechanism operating to maintain the metabolism of the city is (and here he echoes Durkheim) the division of labor, which is a function of the size of the urban population. "The larger community will have the wider division of labor" (1925: 4). With the growth of the division of labor in the city, the population is at once differentiated and brought into close cooperation. A heightening of the community's intellectual life is also indicated, for specialization means essentially that rational methods are increasingly being applied to the solution of communal problems. Largely because they work, then, individuals are caught up in the metabolism of the city. Hence, a study of persons' mobility in space reveals much of the character of their social participation and of the social organization at large.

> The point is that change of occupation, personal success or failure —changes of economic and social status, in short—tend to be registered in changes of location. The physical or ecological organization of the community, in the large run, responds to and reflects the occupational and the cultural. Social selection and segregation, which create the natural groups, determine at the same time the natural areas of the city. (1926: 9)

As a matter of fact, "all we ordinarily conceive as social may be eventually construed and described in terms of space and changes of position of the individuals within the limits of a natural area" (1926: 12). From this, it might seem that the propositions of sociology will ultimately be reduced to a series of statistical equations, since the location and mobility of a population is eminently fitted for description in mathematical terms. This is not the case. Park accepted the interactionist view of society as existing in and through communication. Since communication is an interactive process that changes its constituent units as it is carried on, the sociologist is confronted with a subject matter that is infinitely variable and heterogeneous. This alone weakens the likelihood of a purely statistical study of urban society. The units—urban dwellers—are constantly changed by the processes in which they are involved. There is, therefore, a limit to the fruitful application of ecological method. "Geographical barriers and physical distance are significant for sociology only when and where they define the conditions under which communication and social life are maintained" (1926: 14). And these are not the only barriers that intrude into and qualify the communicative life. Social and psychic distance are also involved. The interrelations of physical, social, and psychic distance give form to the society in which we live by placing limitations upon our communication with one another.

> The world of communication and of "distance," in which we all seek to maintain some sort of privacy, personal dignity, and poise, is a dynamic world, and has an order and character quite its own. In this social and moral order the conception which each of us has of himself is limited by the conception which every other individual, in the same limited world of communication, has of himself, and of every other individual. He is able to maintain them, however, only to the extent that he can gain for himself the recognition of everyone else whose estimate seems important; that is to say, the estimate of everyone else who is in his set, or in his society. (1926: 17)[10]

Such a statement implies, of course, that the crucial struggles for status are waged in face-to-face communication with others. The arena of such a struggle can only be the small circle, and the small circle is progressively disappearing from urban society, according to Park. "The growth of cities has been accompanied by the substitution of indirect, 'secondary,' for direct face-to-face, 'primary' relations in the associations of individuals in the community" (1925: 23). The same forces that destroy the neighborhood in the urban community also destroy other primary groupings. Everything that increases mobility—the growth of transportation and communication systems—has an adverse effect upon primary group life. Increases in literacy and education

---

10 Note the anticipation of the epoch of high mass-distribution by Max Weber (1958: 180–95).

make the newspaper replace conversation. The pursuit of interests supplants behavior motivated by sentiment. In this respect, "money is the cardinal device by which values have become rationalized and sentiments have been replaced by interests" (1925: 16). Actually the entire basis of social solidarity in the economic order has been changed: there remains "in the industrial organization as a whole a certain sort of social solidarity, but a solidarity based, not on sentiment and habit, but on community of interests" (1925: 15–16). According to Park, as a result of this ascendancy of secondary relations and the increased importance of interests in modern urban conduct, the overall organization of the city is characterized by a precarious equilibrium that can be maintained only by a process of continuous adjustment. Urban life progresses from crisis to crisis, and the "psychological moment" replaces the sixty-second minute as a measure of time. The crisis of the city may be counted on the front pages of the daily newspapers and in the stock exchanges. Indeed, the stock exchange is in a perpetual state of crisis so that the behavior of its members is more akin to the behavior of crowds than to the behavior of institutionalized personnel. For Park less dramatically, but nonetheless steadily, the deterioration of primary group life is visible in the readjustments of the family, the church, the school, and the neighborhood. "It is probably the breaking down of local attachments and the weakening of the restraints and inhibitions of the primary group, under the influence of the urban environment, which are largely responsible for the increase of vice and crime in great cities" (1925: 25). This proposition exemplifies nicely the way in which dichotomous thinking has blinded urban sociologists to the function of the primary group in contemporary society. Park knew full well and made explicit in other essays the primary group nature of crime and delinquency. What he meant (but did not say) was that *different* and often unconventional primary groupings had been substituted for the *conventional* ones. He states this brilliantly in his discussion of the political machine, but, even there, primary relationships are viewed (when they are perceived in the context of the city) as rural survivals.

For Park, the entire basis of social control is altered by the rise of cities. He notes (1925: 31) that three fundamental changes are evident:

1. The substitution of positive law for custom, and the extension of municipal control to activities that were formerly left to individual initiative and discretion.
2. The disposition of judges in municipal and criminal courts to as-

sume administrative functions so that the administration of the criminal law ceases to be a mere application of the social ritual and becomes an application of rational and technical methods, requiring expert knowledge or advice, in order to restore the individual to society and repair the injury.

3. Changes and divergencies in the mores among the different isolated and segregated groups in the city.

Perhaps no area of urban life has undergone more drastic readjustment than that of government. The kind of government that had its origin in the town meetings of the early American colonists has no place in the large city. In its stead, two alternatives have emerged: the political machine and the "good government" organizations.

> The political machine is, in fact, an attempt to maintain, inside the formal administrative organization of the city, the control of a primary group.... The relations between the boss and his ward captain seem to be precisely that, of personal loyalty on one side and personal protection on the other.... The virtues which such an organization calls out are the old tribal ones of fidelity, loyalty, and devotion to the interests of the chief and the clan. The people within the organization, their friends and supporters, continue a "we" group, while the rest of the city is merely the outer world, which is not quite alive and not quite human in the sense in which the members of the "we" group are. We have here something approaching the conditions of primitive society. (1925: 35–36)

As over against the political machine, the "good government" organizations are essentially secondary groups rationally oriented to political life in the interest of reform. The two agencies vie with one another for the vote of the electorate.[11]

---

[11] Here Park supplied excellent research leads which were never pursued, so far as we can ascertain, by his students. He established a typical tension in urban life: the struggle between the primary group and the secondary group for the allegiance of the individual. In the political sphere, at least, it seems apparent where the balance rests. It is with the political machine—the primary group. Lincoln Steffens realized this almost fifty years ago, just as the Kefauver Committee rediscovered it in the fifties, and the Watergate Committee discovered it in the mid-seventies. As a precinct captain told one of us in Chicago in 1949: "If you're ever in trouble, don't bother your family. Come in and see me first. We'll fix it up." The primary nature of the political machine has stood the test of time and has prevailed in its struggle with reform. All three of the cases mentioned indicate that there still remains in contemporary politics a strong element of primary group affiliation. The consequences of this fact for urban sociology and social psychology have been, we believe, remarkably overlooked. For a very recent study of this phenomenon see Mike Royko (1971).

The ecological and sociological characteristics of the city are not without their social psychological implications. Social distance and the weakening of primary restraints permit a great diversity of individual expression. Whereas the small community is always peopled by one or two eccentrics, the city consists of a world of "characters" who can always find one another and establish themselves in their own "moral regions." "Because of the opportunity it offers, particularly to the exceptional and abnormal types of man, a great city tends to spread out and lay bare to the public view in a massive manner all the human characters and traits which are ordinarily obscured and suppressed in smaller communities" (1925: 45–46).

With magnificent insight, then, but without logical rigor, Park established a number of propositions describing and explaining city life that considerably broadened the area of theory and research in urban sociology. Implicit in his contributions to the study of the city was a frame of reference for the study of any sociological problem. This, however, was not made explicit until one of his students, Louis Wirth, formulated it for application to the study of urbanism. Park had demonstrated that the city as an empirical event could be investigated in ecological, social-organizational, and/or social psychological perspective. Wirth (1939) clarified these perspectives, commented upon their interdependence, and showed their relevance for the formulation of a systematic theory of urbanism.[12]

LOUIS WIRTH: URBANISM AS A WAY OF LIFE

Wirth's work marks the culmination of what we have been referring to as the classical view of urban sociology. Impressed with the central significance of the city for any interpretation of contemporary civilization, Wirth noted the inadequacy of existing definitions of the city for any disciplined exploration into the nature of urbanism. In Wirth's view, the difficulties of formulating an unambiguous sociological definition of the city are insurmountable, since any particular city seen in sociological context is only more or less urban. Because the past always overlaps with the present, there is no city without rural characteristics.

---

[12] Subsequent to the appearance of Wirth's essay, a publication of Park's (1940) appeared, which also made explicit his formerly implicit frame of reference. Even this attempt, however, was characterized by the shifting varieties of abstraction (for example, the mixture of concrete and abstract categories in a single typology) that abound in Park's work.

To a greater or lesser degree . . . our social life bears the imprint of an earlier folk society, the characteristic modes of settlement of which were the farm, the manor, and the village. This historic influence is reinforced by the circumstance that the population of the city itself is in large measure recruited from the countryside, where a mode of life reminiscent of this earlier form of existence persists. Hence we should not expect to find abrupt and discontinuous variation between urban and rural types of personality. The city and the country may be regarded as two poles in reference to one or the other of which all human settlements tend to arrange themselves. In viewing urban-industrial and rural-folk society as ideal types of communities, we may obtain a perspective for the analysis of the basic models of human association as they appear in contemporary civilization. (1938: 3)

The presence or absence of rural characteristics, in what we are accustomed to refer to as cities, is contingent upon many variables, among which would be included the unique history of the city, its function, the manner in which its population is recruited, and/or the character of the surrounding region. Consequently, census definitions of the city at the time (that is, as any community with a population of 2500 or greater) cannot be employed fruitfully in sociological investigation. A census definition can never guarantee that the institutional structure of communities whose population is less than 2500 is predominately rural-folk. Nor can political boundaries define a city, since it is a sociological truism that the legislated limits of a community never coincide with its natural limits. Other definitions that depend upon single criteria like population density, occupational distributions, physical facilities, and various institutional features also fail to provide the sociologist with an adequate definition of the city. "A sociologically significant definition of the city seeks to select those elements of urbanism which mark it as a distinctive mode of human group life" (1938: 4). It is precisely this that existing definitions have not sought to do.[13]

Accordingly, Wirth established essentially five criteria that a sociological definition of the city must satisfy:

1. Urbanism must be defined as a mode of life.
2. A serviceable definition of urbanism must be generic and not par-

---

[13] For an incisive recent treatment of this issue, see John Gulick (1973).

ticular; that is; the mode of life referred to must not arise out of specific locally or historically conditioned cultural influences.

3. The definition should denote the essential characteristics that cities in our culture have in common. Conversely, the definition should not be so detailed as to include all the characteristics that our cities have in common. Rather, the more significant features of cities, viz., size, density, and differences in the functional type of cities must be included in the definition.

4. (Implicit) The characteristics of cities included in the definition should be as few in number as seems feasible for the deduction of significant sociological propositions.

5. The definition should lend itself to the discovery of significant variations among cities.[14]

We may note that these five criteria suffer from at least two apparent shortcomings. First, although it has been specifically stated that the definition of urbanism must be generic, the extension of the desired definition has been confined to the essential aspects of cities in Western culture (if that is what is meant by "our" culture). This is undoubtedly a result of the fact that, at the time of Wirth's writing, sociological information about cities in other cultures may have been sparse. Second, there are no criteria in Wirth's essay for distinguishing the essential from the nonessential characteristics of cities. Wirth perceived that "some justification may be in order for the choice of the principal terms comprising our definition of the city" (1938: 9); but, in the brief discussion that follows in his essay, no alternative characteristics are considered.

Despite these inadequacies, Wirth has advanced a definition of the city that conforms to the criteria he has established and that is demonstrated to be useful for extending and integrating our sociological knowledge of city life. "For sociological purposes a city may be defined as a relatively large, dense, and permanent settlement of socially heterogeneous individuals" (1938: 8).

If it is postulated that "the larger, the more densely populated and the more heterogeneous a community, the more accentuated the characteristics associated with urbanism will be" (1938: 9), a series of propositions may be deduced about the urban mode of life as it is condi-

---

[14] These are paraphrased and summarized from Wirth (1938: 4–8).

tioned by the interrelated influences of the three selected variables.[15] Each of the three variables—size, density, and social heterogeneity of the population aggregate—is treated separately by Wirth in the effort to distinguish the consequences for social life under circumstances characterized by the relatively high quantitative value of the variables concerned. It becomes at once apparent, however, that the variables are so interrelated that most of the deduced consequences flow not just from any single factor, but from the combined influence of the three. Therefore, our account of Wirth's essay will enumerate only the major consequences discerned in his inquiry rather than discuss the relations between such consequences and each separate variable.

Eight major effects upon human association and social life may be expected to occur in communities that are typically large, and whose population is dense and socially heterogeneous. First, large numbers ordinarily result in an *increase of individual variation* in the population aggregate. This tendency is reinforced under conditions of great density. We may note here that Wirth's conception is close to that of Durkheim. Wirth writes that "an increase in numbers when an area is held constant (i.e., an increase in density) tends to produce differentiation and specialization" (1938: 14). Since social heterogeneity is directly stimulated by density, individual variation would be expected to increase.

Second, large numbers contribute to the *segregation* of population groupings according to various commonly held characteristics such as color, ethnic heritage, economic and social status, or tastes and preferences. This tendency is even more pronounced under conditions of density where physical proximity is socially reflected as distance. "The city consequently tends to resemble a mosaic of social worlds in which the transition from one to the other is abrupt" (1938: 15). Just as the city's population is broken up into distinct natural groupings, so is the personality of the urban dweller divided into compartments.

A third effect of urban conditions is the *segmentalization of personal life.*

---

15 In this respect it is important to note that only three variables were extracted from the definitions of the city as a basis for the deduction of propositions. The variable of *permanence* is given no further role in Wirth's discussion. The point is raised here for two reasons: (1) permanence is undoubtedly as much a variable as size, density, or social heterogeneity of the population aggregate and, as such, deserves some consideration in the essay; and (2) it may be that what we have often regarded as typical urban phenomena (the high crime rate, the low birth rate, and so on) decline as cities become older or "more permanent."

The multiplication of persons in a state of interaction under conditions which make their contact as full personalities impossible produces that segmentalization of human relationships which has sometimes been seized upon by students of the mental life of cities as an explanation for the "schizoid" character of urban personality. This is not to say that the urban inhabitants have fewer acquaintances than rural inhabitants, for the reverse may actually be true; it means rather that in relation to the number of people whom they see and with whom they rub elbows in the course of daily life, they know a smaller proportion and of these they have less intensive knowledge. (1938: 12)

This segmentalization of personal experience is exacerbated by the heterogeneous character of the urban population, for the city dweller is inevitably caught up in varied and sundry social groups.

No single group has the undivided allegiance of the individual. The groups with which he is affiliated do not lend themselves readily to a single hierarchical arrangement. By virtue of his different interests arising out of different aspects of social life, the individual acquires membership in widely divergent groups, each of which functions only with reference to a single segment of his personality. Nor do these groups easily permit of a concentric arrangement so that the narrower ones fall within the circumference of the more inclusive ones, as is more likely to be the case in the rural community or in primitive societies. Rather the groups with which the person typically is affiliated are tangential to each other or intersect in a highly variable fashion. (1938: 16)

The characteristic apathy of many urban dwellers is quite probably linked to the fact that each must compartmentalize one's role-playing to carry on an effective urban existence. It is difficult for the person whose loyalty is claimed by diverse interest groups to decide what is in one's own "best interest," or even to make major decisions at all. The imposition of diverse claims upon individuals renders it difficult for them to see their place in a total scheme of things and frequently results in their disinvolvement from a large segment of the social world.

A fourth effect of urbanism may be termed the *depersonalization of human association*. Wirth has referred to Weber to explain the way in which size and density bring about depersonalization: "Large numbers of inhabitants and density of settlement," he writes, "mean that the personal mutual acquaintanceship between the inhabitants which ordinarily inheres in a neighborhood is lacking" (1938: 11). And this observation is valid despite the fact that the everyday contacts of city life are face-to-face contacts.

> The contacts of the city may indeed be face to face, but they are nevertheless impersonal, superficial, transitory, and segmental. The reserve, the indifference, and the blasé outlook which urbanites manifest in their relationships may thus be regarded as devices for immunizing themselves against the personal claims and expectations of others. (1938: 12)

There is a certain similarity between some of the responses of urban dwellers to the depersonalization of their relationships with others and what might be termed a fifth effect of urban conditions, viz., *sophistication and rationality*. Wirth has noted in this regard that "the superficiality, the anonymity, and the transitory character of urban social relations make intelligible also, the sophistication and the rationality generally ascribed to by city-dwellers" (1938: 12). Not only are sophistication and rationality associated with the large numbers and great density of the typically urban population, but, like the depersonalization of social experience, may also be traced to the socially heterogeneous character of the city. Life in the city is a swiftly mobile life that persistently exposes the urbanite to sharp social contrast and other varied stimuli. Thus, one's awareness of the shifting unstable character of the world at large is enhanced. "This fact helps to account, too, for the sophistication and cosmopolitanism of the urbanite" (1938: 16). Both the depersonalization of social life and enhanced rationality in the city may be interpreted as the subjective reflection of the dominance of secondary groups over primary groups in the urban situation.

It follows that a sixth consequence of the rise of urbanism in a community is *the substitution of formal for informal social controls*. "Under ... urban ... circumstances competition and formal control mechanisms furnish the substitutes for the bonds of solidarity that are relied upon to hold a folk society together" (1938: 11). The large size of the urban population means that the residents rely on representatives rather than on themselves in the political process.

Seventh, Wirth perceived the complexity of social stratification in the city in a manner that has not been followed up by students of stratification but that we shall develop in this book. He pointed out that social stratification in the city is not simply *hierarchical* but also *multidimensional* in nature. Yet he did not observe the importance of nonverbal symbolism in the stratification of urbanites, nor did he detect the "crazy rhythm" of shifting status alignments.

Finally, Wirth noted the enhanced probability of collective behavior in the urban environment. In cities, crowds can materialize from dense anonymity. Results may be tragic, as in the case of Watts in Los Angeles, or merely chaotic, as in the case of crowd behavior in the stock exchange on Wall Street.

These eight consequences of the characteristic size, density, and heterogeneity of urban populations do not exhaust the number set down by Wirth in his essay. Other effects of the city were considered. Some of these have been deliberately omitted from this exposition because they stem from conditions that are found only in modern cities beset by the unique impact of industrial capitalism. In omitting these items, Wirth's own stipulation has been regarded:

> It is particularly important to call attention to the danger of confusing urbanism with industrialism and modern capitalism. The rise of cities in the modern world is undoubtedly not independent of the emergence of modern power-driven machine technology, mass production and capitalistic enterprise. But different as the cities of earlier epochs may have been by virtue of their development in a preindustrial and precapitalistic order from the great cities of today, they were, nevertheless, cities. (1938: 7–8)

CONCLUSION

When the contributions of Park, Simmel, Spykman, and Wirth are assessed to determine whether some consensus upon the common features of modern cities may be revealed, many areas of agreement are at once forthcoming. Each of the four writers agrees, in the first place, that the city is large. No "city" may be said to exist without a large population. Moreover, the city must occupy a relatively large space. Its functions are extended over a large territory far exceeding that defined by its legislated limits, in fact, the exact limits of the city are difficult, if not impossible, to ascertain. As Park put it, they are the product of natural forces. Furthermore, they are in a perpetual state of flux. City boundaries vary with changes in the nature and range of the city's functions; and these variations in function, it may be added, can occur within relatively minute intervals of time. The functions of the city are altered frequently if only by virtue of the fact that the day-to-day activities of its population are distributed differentially over a twenty-four hour period. Despite such obstacles to the precise demarcation of the city's spacial extent, it is clear that the city is large in a physical sense. At least it is typically larger than its legislators have anticipated.

There is complete accord among the sociologists reviewed here that the economic organization of the city is typified by a highly developed and pervasive division of labor. It is this that can explain in structural terms Wirth's choice of social heterogeneity as a criterion for distinguishing the city from other population aggregates. For instance, Park has observed that the specialization of occupations, signifying the development of the division of labor, is often marked by the tendency for each occupation to take on the aspect of a profession in the sense of developing a distinctive ethic. Ethnic differences do not necessarily have to be introduced into the equation to justify Wirth's depiction of the city as a mosaic of social worlds or Park's designation of the city as a composite of natural areas peopled by natural groups with divergent mores. The social heterogeneity of the city can be explained in terms of the division of labor and its ideological ramifications. It is, of course, also manifested in ethnic differences and other differences originating from the diverse ways in which urban populations are recruited. This agreement upon the typical social differentiation of the population of cities supports the sociologists considered here in their further assertion that the city is a locus of contrasting social stimuli. The number, diversity, and transitoriness of urban relationships characteristic of life in the complex environment of the city call out in the urban dweller the typical responses of sophistication and the blasé attitude that distinguish his demeanor from that of individuals living in nonurban milieus. For Park, the clash of stimuli involved in urban relationships is aggravated by the frequent and sudden contact that the mobile urbanite has with many socially distinct groupings. Seen either from the point of view of social organization or of the individual person, then, the city, as a consequence of the division of labor, is complex.

Economic institutions are important for distinguishing urban life because they underlie occupational specialization. In addition, money and its exchange for goods and services, all writers agree, capture in symbolic fashion an important aspect of urbanism. When Park, for example, submitted that the business center is the city *par excellence,* he was merely demonstrating the reversibility of Simmel's contention that the city was the seat of the money economy. The importance of the money economy for depicting the city as a type-phenomenon inheres, as Wirth has said, in the fact that the use of money introduces a new basis of relationship into human association.

> The development of large cities, at least in the modern age, was largely dependent upon the concentrative force of steam. The rise of the factory system made possible mass production for an impersonal market. The fullest exploitation of the possibilities of the division of labor and mass production, however, is possible only with standardization of processes and products. A money economy goes hand in hand with such a system of production. Progressively as cities have developed upon a background of this system of production, the pecuniary nexus which implies the purchasibility of services and things has displaced personal relations as the basis of association. (1938: 17)

Spykman, Park, and Simmel also point to the importance of money exchange for stimulating abstract reasoning among the members of the urban population.

Both Spykman and Park regarded political reform as a distinctive emergent of modern urban life. Spykman, however, looked upon reform as a vehicle that would unleash reason and give it free play in the urban political areas. Park, not quite so optimistic, perceived reform and the political machine as contending forces that had not yet become reconciled.

That the sociologists reviewed above agree upon these distinctive institutional features of city life signals another (and perhaps the most important) area of agreement. This can be found in their discussion of the altered nature of social organization and social control that urban conditions induce. Each writer observed that the opportunity for close social contact is lessened in the city. Despite the fact that social contacts increase in number with increasing urbanization, they are devoid of intimate contact. In their view, the small social circle is disappearing from urban society as secondary relations are substituted for primary relations in every area of life. Neighborhoods become progressively more disorganized. The community is being replaced by associations or interest groups. The solidarity of the family and the church is broken up by the rise of cities. Changes such as these in the nature of social relationships calls forth typical changes in the area of social control. In general, formal controls come more and more to replace the informal control mechanisms. According to these writers, the decreasing significance of the primary group in urban social organization has taken its toll in a vast weakening of moral consensus and has necessitated a reliance upon law to succeed custom as the prime regulating agency of urban life.

It is in observations like these that the influence of Maine, Tönnies, and Durkheim is most readily apprehended. Contract, *Gesellschaft*, and organic solidarity have become identified with urbanism. In the case of Spykman and Park, however, some exceptions to the general rule that secondary relations were destroying the opportunities for establishing primary relations in the city were noted. Spykman, for example, perceived that the nature of primary association is altered under conditions of urbanism in that individuals tend more and more to calculate their membership in intimate groupings.

One dimension of the change in the character of the primary group under the impact of urbanization is to be found in the preponderance of *unconventional* over *conventional* primary groups in certain regions of the city. Many examples of these unconventional groupings, together with a consideration of their importance for the larger social order, are to be found in existing studies of gangs and the criminal underworld. Perhaps another dimension can be found in the implications of Park's discussion of the political machine. Here the notion is suggested that the contexts within which primary relationships are carried on have changed. Specifically, Park's observations indicate that, whereas primary groupings were formerly carried on in informal community organizations and comprised an integral part of those organizations, as urbanization progresses they come more and more to be contained in formal organizational or associational contexts. A fruitful hypothesis to pursue in this area would assert that every formal social structure contains informally patterned relationships of varying degrees of intimacy that permit the exercise of primary controls to regulate the collective conduct of the larger formal organization. But, to liken such informal relationships, as Park has done, to primitive tribal structures or to refer to them as clanlike residues of a bygone age seems indeed farfetched. Or to say that a city is less a city because of this, as Wirth has implied, seems only to impede our understanding of urban life.

Park has somewhere said that the politician in the city is a professional neighbor, and, we should add, this does not necessarily make him any less a neighbor. Another dimension of the altered nature of the primary group might be located precisely in the exchange of intimacy and the building of primary, or at least intimate, social relationships as professional investments that characterize the politician's role and other professional roles in the city. Intimacy is also built up in the city on the expectation of a money return. Relationships established in such specifically urban institutions as the archaic taxi dance hall or the contemporary massage parlor, for example, are purchased, but this does not necessarily mean that they are any the less intimate. History and literature abound with instances of prostitutes who have fallen in love with, and had their love reciprocated by, clients. The professional lover is not *necessarily* any the less a lover—even in the urban society. Studies of the nature and function of such relationships as those mentioned here have been generally neglected by sociologists largely because urban theory has not conceptualized them in terms of any adequate frame of reference.

We have tried to demonstrate in this chapter how the theoretical origins of existing propositions that purport to describe and explain urban life have affected the contributions of specialists in urban sociology. The conceptual distinctions of Maine, Tönnies, and Durkheim between status and contract, *Gemeinschaft* and *Gesellschaft,* and mechanical and organic solidarity, respectively, have been interpreted often as antithetical polar dichotomies in which one pole is representative of rural life and the other of urban life. Such an interpretation seems to apply correctly only to the conceptual scheme of Maine; it must be qualified when applied to the theoretical systems of Tönnies and Durkheim, both of whom viewed the contrasting concepts that they formulated as having a place in the explanation of each other.

The contributions of Simmel, Spykman, Park, and Wirth were discussed as instances of the kind of influence that has been exerted by the more generalized theories of social organization proposed by Maine, Tönnies, and Durkheim. Each of these specialized theoretical contributions to urban sociology was characterized by a view of urban life that singled out its typical polar opposition to rural life. Consequently, the significance of primary or close personal relations for an adequate understanding of urbanism was neglected, glossed over, or obfuscated. Merely because primary relations take on different forms in the context of the city, or because they are apparently outnumbered by more easily identifiable secondary relations, does not necessarily mean that they have decreased in importance or that they have lost their significance. As we shall indicate in the following chapters, the accumulating

evidence for the existence of communal ties within urban settings—
which was gathered by a later generation of sociologists—necessitates a
new paradigm for the study of urban social relations.

REFERENCES

Berle, Adolphe A., and Gardner C. Means. *The Modern Corporation.* New
York: Macmillan Company. 1933.

Bronner, Phillip, Robert Borosage, and Bethany Weidner (eds.). *Exploring
Contradictions: Political Economy in the Corporate State.* New York:
David McKay Co., Inc., 1974.

Cressey, Paul G. *The Taxi Dance Hall.* Chicago: University of Chicago Press,
1932.

Durkheim, Emile. *The Division of Labor in Society.* Translated by George
Simpson. Glencoe, Ill.: The Free Press, 1947.

Fromm, Erich. *Escape from Freedom.* New York: Farrar and Rinehart, 1941.

Gulick, John. "Urban Anthropology." Pp. 979–1031 in John J. Honigmann
(ed.), *Handbook of Social and Cultural Anthropology.* Chicago: Rand
McNally and Company, 1973.

Landesco, John. *Organized Crime in Chicago.* Chicago: Chicago, Illinois, Association for Criminal Justice, 1929.

Mills, C. Wright. "The Competitive Personality." *Partisan Review,* 13 (September–October 1946): 433–36.

Mills, C. Wright. "The Professional Ideology of Social Pathologists." *American Journal of Sociology,* 49 (September 1943): 165–80.

Park, Robert E. "The City: Suggestions for the Investigation of Human Behavior in the Urban Environment." Pp. 1–46 in Robert E. Park, Ernest
W. Burgess, and Roderick D. McKenzie, *The City.* Chicago: University
of Chicago Press, 1925.

Park, Robert E. "Physics and Society." *Canadian Journal of Economics and
Political Science.* 6 (May 1940): 135–52.

Park, Robert E. "The Urban Community as a Spacial Pattern and a Moral
Order." Pp. 3–18 in Ernest W. Burgess (ed.), *The Urban Community.*
Chicago: University of Chicago Press, 1926.

Park, Robert E., and Ernest W. Burgess. *Introduction to the Science of Sociology.* Chicago: University of Chicago Press, 1921.

Riesman, David. *The Lonely Crowd.* New Haven: Yale University Press, 1950.

Royko, Mike. *Boss: Richard J. Daley of Chicago.* New York: New American
Library, 1971.

Simmel, Georg. "The Metropolis and Mental Life." Pp. 409–24 in Kurt E.
Wolff (ed.), *The Sociology of Georg Simmel.* Glencoe, Ill.: The Free
Press, 1950.

Simmel, Georg. *The Sociology of Georg Simmel.* Translated and edited by
Kurt E. Wolff. Glencoe: Ill.: The Free Press, 1950.

Spykman, Nicholas J. "A Social Philosophy of the City." Pp. 55–66 in Ernest W. Burgess (ed.), *The Urban Community*. Chicago: University of Chicago Press, 1926.

Spykman, Nicholas J. *The Social Theory of Georg Simmel*. Chicago: University of Chicago Press, 1925.

Sullivan, Harry Stack. "Psychiatry: Introduction to the Study of Interpersonal Relations." Pp. 98–121 in Patrick Mullahy (ed.), *A Study of Interpersonal Relations*. New York: Hermitage Press, 1949.

Thrasher, Frederick M. *The Gang: A Study of 1313 Gangs in Chicago*. Chicago: University of Chicago Press, 1928.

Tönnies, Ferdinand. *Fundamental Concepts of Sociology*. Translated and supplemented by Charles F. Loomis. New York: American Book Company, 1940.

Weber, Max. "Class, Status, Party." Pp. 180–96 in Hans H. Gerth and C. Wright Mills (trans. and ed.), *From Max Weber*. New York: Oxford University Press, Galaxy Book, 1958.

Wirth, Louis. "Urbanism as a Way of Life." *American Journal of Sociology*, 44 (July 1938): 1–24.

Part Two

Experiencing
City Life

3

The Rediscovery
of Community

A major preoccupation of sociological work has been to question, to examine critically, and often to take issue with commonly held ideologies, images, beliefs, and stereotypes. Some, indeed, have suggested that sociology is an inherently revolutionary discipline, given its frequent concern with testing the validity of long-standing "truisms." Peter Berger underscores this aspect of the sociological consciousness. Regarding what he calls the "debunking" motif of sociological analysis, he writes:

> The sociological frame of reference, with its built-in procedure of looking for levels of reality other than those given in the official interpretations of society, carries with it a logical imperative to unmask the pretensions and the propaganda by which men cloak their actions with one another. (1963: 38)

Among other things, sociologists have questioned long-standing beliefs about the poor, have demonstrated the faulty character of racial stereotypes, have uncovered the "informal" aspects of bureaucratic structures, and have exposed the latent functions of a variety of deviant behaviors. Sociologists have succeeded in showing that shorthand characterizations of the social world frequently oversimplify its complexity. While generalizations about social life help to make more intelligible our individual and collective experiences, such generalizations are, by definition, based upon only selected aspects of social reality. Therefore, a continuing task of the sociological enterprise must be to uncover those features of social life that lie beneath the veneer of accepted knowledge about the world. In some instances we shall come to see the necessity of thoroughly rejecting certain images; in other cases our data will dictate that these images be specified and clarified.

To this general characterization of the goal of sociological research we must add a specification that carries us into the subject matter of this chapter. It is that scientific knowledge accepted as truth when produced may later be found wanting. Indeed, Thomas Kuhn (1967) argues in his book *The Structure of Scientific Revolutions* that scientific progress is founded on demonstrating the inadequacy of prior explanation. There exists, in other words, the risk that our scientific explanations may be partial, incomplete, or wholly illusory. Still more to the point, sociologists, as do all scientists, create images of the social world that are incorrect, misleading, or in need of revision in the face of historical process. Ordinarily these faulty images acquire, largely through continued use, an unquestioned legitimacy as part of a discipline's accepted body of knowledge. Scientists may fail to question unremittingly the continuing truth value of certain of their key ideas. In this chapter we seek to show that the sociological image of the city described earlier in this book represents one such case of a long-standing conceptual misunderstanding.

Recall that in Chapters 1 and 2 we worked to trace out the theoretical and empirical roots of much urban sociology. We documented a tradition that pictures the progressive disappearance of warm, sustaining community social relations. It is a tradition that paints an unceasingly negative picture of life in urbanized areas. Durkheim, for example, saw the industrial centers, the prototype of the organically integrated society, as "epitomizing the social dust heap" (Greer, 1962: 14). Max Weber (1958) in his book *The City* pointed out that the large number of inhabitants and population density (in cities) combine to increase the likelihood of impersonal, anonymous relations. Georg Simmel (1950) saw the "psychic life" of the urban dweller threatened by the overwhelming tempo of his everyday existence.

The theoretical images provided by these writers were given credence in the empirical work of most early American sociologists. Following the tenor of their European predecessors, many sociologists at the University of Chicago saw the growth of cities typified by the substitution of indirect and secondary for direct face-to-face, primary relations. The observations of Robert Park and his students bolstered the belief that the sources of social control represented by the family, the neighborhood, and the local community were largely undermined by the demands of a rational urban existence. In all this writing, the city was on trial. The charge was to be found in the nineteenth-century theoretical conceptions of the city and the overwhelmingly damaging evidence in the observations of the city by Park and others. The verdict seemed nearly a unanimous one: that the city had, indeed, killed community.

There must, of course, be some truth to this sociologically created image. Were it glaringly incorrect and thoroughly contrary to our commonsense experience of city life, it would have been quickly rejected. We prefer to say that such a view has a relative validity. No one can doubt that the city is different in important respects from the small town. The city *is* "a relatively large, dense and permanent settlement of socially heterogeneous individuals" (Wirth, 1938). We maintain, however, that too rigorous a comparison of urban and small-town life has led to an incomplete picture of urban social relations.

The tendency to see the two types of social organization (small town and city or *Gemeinschaft* and *Gesellschaft*) as opposites, as examples of what the other is not, badly obscures elements of both. Forms of social organization are not static, but are in a continual state of process. In looking at urban life, then, the focus ought not to be on whether various features of human relations are existent or nonexistent in some absolute sense, but instead on how they may have been, or are in the process of being, modified and transformed. We should not ask whether primary relations exist in cities just as they do in small towns. The question is a comforting one in that it yields a clear, decisive answer—

certainly they do not! At the same time the question is misleading. It does not cause us, or allow us, to understand how primary relations in cities have assumed new forms.

Strong social bonds and a distinctively integrated group life *do* exist among urbanites. They are simply not quite so obvious, not quite so easy to observe. They must be uncovered, discovered. Our argument in the pages to follow centers on the idea that we must reconceptualize our long-held sociological beliefs about the nature of urban community. We shall work to show that "a lively primary group life survives in the urban area, and primary controls are effective over wide segments of the population. The alleged anonymity, depersonalization, and rootlessness of city life may be the exception rather than the rule" (Wilensky, 1966: 136). As a first step in establishing the validity of this position, we must consider the use made by social scientists of the idea of community.

THE CONCEPT OF COMMUNITY

The concept of community has been a troublesome one in sociology. It has come to be applied to such a wide diversity of situations, settings, and forms of group life that it has lost much of its distinctiveness as an analytical tool for investigation. We speak, for example, of rural communities, urban communities, neighborhood communities, and communities of scholars. We have come to use the term in its most generic form to describe any collectivity of persons sharing values, ideas, or life styles in common. The difficulties of its usage were particularly highlighted in a 1955 article by the sociologist George Hillery, who documents ninety-four separate definitions offered by sociologists for the concept of community. Perhaps we should not find such disagreement surprising, since sociologists work from a number of different theoretical perspectives and adopt (if even unwittingly) the definition that is most congenial to their theoretical outlook (see Lodahl and Gordon, 1972). We submit, however, that despite this general confusion, an analysis of some of the most widely accepted definitions of community reveals common themes.

Roland Warren (1972: 9) has, for example, considered community to be "that combination of social units and systems which perform the major social functions having locality relevance." Warren goes on to specify the social functions that he has in mind. He suggests that a community must function to produce and to distribute the goods and services necessary for the maintenance of a particular locality. A community must, as well, generate *social control* mechanisms to insure a predictable behavioral order. Third, a community must provide *institutional sources for social participation* by its members (churches, schools, businesses, recreational facilities, and the like). Finally, a community must be a context in which individuals find the *mutual support provided by a primary social relationship.*

Other writers put greatest emphasis on one or another specific criterion. Talcott Parsons (1959), whose life's work has been to understand the interdependence between the various units of a society, emphasizes the nature of *social systems* shared by a population of persons inhabiting a common geographical location. Marvin Sussman (1959) puts greatest stress on the structure of community interactions allowing persons to meet individual needs and resolve collective group problems. There is, as well, a long history of research on largely nonurban communities that has become part of the tradition of American sociology. In a series of community case studies (Lynd, 1929; 1937; Warner and Lunt, 1941; West, 1945; Seeley et al., 1956; Vidich and Bensman, 1958; Redfield, 1955), we find greatest attention given to the shared institutional and cultural realities of a geographically identifiable population. As symbolic interactionists we find appealing a number of studies that have emphasized the nature of social interaction as a primary feature of community life. Kaufman (1959) and Martindale (1958) deemphasize the spacial or territorial basis for community. Instead, they describe community in terms of networks of interaction or "interactional fields."

We could continue to list a large number of definitions that slightly differ from one another. At this point, however, it seems fair to say that the three elements most consistently found in the literature as important features of community life are the following:

1. Community is generally seen as delineated by a geographically, territorially, or spacially circumscribed area.
2. The members of a community are seen as bound together by a number of characteristics or attributes held in common (values, attitudes, ethnicity, social class, and so on).
3. The members of a community are engaged in some form of sustained social interaction.

We have ordered these three general characteristics as determined by the frequency with which they are mentioned as criteria for the existence or nonexistence of community. That is, there seems to be some uniform agreement among social scientists that, at the very least, a population of persons must share a clear spacial or ecological structure before a community can be said to exist. An examination of Hillery's findings show that the criterion of a geographical area shared by some population is to be found, either explicitly or implicitly, in virtually all ninety-four definitions. This is, once more, not unexpected, since the tradition of sociological thought about the city finds its origin in a silent comparative reference to the geographically well contained rural or peasant community. If the members of some collectivity are able to generate a degree of communal cohesion, if persons are to share a common set of values, if there is to exist a mutual concern for individual needs, if warm primary relations are to develop, it is likely to happen to persons who share a common physical space. Geographical stability, given this image of the peasant community, appears as the *sine qua non* of community life. This is a central point because we believe that a good part of our difficulty in fully comprehending the nature of city life stems from sociologists' past overreliance on geographic or spacial variables. To see how this is so, we must examine a theory that has particularly dominated sociological investigation of urban life. We must look to the work of those who analyzed the city in primarily ecological terms.

ECOLOGICAL CONCEPTIONS OF
URBAN COMMUNITY

As noted in earlier chapters, classical European writers approached the city from the viewpoint of its institutional structures—its division of labor, its economic system, and the like—and largely engaged in secondary analyses of historical and ethnographic data gathered previously by other investigators. Georg Simmel departed somewhat from this approach through his reliance on imaginative introspection. Even in his case, however, we find no systematic observational studies on specific urban institutions, populations, or communities. European thinkers, while residents of major urban areas themselves, tended to view the city from a distance. Only with the emergence of the Chicago School of Sociology does the notion of the city as a "research laboratory" develop. It was largely under the influence of Robert Park, a former journalist, whose previous work sensitized him to the necessity for first-hand observation of the human drama, that researchers began to investigate various "slices" of urban life. The spirit of much of the work done during this period is caught in Park's methodological directive to his students:

> You have been told to go grubbing in the library thereby accumulating a mass of notes and a liberal coating of grime. You have been told to choose problems wherever you can find musty stacks of routine records based on trivial schedules prepared by tired bureaucrats and filled out by reluctant applicants for aid or fussy do gooders or indifferent clerks. This is called "getting your hands dirty in real research." Those who counsel you are wise and honorable; the reasons they offer are of great value. But one more thing is needful; first-hand observation. Go and sit in the lounges of the luxury hotels and on the doorsteps of the flophouses; sit on the Gold Coast settees and on the slum shakedowns; sit in the orchestra hall and in the Star and Garter Burlesque. In short, gentlemen, go get the seats of your pants dirty in real research. (McKinney, 1966: 71)

It was not enough, however, that these researchers share a common methodological orientation. Park's further contribution was to delineate a set of theoretical questions that gave these separate investigations a uniform purpose and direction. In 1915 Park wrote a position paper in which he raised a set of research questions that became the focus for a generation of urban sociologists. Among other questions, Park asked: "What exactly makes cities grow? Is there a natural patterning to city growth and population distribution? What is the structure of urban neighborhoods? How do social institutions change with the growth of cities?"

These questions, in short, caused researchers to focus their investigations on the ecological structure of the city. The commitment to view the city in ecological terms provided the theoretical impetus for nearly all the research conducted at Chicago between 1915 and 1940. Ecology became the theoretical thread that would ultimately hold together the comprehensive image of urban life that Chicago sociologists were working to produce. One of the most influential of the early ecologists, R. D. McKenzie, specified the goal of ecological investigation this way:

> The spacial and sustenance relations in which human beings are organized are ever in the process of change in response to the operation of a complex of environmental and cultural forces. It is the

task of the human ecologist to study these processes of change in order to ascertain their principles of operation and the nature of the forces producing them. (1925: 167)

Although a formal theory of ecology was not to be spelled out until 1950 with the appearance of Amos Hawley's work *Human Ecology: A Theory of Community Structure,* urban ecologists shared from the beginning the view that human community life was essentially analogous to the structure of other biological communities. Human beings, like any other organism, must somehow adapt to the particular environmental contingencies that they daily face. Community was understood to be "the patterns of symbiotic and commonalistic relations that develop in a population; it (community) is in the nature of a collective response to the habitat; it (community) constitutes the adjustment of organisms to the environment" (Hawley, 1950: v).

Equipped with a common methodological and theoretical base, a number of researchers conducted studies of subgroups or subcommunities within the city. In each case, the concern was to discover the kinds of adaptations made by communities of persons to their particular urban environments. It was a time of great activity and research productivity. In characterizing these researches, Howard Becker (1970: 421) describes each as constituting one piece in a total mosaic of urban life. "Individual studies can be like pieces of mosaic and were so in Park's day. Since the picture of the mosaic was Chicago, the research had an ethnographic, case history flavor, even though Chicago itself was seen as somehow representative of all cities." These studies were important because their collective force was to show that urbanites did not very well adapt to the contingencies placed on them by the urban environment. Consider the tone of some of these better-known ethnographies.

Harvey Zorbaugh (1937) documented the extreme personal demoralization and destructive impersonality of Chicago's rooming-house district. The large proportion of persons in this area were transients; they were without families and without personal ties. As described by Zorbaugh, it was an area in which social controls had virtually disappeared. It was clear that here no "normal" community life could develop. Nels Anderson (1923) documented the pathology-producing effects of city life in his analysis of "homeless men." The hobo, living in a rootless, impersonal urban "jungle," was somehow symbolic of what the urban world was making of many. Paul Cressey (1932) focused his attention on immigrants to the city of Chicago. He painted a nearly pathetic picture of persons so starved for personal relations that the "taxi dance hall" (a ballroom in which one purchased tickets to dance with women for a specified time) could become a viable urban institution. In addition, a series of studies related a variety of social problems to urban existence. Ernest Mowrer (1927) argued that family disorganization, as reflected in divorce statistics, could not be disassociated from the general decline of primary group controls and increasing individualization in the city. Frederick Thrasher (1926) seemed to provide evidence of the city as a cause of behavioral disorder in his investigation of over 1300 gangs in the city of Chicago. Faris and Dunham (1948) documented varying rates of mental illness in different ecological areas of the city. They showed that rates of mental illness systematically declined as one traveled from the central city to the periphery of the city. They claimed that their study established the fact that "insanity, like other social problems, fits into the ecological structure of the city." In much the same fashion, Clifford Shaw (1966) demonstrated that rates of juvenile delinquency varied with the ecological structure of the city.

These works did, indeed, have a flavor to them. Despite their failure, by and large, to produce comprehensive theories about the city, despite their pretensions to objectivity, and despite the ministerial moralisms directed at the "pathologies" of city life that "infected" their pages, these works succeeded in doing what good ethnographies ought to do. They gave the reader a "gut" feeling for relatively unknown aspects of urban life. We could empathize with the hobo; we could begin to understand how immigrants coped with their new urban status; and we were provided an intimate picture of such diverse groups as waitresses, juvenile thieves, gang members, ghetto dwellers, and the wealthy.

Taken together, these works contributed to the development of "social disorganization" as an academically respectable field of inquiry during the 1930s and 40s. We should also add that these studies seemed to provide confirmation for the more general ecological theory of city growth proposed by the sociologist Ernest Burgess (1925). Burgess developed a picture of urban growth and process by focusing on the spacial distribution of population numbers and patterns of geographical mobility in the city. The assumption underlying Burgess' work is the central tenet of urban ecological analysis generally. It is that the typical spacial order of any city is a product of, and reflects, the moral order. Still more explicitly, Burgess tried to show that city growth eventuated in the development of a number of "natural" ecological areas. Much of his work is devoted to describing these natural areas, which, he believed, would mark the growth of any city. Based on his investigation of Chicago, Burgess' argument was for a growth pattern best characterized by a series of concentric circles or concentric zones. We can describe the natural areas specified in his concentric circle hypothesis.

The first that clearly comes into focus is the *center of the city*. The modern city grows up around the market. Here we find the greatest density and mobility of population. Mobility is especially great because of the existence of mass transportation that easily shuttles persons into and out of the central city. For the early ecologist, the central business sector, with its continuous activity, tightly packed buildings, and emphasis on rational pecuniary social arrangements, is seen as the city *par excellence*. It is the central business district with its banks, department stores, hotels, theatres, museums, and so on, that most readily comes to mind when most of us think about the city.

As Burgess describes it, we find around the city center a *zone of transition*. It is in this ecological area (composed of warehouses and slums) that vice, poverty, depersonalization, and social disorganization are most pronounced. That Chicago sociologists had a particular fascination with this "natural area" is evidenced by the number of ethnographies conducted of life in it. Here were found Zorbaugh's rooming houses, Cressey's taxi dance hall, Anderson's hoboes; here also were the highest rates of delinquency, mental illness, and family disintegration. Beyond the zone of transition, there is a *zone largely populated by workingmen's families*. This was a primarily residential area composed of second-generation immigrants. They were persons who still found their employment in the center of the city but who had been able to "escape" from the zone of transition. Still further toward the periphery of the city, we find another *residential zone populated largely by middle-class persons* living either in single dwellings or well-maintained apartment buildings. Finally, Burgess described a *suburban zone* composed of economically advantaged, geographically stable, upper-class commuters to the city. This conception of naturally produced ecological areas in the city can be expressed in graphic form, as in Figure 3–1. Burgess' hypothesis aroused tremendous controversy among his contemporaries. Homer Hoyt (1937), for example, suggested that cities did not take on the ecological pattern suggested by Burgess. Rather, he thought, cities grew in sectors along the main lines of transportation. His model of the city, then, consisted of a series of sectors or bands that

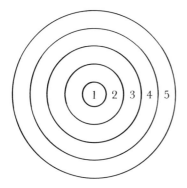

1. central business district
2. zone of transition
3. workingmen's houses
4. middle-class residences
5. commuter zone

FIGURE 3–1

followed economic activity. He also suggested that residences clustered along the boundaries of bands. Rather than a concentric zone configuration, therefore, the city was pictured more like a starfish or spoked wheel. The disagreement still did not stop with these two descriptions. Later Harris and Ullman (1945) argued that neither the concentric zonal or sector hypotheses best fit the natural ecology of the city. They provided yet another model that posited the existence of "multiple nuclei," each nucleus representing a specific concentration of specialized activities growing up around facilities in that nucleus. The basic premise of the multiple nuclei theory is that similar kinds of activities tend to be drawn together while dissimilar activities are repelled.

It is not, however, our purpose to indicate the full complexity of these debates. We may see that, regardless of dissimilarities in the particular configurations, all the descriptions remain wholly ecological in nature. The presumption is that cities, and the specific communities contained within them, can be understood in terms of the economic and social activities and the demographic characteristics of the population inhabiting a natural ecological area. This was the guiding hypothesis of each of the separate studies reviewed earlier.

In all fairness to these ecological conceptions or characterizations of the city, we should say a few more words about what Burgess and others hoped to accomplish through their ecological constructions. It has, for example, been suggested that Burgess' hypothesis was incorrect for a number of reasons. First, it was generated by looking at the city of Chicago in the 1920s. Burgess' critics question the representativeness of that city. Second, more contemporary urbanologists have claimed that his ideas do not apply to today's cities. It is increasingly the case today that cities are carefully planned. Burgess described a city that, to that point, had grown "naturally" without any outside planning intervention. The idea of planned cities could not, of course, have entered into Burgess' formulations, since the implementation of urban planning, particularly in the U.S., is rather recent. To some extent, however, these criticisms misunderstand Burgess' intent.

Burgess was considerably more sophisticated than these fellow critics allow. He did, after all, live in Chicago and was obviously aware that Lake Michigan, for example, cut into the symmetry of his concentric zones. In other words, Burgess himself knew that he was not describing a city in absolute, actual terms. He was, rather, creating what sociologists refer to as an *ideal type*. As noted in Chapter 1, an ideal type is a tool to help social scientists ask questions about phenomena as they engage in analysis. As social scientists construct their ideal type, they recognize that it is an intellectual invention of sorts. They realize that there is nothing in the real world perfectly fitting their ideal picture. Instead the ideal type becomes a kind of yardstick against which what does exist in the real world can be evaluated. The ideal type, we might say, represents a series of assumptions about the organization of social life. After we specify these assumptions, we can ask: "How may we expect things to look given these assumptions?" For Burgess, as for other ecologists, their explanations, their ideal types, their images of the city rested on three basic assumptions:

1. Individuals do not act alone. They act collectively in aggregates. Such aggregates are usually organized in social terms.
2. Behavior and social organization is rational and can be described as such.
3. Actors all have adequate knowledge of market and economic processes and will use space in the city based on that knowledge.

Burgess was proposing that *if* people, in fact, behave rationally, have knowledge of the market for social space, and behave as part of an aggregate, then we should see cities developing in such and such a manner. Burgess, like other ecologists, was interested in isolating the factors that would account for city growth and thereby would account for the social organization of communities in the city. It is our position that these ecological assumptions and emphases are inadequate and have constrained our understanding of urban communities. Let us consider how our symbolic interactionist approach leads us to critique the ecological perspective that we have recently been describing.

ECOLOGY AND HUMAN BEHAVIOR

We see a number of flaws in the ecological position that may have contributed to inadequate conceptions of urban community life. Ecologists seem either to forget or to disregard the fact that space has *meaning* for people. If we are to develop ideal types, we must be careful to create as close a fit between our assumptions and empirical reality as is possible. We disagree with the ecological assumptions that we have named simply because it seems clear that individuals do not behave only in terms of the sheer economic value of space. More frequently, we suggest, persons relate to their social space in sentimental or emotional terms. This point has, of course, been amply documented in the relatively recent works of the anthropologist Edward Hall (1969) and the social psychologist Robert Sommer (1969). Both show enormous cultural differences in persons' attitude toward the uses of physical space. Theirs is a compelling argument that the "meaning" of social space cannot be conceived only in economic/geographic terms.

Ecologists concentrate so much on the physical features of city space that they have relatively little to tell us about behavior and social organization. We learn little from ecological theory about the social psychology of city life. As symbolic interactionists, we see the need to assess the relationship between space, the symbolic meaning attached to space, and so human behavior itself. The sentimental value attached to urban space has, for example, been clearly documented in the writings of the sociologist Walter Firey (1945). He shows that Beacon Hill in Boston is not merely a spacial area to be fitted into a concentric circle, zone, or nucleus. If we wish to understand Boston as a city, we must consider the symbolic value, the history, the meaning attached to its various spacial features. Boston's Beacon Hill community does not exist merely because persons share a common ecological space that serves a set of rational individual and collective economic functions. The community's existence is more bound up in the mutual symbolic value placed on that territorial area. Firey expresses the issue this way:

> It is the dynamic force of spacially referred sentiments, rather than considerations of rent, which explains why certain families have

chosen to live on Beacon Hill in preference to other in-town districts having equally accessible location and even superior housing conditions. There is thus a non-economic aspect to land use on Beacon Hill, one which is in some respects actually diseconomic in its consequences. (Firey, 1945: 144)

We may extrapolate from Firey's argument. It is the sentiment attached to urban areas; it is the whole range of meanings attached to urban areas (and here we must, of course, include economic meanings) that essentially determines the shape and social organization of cities.

In extending this discussion, we must be very careful in our assessment of natural ecological boundaries. Ecologists tend to see certain features of the landscape as creating natural barriers. Surely, for example, we cannot consider city rivers merely as barriers or boundaries. There is more involved than that. Rivers may be related to, and thought about, as objects of beauty, as focal points for recreation, and possibly as central to persons' images of the city as a whole. It is not the boundary itself that alone determines forms of social organizations or communities. It is, rather, how we think about, interpret, and give meaning to these natural barriers. We must ask whether physical barriers are also *social barriers*. The description of something (railroad tracks, rivers, and the like) only as a physical barrier may cause us to read the sociology of the city incorrectly. It is true that an empty space may constitute a line of demarcation in a city, but it is equally possible that the same empty space might become a playground and therefore have the effect of extending patterns of interaction in the city. Unless we consider the use, the meaning, the symbolic significance, and frequently the sentiments and emotions attached to various features of the city's topology, we shall incorrectly understand patterns of interaction in the city, and by definition, therefore, incompletely understand the city's social organization.

This leads us to our second general criticism of ecological conceptions of the city. Too great an emphasis on spacial patternings without equal attention to the nature of social interaction between persons both within and beyond specific geographical areas of the city may be misleading. We must recall at all times that communities are composed of human beings actually or potentially interacting with one another. The limitations of a purely ecological approach are seen when we look to the relationship between geography and social interaction. If we agree that one of the elements of human community is social interaction, we must ask whether that interaction can be fully understood in terms of clear spacial demarcations.

If we were to find that social relations between urbanites transcend naturally occurring or arbitrarily defined ecological boundaries, this would be good reason for rethinking or reevaluating the territorial basis for community. We are proposing that society, or in the more limited sense, community, exists in and through human communication. Communication is, of course, an interactive process. Further, we can say that any interactive process changes its constitutive elements in every interaction. In each contact the identities of the participants are inevitably changed somewhat. Therefore, as patterns of communication and interaction change, the basis of community shifts as well. Urban units (the community being a central unit) are constantly changed by the process through which they are created—human interaction. The kind of dialectical process that we are describing places a limit on a purely ecological or geographical conception of community. To understand fully the nature of urban social arrangements, we have at the same time to understand the shifting patterns of communication that continually transform them.[1] Form and his colleagues (1954) have shown, following this line of thought, the inadequacy of purely ecological definitions of human community.

They begin their analysis of one city by drawing a topological map showing both natural barriers or boundaries (hills, rivers, empty spaces and so on) and boundaries imposed by technology (bridges, buildings). This is one approach taken by ecologists in distinguishing various city areas. Next, they look closely at the demographic characteristics and spacial distribution of the population in the city. The purpose of this exercise is to see more clearly the relationship between the purely topological boundaries earlier described and the racial, social, ethnic and economic composition of populations. These two elements (topological and demographic), in combination, we have noted, are traditionally used to delineate the boundaries of city communities. The task, in other words, is to see if there is any fit between the topological characteristics of the city and the distribution of its population. The third

---

[1] It may not be entirely fair to Park to criticize human ecology for ignoring social interaction. In fact, his studies did include consideration of social interaction, and Park did define society as involving social interaction. Although ecologists talked about "community" as being in some sense subsocial (a view that derives from the intellectual origins of the human ecological studies), much of what in fact was done did include the "societal" or interactional aspects. See Chapter 1, pp. 42–43.

possibility for demarcation (and the one that is of greatest interest to us here) was obtained by measuring the extent to which persons interacted or communicated with each other over the city space. In effect, the researchers created three maps of the city—a topological, a demographic, and an interactional map—and then looked to see how much overlap existed among the three. Their finding: there was practically no correspondence among the three maps; there was virtually no overlapping.

Let us try to make clear the import of this lack of correspondence among social interaction, demography, and the physical features of the city. It makes plain the difficulty of drawing arbitrary lines of demarcation in cities that will presumably alert one to the existence or nonexistence of community. The matter is just not that simple. Perhaps one of the reasons that urban sociologists came to the conclusion that there were few viable urban communities was their failure to see the inadequacy of purely ecological conceptions of social organization. One cannot determine the existence of community by simply chopping up the city with arbitrary lines of demarcation.[2]

Other researchers, dissatisfied with assumptions about social relationships and interaction implicit in ecological theory, have sought out better ways to identify and to describe urban subcommunities. One central direction of this research has been the continuous development since 1949 (Shevsky and Williams, 1949) of a method called *social area analysis*. Social area analysis is a method for the "systematic analysis of population differences between urban subcommunities" (Bell, 1965). Using published data on an areal unit called the census tract (each census tract contains between 3000 and 6000 persons), researchers then create indices of each tract's *socioeconomic status* (based on such indicators as rent, education, and occupation), *familism* (based on such indicators as fertility ratios and women not in the labor force), and *ethnicity* (based on such indicators as race and nativity). The scores on each of these indices is standardized such that they range from 0 to 100. Once all of the census tracts in a particular metropolitan area have been scored according to these three characteristics, it becomes possible

---

[2] While making this general criticism, we do not wish to imply that there is never any linkage between the city's ecology and patterns of behavior. Recall that sociologists at Chicago documented a correlation between distance from the city center and the occurrence of such behaviors as mental disorders and juvenile delinquency. This is not to say, however, that the correspondence is perfect or that "subsocial" explanations are valid.

to delineate distinct social areas within the city. One such social area, for example, would be constituted by all those census tracts with high scores on all three indices; another social area might be composed of tracts scoring low on all indices. In a review essay on the subject, Wendell Bell (1965) describes how thirty-two separate social areas may be identified, each representing a unique configuration of the three central indices we have described.

Once the social areas in a city have been specified, researchers may consider how they vary from one another in any of a number of respects. Studies based on the method of social area analysis have uncovered many orderly patterns within cities. Research indicates, for example, that social areas vary widely and systematically on such factors as persons' social participation, their membership in formal organizations, and their sense of community identification. Those living in different social areas, in other words, differ consistently on a whole range of attitudes, beliefs, and behaviors. Moreover, the patterns uncovered in one city appear relatively constant when the same method is applied to a number of cities.

There is an important idea to be drawn from our brief discussion of social area analysis. The method and the findings derived from it are congenial to the point of view that we have been advocating for the last few pages. We say this because the census tracts composing an identified social area need not be contiguous to each other; they may be spread out through the city space. Work done using social area analysis stands as further empirical confirmation that urban communities need not have a specific territorial locus.[3]

There is another step to be taken in achieving a better understanding of the sense of community felt by many city persons. At this point we want to suggest that there may be subjective community identifications that simply cannot be accounted for through the use of "objective" criteria for defining community. Sociologists have long known that actual membership in one or another group may be less important than an identification with that group. We know, for example, that if we wish to explain certain social behaviors related to a person's social class position, it may be less important to know the person's objective class position (as measured, for example, by occupation, education, and income) than to know the social class with which the individual iden-

---

[3] For some examples of recent empirical studies of the "factorial ecology of cities," see the collection of studies edited by Schwirian (1974).

tifies. Reference-group theory in sociology is based on the idea that persons' objective social statuses, attributes, and group affiliations may be less important than their *interpretations* of these same elements. W. I. Thomas' dictum that "what persons define as real is real in its consequences" is, we think, applicable to persons' constructions of their lives as urbanites. A sense of community may reside in a person's feelings of identification with a city. Such identification cannot be appreciated by simply documenting urbanites' structural positions.

SUBJECTIVE COMMUNITY IDENTIFICATION: NONTERRITORIAL BASES OF URBAN COMMUNITY

In an article titled "City Shoppers and Urban Identification," Gregory P. Stone (1954) provides evidence for an idea that we have advocated at several points. It is that anonymity is certainly enhanced in the urban environment, but that, in time, some urban impersonal or anonymous contacts tend to become personalized. The finding of Stone's study is that persons need not be members of a community in some objective sense in order to achieve an identification with it. He begins his investigation by noting that there are various "types" of city shoppers. There are, for example, those who adopt an orientation toward stores that is wholly economic. These persons treat the marketplace in rational, pecuniary terms. This approach to the marketplace is consistent with the classical image of the city that sees virtually all human relations circumscribed by rational considerations of profit. He names two other types of shopper (apathetic and ethical shoppers) that will not concern us here. Importantly—and this type becomes the focus for Stone's analysis—there are shoppers who *personalize* their relationships with store clerks or personnel. This last type of shopping orientation would not be easily predicted by the typical picture of the depersonalized nature of relationships in urban sectors. With further investigation Stone discovered that individuals who personalized their shopping relations with store clerks typically had relatively little access to channels of participation in the larger community.

For these persons, the quasi-intimate contacts created through shopping operated as a kind of substitute for true participation in the community; shopping was a way of identifying with a community. Stone found that a large proportion of those whom he characterized as "personalizing" shoppers had no or few objective ties to the local community. They either had resided in the community for only a short time or had few friends in the local community. In short, Stone argued that shopping provides the opportunity for some to develop a subjective identification with a community although they are not part of the community by some set of objective standards. We find a situation that provides strong ties for people where we might not have expected such ties to exist. We begin to see that, in the urban context, shopping serves an integrative function every bit as important as the more overt function of buying goods. Stone makes the plausible conclusion that the personalization of relationships in the market makes for a subjective identification with the larger community. This is, we might add, an identification that simply would not be seen if we examined only places of residence. Let us reiterate the significance of this study in somewhat more theoretical terms.

This work seems to be saying, as we have been arguing, that human beings are eminently capable of transforming their environments in important ways. Although the conditions of urban life may seem conducive to impersonality and rationality, persons can tolerate only so much of this impersonality. Perhaps at the height of feelings of depersonalization and lack of integration, persons will seek out alternatives in the environment to provide them with just the kinds of relationships that seem denied them. The marketplace, and particularly the small store, becomes a source for sustained human relationships— for community identification. Should we fail to see how new networks of interaction are created in the urban situation, we shall too quickly leap to the conclusion that there are none at all.

It is important, as well, to cite the policy implications of findings like Stone's. Once we see that the small store acquires a new symbolic meaning in the urban context, we must be careful in our planning. We must be cognizant that economic agencies in urban areas play a very important function other than the purely economic function. Small stores, taverns, cafes, and the like are not just places to purchase goods; they also constitute meeting places for neighborhood residents and crucial communications centers for informal news about the community. The demolition of such stores does not just eliminate a few more buildings from the community but may also rupture the entire fabric of social life in that neighborhood.

This argument is of considerable importance for those engaged in redesigning urban places. Our attention is called to the fact that there is more to consider than the physical shape of a building before the decision is made to do away with it. We might, for example, put this in the context of building shopping centers in the city. Planners too frequently create their ideas for city change using the suburbs as their model. The preference becomes to build a large shopping center in place of the "Ma/Pa" small store. One argument is that small businesses are dying anyway and that it is reasonable to hasten the process by engaging in a kind of social euthanasia. We quarrel with the idea that small businesses inevitably must die. It may very well be true that there is a big turnover in small businesses. We must, however, also look at the statistics showing an enormous constancy in the percentage of the labor force involved in small businesses. There is always another Ma and Pa on the outside waiting to take over small community businesses. The more important point that we wish to make is this: Planners going into an area should not tamper with the existing institutions because change would better fit their own aesthetic conception of what the city should look like. We have to understand the crucial importance of some of these institutions in providing a platform on which a substantial number of urban residents build their identities.

The establishment of shopping relations is certainly not the only basis for subjective urban community identification. As a matter of fact, the findings of the city shoppers study is important only if it sensitizes us to other sources of community identification that transcend spacial boundaries. As another example, we shall examine the function of institutions like sport in the modern urban center.

Based on a quota sample investigation of 515 persons, Gregory Stone (1968: 8) offers some evidence that "involvement with spectator sports makes for subjective identification with the larger community under objectively improbable conditions." By "objectively improbable conditions" Stone meant that subjective identification with the urban community through sports would be highest for those who were, according to purely objective criteria, least integrated into the urban community (those who had been residents in the city for the shortest time, those who had the fewest number of friends in the community). Once more, the theoretical point that we made earlier seems to be sustained by the data; namely, that persons produce a symbolic transformation of urban institutions so as to provide themselves a source of identification that is not available to them through routine sources of community involvement.

Sports teams should be thought of as collective representations of the larger urban world. Teams represent that world. Significant

then are the names of teams. Such names have in the past designated urban areas.... Identification with such representations
may be transferred to identification with the larger communities
or areas they represent. (Stone, 1968: 10)

We have offered two examples of urban institutions that serve the
unintended function of providing urbanites a source of identification
with urban community. Sport and the marketplace may be identified
as two sectors of the urban world that must be studied in order to
understand how urbanites produce an involvement in the urban world
that maintains their separate identities, that injects a personal quality
into a situation where it would otherwise not seem to exist. There is
an important point that comes out of the brief analysis we have made
here. It is that the urban world is organized. There is a clear social
organization produced by urbanites through their transformations and
usages of urban institutions. We repeat that such organization is not so
easily seen because its source is to be found in unsuspected settings.

Institutions such as sport and the marketplace are not the only bases
for subjective community identification. R. Richard Wohl and Anselm
Strauss (1958) alert us to the idea that specific objects in cities become
symbolic representations of the whole city for its inhabitants. City
dwellers build up a sentiment and emotion for these meaningful "city
objects." Urbanites come to feel a fondness for such objects as trees,
buildings, particular street corners, rivers, and parks. Some of these
objects become, in fact, synonymous with the city itself. We need only
show persons New York's skyline, or San Francisco's Golden Gate
Bridge, or New Orleans' French Quarter, and the city will be quickly
identified by most. For those who live in these respective cities, such
objects and places do not merely identify the city, they are also sources
for personal identification with the city. "The city, then, sets problems
of meaning. The streets, the people, the buildings, the changing scenes
do not come already labelled. They require explanation and interpretation" (Wohl and Strauss, 1958: 572).

As we speak, then, of subjective identification with the urban community, meaning to indicate that (just as Robert Park maintained) the
city is "state of mind," so also must we consider community a psychological production. Communities do not exist unless they are collectively identified as such. Nothing has any meaning until we invest it
with meaning. It is not enough to offer simple objective criteria for
community. To say that subjective community identification is possible
is to reiterate a previously made point: We do not live in communities

as much as we live in our interpretations of community. Our continuing assertion that community identification does not depend solely upon residence in a well-defined ecological area of the city flows from this theoretical position.

PARTICIPATION IN URBAN COMMUNITIES

To our already accumulated evidence for the existence of nonterritorially based sources of community identification, we should add the findings of those researchers who, using more structured quantitative procedures, have generated a large volume of data on "participation" in the urban community (Axelrod, 1956; Greer, 1956; Bell and Force, 1956; Bell and Boat, 1957; Komarovsky, 1946). The focus of these studies has been to document the frequency with which neighbors visit one another in cities, the extent to which urbanites join voluntary organizations, the patterns of interaction among family members, and the structure of informal social relations in large cities.

These studies, nearly all written in reaction to Wirth's view of urbanism or interpretable in that way, are in essential agreement that the degree of secularization and disorganization supposedly typifying urban communities has been greatly exaggerated. Once more, evidence from these investigations focusing on various levels of the urban community, from the local neighborhood to formal work organizations, reveal that urbanites operate within an extensive network of interactional involvement. The evidence keeps accumulating, in short, that it is unfair, misleading, at best partial to picture city dwellers as leading desperately lonely, isolated, segmented lives. We can briefly cite some of the major findings of this research.

Working explicitly with the frequent contrast made between city and rural settings, the sociologists Otis Dudley Duncan and Albert Reiss (1956) compared patterns of relatively intimate friendship relations in both urban and rural situations. They found that urban persons have many more such friendship contacts than their rural counterparts do. The ratio of these friendships to the total number of contacts that persons have is, of course, much lower in the city, since urbanites have many more contacts. The fact remains that the absolute number of primary friendship contacts is considerably larger for the urbanite than for rural persons. As we might expect, the work place is an important source of primary contacts in the city. The relationship between city living and personal contacts must, however, be somewhat specified. Such specification can be found in the research of Smith, Form, and Stone (1954).

One of their basic findings is that intimacy in neighborhoods varies with the relative status of the neighborhood; that is, more intimate contact increases as we move from neighborhoods in the inner city to neighborhoods more on the periphery of the city. This finding must be viewed with some caution. The intent of the research was to measure "local intimacy." It would first seem that working-class families (those in neighborhoods closer to the central city) have fewer intimate contacts than do higher-status families farther away from the city center. The authors point out, however, that working-class families are generally more mobile within the city space than are higher-status families. It may very well be, then, that lower-status families simply have a more geographically dispersed network of friends. It is a network that does not get "picked up" by a measure of *local* intimacy.

In his own review of much of the accumulated literature on the subject of urban participation, Scott Greer (1964: 91ff.) relates the following general patterns: kinship patterns are extensive and important sources of primary relations for urbanites; persons typically have some friends in their immediate neighborhood, but these ties are not the most significant for the average person; there is a fair amount of involvement in voluntary formal organizations. "Informal participation in friendship relations, with individual friends or friendship circles, is an extremely frequent occurrence," and "somewhat unexpectedly" persons do not much associate with work associates off the job. One point can be made from the literature that we have been briefly discussing. It is that urbanites have many close associations; they are not, as the stereotype would have it, living isolated, anonymous existences.

SEEING COMMUNITY ORGANIZATION

We have tried to show how a purely ecological theoretical perspective may be an obstacle to capturing the full range of meanings, identification, and social relations possible in urban areas. In taking this position, we do not mean to imply that viable geographical communities are nonexistent in the city space. Such an implication would be contrary to the evidence provided by a number of urban community studies. These studies show that there is frequently a clear social organization in situations first appearing wholly "disorganized." It is somewhat ironic that the very factors taken by Chicago ecologists as indices of disorder are used in these studies to demonstrate the existence of an ordered community social life. As mentioned earlier, Frederick Thrasher studied over a thousand gangs in the city of Chicago. In this work, and in sociological work generally, the gang has always been viewed as a most visible and distressing symbol of urban disorganization. The documenting of Chicago gangs further worked to validate the developing image of the city as the progenitor of social pathology. It was not until the publication of William F. Whyte's *Street Corner Society* that the gang could be seen to reflect a community's organization rather than dissolution.

In still later studies, the ecological area presumably representing the very epitome of disorder—the urban slum—is shown to possess a most distinctive "moral order." In order to see this order, however, we must sometimes be willing to question what first appears obvious. It seems obvious, for example, that the more organized crime in an area the more disorganized must be that area. In order to illustrate the necessity of questioning such seemingly unassailable ideas, we ask you to consider the following examples.

In his autobiography (1931) Lincoln Steffens tells of the following incident. His billfold having been stolen in a New York subway, Steffens complained to city officials. That very evening his wallet was returned to him intact. In this case, organized criminals were responsible for the quick retrieval of an important individual's stolen property. The quick retrieval obviously demanded a high level of social organization that is typically not visible to us. The organized criminals did not want too much of this free-floating crime taking place because it potentially put too much heat on them. In other words, we frequently find organized criminals becoming one of the major organs of *social control* because they cannot tolerate unorganized crime, which causes a public clamor and makes things difficult for them. A second example illustrates the same point.

In the summer of 1966 New York was experiencing the threat of a severe struggle in Brooklyn between Italian and black gangs. The situation was further complicated by the development in the affected areas of a Jewish vigilante group—the Maccabees—who began to patrol the area at night in order to prevent or reduce muggings, robberies, and "rumbles." Despite their efforts, the whole situation threatened to get out of hand. A solution was provided to the problem. How was the difficulty stopped? The local rabbi in charge of the vigilante group, together with a city officer, approached a leader of a criminal organization—one of the top racketeers in the city. They explained that the juvenile warfare going on was threatening the community and had to be stopped. The very next day the Italian juveniles left the area and went back to their own communities, ceasing their attacks on the black gangs in the city. The result of this solution was an enormous outcry in the newspapers as people asked what kind of city had to rely on organized criminals to produce and maintain community order. We propose that such a city is a highly organized one. In short, once we are willing to look at certain social forms from unfamiliar angles, we may come to perceive those forms differently and more clearly. A number of urban community studies written since 1943 look at the community from such unfamiliar angles. The accumulated evidence from these researches further causes us to question the image of the urban center as the source of unremitting anomie.

In 1943 William F. Whyte published his now classic study of Boston's North End. We can turn to Whyte's own words to describe how his study began:

> I began with the vague idea that I wanted to study a slum district. Eastern City provided several possible choices. In the early weeks of my Harvard Fellowship I spent some of my time walking up and down the streets of various slum districts of Eastern City and talking with people in social agencies about these districts. . . . I made my choice on very unscientific grounds: Cornerville best fitted my picture of what a slum district should look like. Somehow I had developed a picture of run-down three to five story buildings crowded together. (Whyte, 1943: 283)

The fact that from a very early point Whyte saw the need to investigate this "slum" community through direct participant observation was not, we think, merely incidental in allowing him to make certain discoveries about its structure. He eventually became a member of the community for more than two years. So much so did he see the need to integrate himself into the community that he worked during that time to learn Italian. We call attention to the method employed by Whyte because it has implications for some of the arguments that we have been making in this chapter and will continue to make throughout the book. We have been advocating the necessity of coming to understand how persons themselves experience and give meaning to their lives as city dwellers. Unless we come to understand how persons define their own behaviors and the environment in which they produce those behaviors, we shall incompletely comprehend their lives. If the goal of symbolic interaction is to uncover these meaning structures, then we must be careful not to impose our meanings as researchers onto those whom we study. We advocate direct participant observation as the method best allowing the researcher to remain true to this task of "seeing the world from the perspective of those studied," providing that the investigator does not lose sight of history.

Primarily through chance, Whyte made friends with several members of a street-corner gang that "hung around" the area. His entrée to this group was provided through one person in particular, Doc, who was the leader of the gang and whose confidence Whyte gained. This gang became the central focus of Whyte's research over the two-year period that he studied Cornerville. While the study of one gang of ten–twelve persons seems a very limited focus for two years' work, it became apparent to Whyte after a short time that he could see many facets of the community reflected in the gang. The gang became a kind of lens through which Whyte would come to see the *highly organized* nature of this urban community. In terms of some of the points that we have already made in this chapter, Whyte came to see that the gang was only one part of a highly elaborated system of social networks in the community and, itself, an important source of personal identity for its members. It soon became obvious to Whyte (a point not easily accessible to the outsider who merely views the community from a distance) that the gang was tightly linked to other institutional sectors of the community—especially the political structure and organized crime.

Whyte eventually came to see that the community was rather tightly held together through a system of developed obligations and reciprocities. These findings, which still hold true today, have important implications for the way that we look at urban community life. Whyte's findings led to a complete reorganization of our usual conceptions of "slum" areas. He came to recognize that one cannot define an area of the city as a slum only in terms of its physical characteristics. Rather, we have to consider whether there is an order, a social organization, a pattern of interactions that holds the area together regardless of its physical appearance. We must realize that slum means much more than physical deterioration. The essence of community lies in the kinds of social bondings described and documented by Whyte. We reiterate that the social organization discovered by Whyte is not readily obvious without investigation. Once we look carefully at certain areas of the city, we shall find viable communities that might otherwise escape us.

The same lesson is repeated in other community studies. Herbert Gans (1962), studying the West End of Boston, found much the same situation that Whyte did. It is interesting that Gans titled his book *The Urban Villagers*. The choice of title indicates exactly the point toward which we are moving in this chapter. We need not mourn the passing away of the small peasant community or village. The social bonds of city dwellers are as meaningfully "cemented" as those of small-town inhabitants. Gans pointedly shows in his work that an awareness of this fact by city planners would help to minimize the residential upheaval and forced relocation of many urban residents. A city is not just a collection of physical dwellings. The physical objects that constitute the "worlds" of city people are often endowed with meanings that pass unnoticed by city planners—specialists in engineering and architecture —who are often insensitive to the "social technology" and "architecture" of social arrangements that prevail in a given community.

Gans, like Whyte before him, laid bare the strong internal organization of the West End despite its outward physical appearance as a slum. He saw the strong family life that existed in this area. He saw the way that families and friends congregated in each others' homes. He saw people laughing around kitchen tables. He saw the care exhibited toward each others' children. These things, we wish to express once more, are not seen unless one does, in fact, get inside the rather run-down looking buildings in the area. Gans also saw the sentiment and emotion felt by these people for their community. By a "heap of living," as the saying goes, they had made their houses "homes." Their lives, their friendships, their sense of identity were tied up in that community. And yet they were forced to move out so that the redevelopment agency in the city could do away with another slum. The quality of the emotional attachment felt by residents of the West End of Boston was caught in the title of a paper by Marc Fried (1963), who described their "Grieving for a Lost Home." In another article Fried and Gleicher investigated sources of residential satisfaction in the West End, and part of their summary underscores the importance of urban dwellers' sentiments for the community:

> The residential area is the region in which a vast and interlocking set of social networks is localized. And . . . the physical area has

considerable meaning as an extension of home, in which the various parts are delineated and structured on the basis of a sense of belonging. These two components provide the context in which the residential area may so easily be invested with considerable, multiply determined meaning. (1961: 315)

The evidence necessary to overturn the conviction of the city's slaughter of community continues to mount with somewhat more recent investigations of community life. Gerald Suttles (1968) in his book aptly titled *The Social Order of the Slum*—an observational study of the Addams area of the Near West Side of Chicago—further supports our contention that intense and careful observation is absolutely necessary for discovering the less visible components of community social arrangements. Suttles' own close observations allowed him to make the convincingly strong case that there exists a clear "moral order" in this "slum" area. It is a moral order rooted in the personalized relationships that members of the community have with one another. It is a moral order derivative of persons' needs to come to grips with a "dangerous and uncontrollable outer world" (1968: ix).

It is particularly useful that Suttles shows the possibility of combining an ecological approach to the study of community with a sensitive attention to the internal, cultural, and symbolic meaning structures established by the residents. He offers further certification for our earlier assertion that various urban institutions importantly foster channels of communication and, hence, community solidarity. The Addams area was particularly an interesting context for investigation since it is an ethnically segmented community. The area is ecologically separated into a number of neighborhoods, each of which is ethnically homogeneous. The four major groups constituting the area as a whole were a black group, an Italian group, a Mexican group, and a Puerto Rican group.

Suttles' argument is that, despite the fact that these groups are segmented by a number of ecological, institutional, and cultural factors, this segmentation can be described as *ordered* segmentation. He means to say that discontinuities and conflicts between groups do not necessarily preclude consensually held needs, goals, and interests. It would be contrary to common sense to disregard cultural, political, and racial conflict in the city. Such differences obviously exist. Suttles asks us, however, not to leap from our observations of these overt differences to the conclusion that there is no underlying social organization or order in the community. The well-worn metaphor that warns us against looking only at the tip of the iceberg applies most directly to community life. We have too frequently assumed that a community existed only in what could be readily seen—in Suttles' case it was conflict and cultural differences that stood out on first inspection. More detailed observation alerts us to the faulty assumption that conflict immediately signals social disorganization.

In a recent, much-read work, the anthropologist Eliot Liebow (1967) offers further evidence to support our earlier contention that certain urban institutions (taverns, pool halls, laundromats) come to have a function as "informal communications centers, forums, places to display and assess talents, and staging areas for a wide range of activities, legal and illegal, and extralegal" (1967: viii). *Tally's Corner* is an especially revealing study because it documents the wide-ranging patterns of communication between persons in an urban black ghetto, an area of the city generally considered wholly lacking in any social organization. In some ways we may construe Liebow's work as a kind of replication of William Whyte's study done some thirty years earlier. Liebow studied in depth, like Whyte, a rather small group of street-corner men. And, like Whyte, Liebow documented a tightly and elaborately established network of primary, face-to-face relationships. It is, further, through an examination of these relationships that broader features of the community are revealed. The underlying relations between fathers and their children, husbands and wives, and patterns of friendship give an order to what often appears from the outside as a disorganized, chaotic situation. The necessity of creating and sustaining personal, identity-fostering relationships is especially great for the persons described by Liebow—black persons facing a continually hostile world that helps to sustain a cycle of economic failure in their lives. Under these conditions the production of a strong network of primary social relations becomes all the more imperative. Liebow expresses well the sense of community that we have been proposing in this chapter:

> More than most social worlds, perhaps, the streetcorner world takes its shape and color from the structure and character of the face-to-face relationships of the people in it. Unlike other areas of our society, where a large proportion of the individual's energies, concerns and time are invested in self-improvement, career and job development, family and community activities, religious and cultural pursuits, or even in broad, impersonal social and political issues, these resources in the streetcorner world are almost entirely

given over to the construction and maintenance of personal relationships.

On the streetcorner, each man has his own network of these personal relationships and each man's network defines for him the members of his personal community. His personal community, then, is not a bounded area but rather a web-like arrangement of man–man and man–woman relationships in which he is selectively attached in a particular way to a definite number of discrete persons. In like fashion, each of these persons has his own personal network. (1967: 162)

Of writers commenting on the nature of urban community, Jane Jacobs (1961) has had perhaps the most visibility and likely, therefore, the most impact. In her *The Death and Life of Great American Cities* Jacobs strongly calls into question a number of assumptions held by city planners about the nature of urban life. In her view, city planners do not appreciate the vibrant qualities that cities possess. The qualities of the city that are distasteful from the perspective of the city planner were the very same qualities that Jacobs found desirable about cities. As she saw it, city planners wanted, in effect, to do away with cities, decentralize cities, spread cities out, create a number of small towns in place of the urban complex. Like many urban sociologists, city planners held, in Jacobs' assessment, a rural bias. Cities were to be dealt with by making them less urban, more like rural settings. The idea was, in general, to keep people off the streets, create underground streets, create large open spaces in cities, and so on. In short, urban planners seemed to find the large size, density, and heterogeneity of the city as negative dimensions. Jacobs, alternatively, tried to cite the uses and benefits of these same factors.

Jacobs saw the inherent orderliness of cities that planners seem to have missed. Speaking of the North End of Boston, for example, she indicated the incorrect image held by city planners. Given their biases, everything was wrong with that area. It was taken as typical of the urban slum with its high population density, older buildings, children playing in the streets, and the like. What urban planners seem to have missed, just as they missed it in the West End of Boston, was the meaning of the area held by its residents and the way that this area of the city worked on a day-to-day basis. Jacobs has this to say about the North End:

The streets were alive with children playing, people shopping, people strolling, people talking. Had it not been a cold January day, there surely would have been people sitting. The general street atmosphere of buoyancy, friendliness and good health was so infectious that I began asking directions of people just for the fun of getting in on some of the talk. (1961: 9)

Jacobs does not see the effects of size, density, and heterogeneity in negative terms. Rather she sees the city as an intensely human place —a place potentially, if not actually, full of vitality, sensibility, joy, and sociability.

CONCLUSION

Our review of some of the more recent literature causes us to recognize that we miss much in our analysis of city life by evaluating its quality in terms of the existence or nonexistence of clear ecological communities. While there is evidence that such community forms exist (Whyte, 1943; Gans, 1962; Suttles, 1968), they simply do not fully encompass the lives of the majority of urban persons. The relative disappearance of the "village" community type should not make us leap to the immediate conclusion that urbanites live "nonsocial" existences. To the contrary, it has been our position that community still exists. It has simply taken a different form. If the essence of any community lies in patterns of warm, intimate interactions, then communities are to be found in cities.

We find it reasonable to characterize urban life in terms of a number of individual, personal, or intimate communities. Persons, we think, owe allegiance less to a particular territory than to a network of social relationships that is without boundaries. This idea leads us to see that there are as many urban communities as there are urban persons. Some have more extensive interactional networks than others, and some obviously have overlapping networks; but we are unlikely to find two personal communities that will be identical.

Once we put greatest emphasis on urbanites' interactional social circles, we find that we are no longer bounded or restricted in our view of what human community is or can be in the city. The view of community as a complex network of interpersonal relations allows us to see other features of the urban social world. We must consider that urban social relations are, like any other set of human interactions, in a continual state of change, transition, or process. We have seen that the rediscovery of community depends on the analyst's ability to look at the world in a new way. Community is alive; it is our old conceptions of community that no longer have any viability.

We have also detailed why this transformation in the nature of community became necessary. As the city becomes progressively more impersonal, persons must create new sources of sentiment, meaning, and identification. As persons' needs demand it, they will assign new meanings to objects and make different usages of existing institutions. We have seen how the marketplace is used by some as a source for identity fostering relationships. We have briefly discussed the possibility that institutions, like sport, may become the basis for subjective community identification. Our analysis is based on the presumption that persons are active participants in the construction of their social worlds.

We may also see how technological developments facilitate the kinds of interactional arrangements that we are describing. As technology develops, it is possible to create interactional networks that are literally boundless geographically. We are, for example, thinking of the use of the telephone in maintaining interactional circles of primary relations among geographically dispersed persons. The telephone company recognizes this, of course, as evidenced by the content of some of their television advertising. The status of the characters may change, but the theme of the ads is much the same. They always show the deep gratification received by those who, because of the relatively cheap rate of phone communication, are able to maintain contact over large spaces with intimate others.

The worth of thinking about communities as bounded by interactional rather than spacial variables is nicely illustrated in an ingenious experiment conducted by Stanley Milgram (1972). Milgram tries to show that social structures are composed of a number of overlapping circles of friends and acquaintances. In order to see just how these overlapping networks of interaction operated, Milgram worked out an experimental method to determine the line of acquaintance linking any two persons chosen at random.

The method he adopted worked as follows: Milgram picked out a person on the East coast who became the "target" for a number of other persons some distance away (in Kansas and Nebraska). Each person participating in the study was given the name and certain selected demographic information about the target person. They were given a folder and told that the object of the experiment was to get that folder to the target person as quickly as possible. The most important rule that each of these persons had to follow was the following: "If you do not know the target person on a personal basis, do not try to contact him directly. Instead, mail this folder ... to a personal acquaintance who is more likely than you to know the target person. ... It must be someone you know on a first name basis" (Milgram, 1972: 294). Milgram's intent, in other words, was to find out how many links it would take to reach the target person, if he could be reached at all.

The somewhat startling finding of this experimental procedure was that the median number of linkages necessary to reach the target person was only five. Milgram's experiment suggests that we are all embedded "in a small world structure." In terms of the arguments that we have made in this chapter, we agree with Milgram's own assessment of the potential importance of his study.

> [The study] reveals a potential communications structure whose sociological characteristics have yet to be exposed. When we understand the structure of this potential communications net, we shall understand a good deal more about the integration of society in general. While many studies in social science show how the individual is alienated and cut off from the rest of society, this study demonstrates that, in some sense, we are all bound together in a tightly knit social fabric. (Milgram, 1972: 299)

The tradition of classical sociological thought is to see, as we have mentioned, the source of integration in one's rootedness to a clearly discernible geographical area. That is perhaps why the image of the peasant community for so long clouded our notions of possible sources of integration as well as our conceptions of those situations in which integration of individuals simply did not exist. A reconception of that image is implied by Milgram's work and has been the general concern of our efforts throughout this chapter.

REFERENCES

Anderson, Nels. *The Hobo.* Chicago: University of Chicago Press, 1923.

Axelrod, Morris. "Urban Structure and Social Participation." *American Sociological Review,* 21 (February 1956): 13–18.

Becker, Howard. "The Relevance of Life Histories." Pp. 419–28 in Norman K. Denzin (ed.), *Sociological Methods.* Chicago: Aldine, 1970.

Bell, Wendell. "Urban Neighborhoods and Individual Behavior." Pp. 235–64 in Muzafer Sherif and Carolyn Sherif (eds.), *Problems of Youth.* Chicago: Aldine, 1965.

Bell, Wendell, and Marion T. Boat. "Urban Neighborhoods and Informal Social Relations." *American Journal of Sociology*, 62 (January 1957): 391–98.

Bell, Wendell, and M. Force. "Urban Neighborhood Types and Participation in Formal Associations." *American Sociological Review*, 21 (February 1956): 25–34.

Bell, Wendell, and Maryanne T. Force. "Social Structure and Participation in Different Types of Formal Associations." *Social Forces*, 34 (May 1956): 345–50.

Berger, Peter. *Invitation to Sociology*. Garden City, N.Y.: Doubleday, 1963.

Burgess, Ernest W. "The Growth of the City." Pp. 47–62 in Robert E. Park, Ernest Burgess, and R. McKenzie (eds.), *The City*. Chicago: University of Chicago Press, 1925.

Cressey, Paul G. *The Taxi Dance Hall*. Chicago: University of Chicago Press, 1932.

Duncan, Otis Dudley, and Albert Reiss. *Social Characteristics of Urban and Rural Communities*. New York: John Wiley, 1956.

Faris, Robert E. L. *Social Disorganization*. New York: Ronald Press, 1948.

Faris, Robert E. L., and H. W. Dunham. *Mental Disorders in Urban Areas*. Chicago: University of Chicago Press, 1939.

Firey, Walter. "Sentiment and Symbolism as Ecological Variables." *American Sociological Review*, 10 (April 1945): 140–48.

Form, William H., Joel Smith, Gregory P. Stone, and James Cowhig. "The Compatibility of Alternative Approaches to the Delimitation of Urban Sub Areas." *American Sociological Review*, 19 (August 1954): 434–40.

Fried, Marc. "Grieving for a Lost Home." Pp. 151–71 in Leonard Duhl (ed.), *The Urban Condition*. New York: Basic Books, 1963.

Fried, Marc, and Peggy Gleicher. "Some Sources of Residential Satisfaction in an Urban Slum." *Journal of the American Institute of Planners*, 27 (November 1961), 305–15.

Gans, Herbert. *The Urban Villagers*. New York: The Free Press, 1962.

Greer, Scott. *The Emerging City: Myth and Reality*. New York: The Free Press, 1964.

Greer, Scott. "Urbanism Reconsidered: A Comparative Study of Local Areas in a Metropolis." *American Sociological Review*, 21 (February 1956): 19–25.

Hall, Edward T. *The Hidden Dimension*. Garden City, N.Y.: Doubleday, 1969.

Harris, Chauncy D., and Edward L. Ullman. "The Nature of Cities." *The Annals of the American Academy of Political and Social Science*, 242 (November 1945): 7–17.

Hawley, Amos. *Human Ecology: A Theory of Community Structure*. New York: Ronald Press, 1950.

Hillery, George A. "Definitions of Community: Areas of Agreement." *Rural Sociology*, 20 (June 1955): 111–23.

Hoyt, Homer. "City Growth and Mortgage Risk." *Insured Mortgage Portfolio*. U.S. Federal Housing Administration, 1937.

Jacobs, Jane. *The Death and Life of Great American Cities.* New York: Random House, 1961.

Kaufman, Harold F. "Toward an Interactional Conception of Community." *Social Forces,* 38 (October 1959), 8–17.

Komarovsky, Mirra. "The Voluntary Associations of Urban Dwellers." *American Sociological Review,* 11 (December 1946): 686–98.

Kuhn, Thomas. *The Structure of Scientific Revolutions.* Chicago: University of Chicago Press, 1967.

Liebow, Eliot. *Tally's Corner.* Boston: Little, Brown, 1967.

Lodahl, Janice B., and Gerald Gordon. "The Structure of Scientific Fields and the Functioning of University Graduate Departments." *American Sociological Review,* 37 (February 1972): 57–72.

Lynd, Robert S., and Helen M. Lynd. *Middletown: A Study in Contemporary American Culture.* New York: Harcourt, Brace, 1929.

Lynd, Robert S., and Helen M. Lynd. *Middletown in Transition.* New York: Harcourt, Brace, 1937.

Martindale, Don. "Prefatory Remarks: The Theory of the City." Pp. 9–62 in Max Weber's *The City.* Translated by Don Martindale and Gertrud Neuwirth. New York: The Free Press, 1958.

McKenzie, R. D. "The Scope of Human Ecology." Pp. 167–82 in Ernest Burgess (ed.), *The Urban Community: Selected Papers from the Proceedings of the American Sociological Society.* Chicago: University of Chicago Press, 1925.

McKinney, J. *Constructive Typology and Social Theory.* New York: Appleton-Century-Crofts, 1966.

Milgram, Stanley. "The Small World Problem." Pp. 290–99 in Leonard Bickman and Thomas Henchy (eds.), *Beyond the Laboratory: Field Research in Social Psychology.* New York: McGraw-Hill, 1972.

Mowrer, Ernest. *Family Disorganization.* Chicago: University of Chicago Press, 1927.

Park, Robert E. "The City: Suggestions for the Investigation of Human Behavior in the Urban Environment." In Robert E. Park, *Human Communities.* New York: The Free Press, 1915.

Parsons, Talcott. "The Principal Structures of Community." In C. Friedrich (ed.) *Community.* New York: Liberal Arts Press, 1959.

Redfield, Robert. *The Little Community.* Chicago: University of Chicago Press, 1955.

Schwirian, Kent P. *Comparative Urban Structure: Studies in the Ecology of Cities.* Lexington, Mass.: D. C. Heath, 1974.

Seeley, John R., R. Alexander Sim, and Elizabeth W. Loosley. *Crestwood Heights.* New York: Basic Books, 1956.

Shevsky, Eshref, and Marilyn Williams. *The Social Areas of Los Angeles: Analysis and Typology.* Berkeley, Calif.: University of California Press, 1949.

Shaw, Clifford. *The Jack Roller* (2nd ed.). Chicago: University of Chicago Press, 1966.

Simmel, Georg. "The Metropolis and the Mental Life." Pp. 400–27 in

K. Wolff (ed.), *The Sociology of Georg Simmel*. New York: The Free Press, 1950.

Smith, Joel, William H. Form, and Gregory P. Stone. "Local Intimacy in a Middle-Sized City." *American Journal of Sociology*, 60 (November 1954): 276–84.

Sommer, Robert. *Personal Space*. Englewood Cliffs, N.J.: Prentice-Hall, 1969.

Stone, Gregory P. "City Shoppers and Urban Identification: Observations on the Social Psychology of City Life." *American Journal of Sociology*, 60 (November 1954): 276–84.

Stone, Gregory P. "Urban Identification and the Sociology of Sport." Paper presented at the annual meeting of the American Association for the Advancement of Science, 1968.

Sussman, Marvin (ed.). *Community Structure and Analysis*. New York: Crowell, 1959.

Suttles, Gerald. *The Social Order of the Slum*. Chicago: University of Chicago Press, 1968.

Thrasher, Frederick M. *The Gang: A Study of 1313 Gangs in Chicago*. Chicago: University of Chicago Press, 1926.

Vidich, Arthur, and Joseph Bensman. *Small Town in Mass Society*. Princeton, N.J.: Princeton University Press, 1958.

Warner, W. Lloyd, and Paul S. Lunt. *The Social Life of a Modern Community*. New Haven: Yale University Press, 1941.

Warren, Roland L. *The Community in America*, 2nd ed. Chicago: Rand McNally, 1972.

Weber, Max. *The City*. Translated and edited by Don Martindale and Gertrud Neuwirth. New York: The Free Press, 1958.

West, James. *Plainville, U.S.A.* New York: Columbia University Press, 1945.

Whyte, William F. *Street Corner Society*. Chicago: University of Chicago Press, 1943.

Wilensky, Harold L. "A Second Look at the Traditional View of Urbanism." Pp. 135–47 in Roland L. Warren (ed.), *Perspectives on the Urban Community*. Chicago: Rand McNally, 1966.

Wirth, Louis. "Urbanism as a Way of Life." *American Journal of Sociology*, 44 (July 1938): 1–24.

Wohl, R. Richard, and Anselm Strauss, "Symbolic Representation and the Urban Milieu." *American Journal of Sociology*, 63 (March 1958): 523–32.

Zorbaugh, Harvey. *The Gold Coast and the Slum*. Chicago: University of Chicago Press, 1937.

4

The Social Organization
of Everyday City Life

Our task of specifying or amending long-standing images of city life
is not yet completed. In the last chapter we chiefly considered how certain sociological images of community life have limited our understanding of urbanites' relations with one another. We discussed at
some length the necessity of viewing "community" in terms of the
range of meanings, sentiments, and feelings constituting persons' own
images of their lives in cities. We should have achieved, to this point,
a better understanding of how sustaining patterns of interaction de-

velop in cities—networks of social interaction that are not bounded spatially. We should better appreciate, by now, the subtle ways in which urban community life is organized. We should recognize, as well, how urbanites use city institutions to achieve a source of identification with each other and with the city itself.

There is, however, a conspicuous aspect of urban life that our conceptualizations developed thus far do not fully prepare us to understand. We have not yet thought about how city persons deal with, make sense of, or manage anonymous public encounters. If, as symbolic interactionists, we see it as a major goal of sociological inquiry to capture those whom we study "in their own terms," then we must ask how urban persons perceive and interact with fellow urbanites on a day-to-day basis in public places. Urbanites do, after all, come into contact with vast numbers of persons daily on city streets, on public conveyances, waiting in lines, and so forth. As we explained earlier, Simmel (1950) saw the everyday tempo of city life as importantly affecting the social psychology of urban persons.

There are, then, a number of questions that a focus on public city encounters leads us to ask: In what ways do urbanites see themselves constrained by the urban scene? In what ways might the anonymity of daily life provide urban persons with a greater freedom than might be found in the relative intimacy of nonurban settings? What are the perceived risks in establishing relations with strangers in the urban milieu? How do urbanites deal with the potential overload of stimuli that they are forced to confront daily? How do spacial configurations unique to the urban context shape our view of ourselves and our relations with others? Is there a clear normative structure to anonymous encounters? In general, the guiding question for this chapter is: In what ways are urban persons relating or failing to relate to one another in anonymous public settings?

An abiding image of the city stresses the failure of urbanites in public places to treat each other with any degree of civility. The litany of complaints about the insensitivity that urbanites show toward one another is long. Adjectives like *uncivilized, uncaring, indifferent, reserved, uncommunicative,* and *blasé* are frequently used to describe urbanites' attitudes toward one another. Visitors to large cities claim that it is frequently difficult to find someone willing to give simple directions. Urbanites seem to treat each other as adversaries, frequently competing for scarce resources—seats on subways, parking spaces, cabs, or places in line. Persons bump into one another on crowded streets, barely acknowledging the unwelcome contact. In the extreme this un-caring attitude is seemingly established by the failure of urbanites to intervene even in those cases where persons are in desperate trouble. The 1964 murder of Kitty Genovese on a New York street as several persons watched is taken by some as exemplifying the total lack of responsibility for each other that persons feel in urban public places. This image is shared by the anthropologist Edward Hall (1969: 174), who claims that "virtually everything about American cities today ... drives men apart, alienating them from each other. The recent and shocking instances in which people have been beaten and even mur-dered while their neighbors looked on without even picking up a phone indicates how far this trend toward alienation has progressed."

As previously, we do not claim that this image is thoroughly incor-rect, rather, it is overstated. It needs specification. It does not ade-quately enough explain how city life is possible in any form. We must come to understand how, in the face of this presumably "chaotic" urban place, persons manage to get along at all. To this end we must get beyond loose description of everyday urban life. We must analyze the daily situations faced by urban persons, the way those situations are defined, and how they are ultimately dealt with.

EVERYDAY INTERACTION:
A NEGLECTED ASPECT OF CITY LIFE

It has largely been only in the last decade that the study of everyday public behavior has become a major area of sociological inquiry. In a number of books written since 1959, Erving Goffman (1959, 1961, 1963, 1971, 1974) has been influential in showing the utility of frameworks for ordering a variety of everyday encounters. Goffman is not gen-erally considered an urban sociologist, and his work is infrequently cited in the context of a discussion of urban sociology. Nevertheless, to the extent that many of the examples appearing in his writing on everyday public interactions are drawn from urban contexts, it is im-portant to consider his theoretical ideas here. With regard to the soci-ological importance of studying everyday behaviors, Goffman says this:

> Although this area (the study of behavior in public and semi-public places) has not been recognized as a special domain for sociological inquiry, it perhaps should be, for the rules of conduct in streets, parks, restaurants, shops, dance floors, meeting halls, and other

gathering places of any community tell us a great deal about its most diffuse forms of social organization. (1963: 4)

The omission of "everyday social interaction" as a major area of sociological inquiry generally—and urban sociology more particularly —is a curious one. We say this because even those theorists who attempt the analysis of large institutional arrangements in a society must have some guiding model of the nature of microsocial interaction. One writer (Wilson, 1970: 697) has made this point by stating that "the process of interaction is . . . at the logical core of sociological interest, even though for some purposes, particularly of a macrosociological sort, this is often left implicit."

It is a major premise of this book, and a major underlying theme of symbolic interaction, that one cannot fully understand the operation of any large institutional complex (a school, a business organization, an army, a city) without paying attention to the ways in which the individuals who make up those institutions are defining and making sense of them. Sociologists frequently lose sight of the fact that institutions are composed of acting, thinking, defining, interacting human beings. The study of face-to-face interaction is not, therefore, simply an exercise motivated by idle curiosity. "Any understanding of human behavior at whatever level of ordering or generality must begin with and be built upon an understanding of everyday life of the members performing those actions" (Douglas, 1970: 11).

If, as we suggest, the study of everyday interactional routines is such an important matter, why has it been so thoroughly neglected by urban sociologists? One reason may be that in most public urban situations, individuals do not appear to be interacting with one another. In anonymous urban situations they seem to avoid one another, closing themselves off from direct communication. Urbanites frequently hide behind newspapers. They normally avoid excessive eye contact as an invitation to interaction. They maximize their "personal space." To be sure, any interaction that may occur seems to be of a most transitory, ephemeral sort. They are encounters constructed around a question asked and an answer given, an accidental bump and an "I'm sorry." These are interactions without a career. They have no past and hold little possibility of a future. Urbanites seem to shun involvement with others at nearly all cost. They watch passively as a person is beaten up on the street. They pass by derelicts lying in gutters. They seem to look upon any direct encounters with others as fraught with danger. City dwellers, in sum, appear distrustful, if not fearful, of contact with others. Hence, the logical question: "How can one study public urban interactions when no such interaction is occurring?"

One of the things we shall try to show here is that those who hold to this view have too narrow an idea of social interaction. Interaction encompasses more than direct *verbal* communication. We advocate a view that interaction is occurring in any social situation in which persons are acting in awareness of others and are continually adjusting their behaviors to the expectations and possible responses of others. Our definition, for example, would cause us to see *avoidance* as a form of social interaction. As we shall see, there are occasions, particularly in urban settings, when persons must communicate to others that they wish to avoid communication. In the typical urban street situation it appears that persons have nothing to do with each other, that persons on subway cars bear no relation to one another, and so on. By looking closely at the behavior of persons in such contexts, we see that the operation of our everyday behavior as urbanites demands a high degree of cooperation. We must question the assumption that urban interactions are haphazard, unordered, or altogether nonexistent. Immediately we may assert that persons in public places cooperate with one another if for no other reason than to preserve and sustain their social identities. The "moral" task of preserving both one's own and others' public images is most detailed in Goffman's writings.

IDENTITY AND INTERACTION

Goffman is primarily responsible for what has come to be known as the "dramaturgical" view of interaction. In our previous discussions we argued that people are not merely passive agents, simply abiding by fixed meaning structures. Persons, rather, are always in the process of defining and redefining one anothers' acts, and they are continually interpreting and assigning meanings to the situations in which they are behaving. The dramaturgical view of interaction developed by Goffman clearly falls within a symbolic interactionist frame of reference. Goffman is sympathetic to the idea that persons must interpret the interactions in which they find themselves, that they must forge out meanings in the encounters in which they participate. In Goffman's work, and central to the dramaturgical model, certain aspects of this process are emphasized. Beyond being a role-taker and a meaning interpreter, Goffman sees persons as continually *manipulating* meanings in interaction.

Goffman sees persons as continually fostering impressions of themselves (the model is sometimes referred to as an "impression-management" model). Persons are always to some degree systematically excluding information about themselves that might be damaging in any particular social encounter. For Goffman human beings are always "on" in the theatrical sense. He views persons as primarily concerned with their appearances. It matters little what one *actually* is. What really matters is what one *appears* to be, because it is on the basis of appearances that persons will formulate their definitions of the situation. In other words, actors always have some motive for trying to control the definition of the situation that others will come to have.

In the analogy suggested by a dramaturgical view of interaction, the essential reality of life becomes a series of fostered roles, and society becomes a theatre in which all are actors engaged in a perpetual play. Goffman's view results from his taking seriously Shakespeare's claim that "All the world's a stage and all the men and women merely players."

There are a number of major assumptions underlying such a view of human relations. Because of space limitations we shall not attempt to discuss them all. We must, however, note what is clearly the major assumption underlying this model. Basic to the dramaturgical model is the view that people are continually guided in their behavior by the need for approval. Goffman sees us as anxious to receive social approval for our acts. The approving agreement of others helps to confirm the images that we have of ourselves. We want to be seen as social, as proper, as worthwhile persons. People coming together are always trying to present their best "faces" in an attempt to win recognition and approval from others. Goffman does not see us as having only one identity. We have, rather, a repertoire of identities, and we choose from among these the identity that will make us appear as most proper in front of a particular audience.

Given this characterization of human life, we can begin to see the tentativeness, fragility, and risks that may be involved in any social interaction. In the beginning of his first major work, *The Presentation of Self in Everyday Life,* Goffman (1959) understandably argues that if we are always managing impressions in order to appear as proper, then there is a major risk to be run in any social interaction. There is the unremitting possibility that the images and identities presented to others are subject to disruption. Any interaction is likely to be suddenly punctured by events that cast new and unfavorable light on us. There is always the possibility that our presented self-image will be disconfirmed by public events. Given such a model, it is no mystery why the dramaturgic analyst's work frequently focuses on the commission of improprieties by persons. The study of public deviance is a necessary research concern. It is by studying those situations in which something goes awry that we are informed about the processes through which order is normally maintained.

For Goffman (and this is a theme that runs through a good deal of his work), individuals in public places work to insure their "properness" by carefully monitoring the nature of their "involvement" with others. To the extent that those in public places wish to be seen as proper by those around them, they are clearly taking one another into account in producing their own behaviors. The silent, internal question that persons must continually raise for themselves is: "What is sufficient presence or involvement in various social context?" More directly of interest for us is an assessment of what constitutes appropriate situational involvement in urban, anonymous public situations. The decision made by persons in public regarding the proper extent of their involvement with others hinges on an important feature of urban public life—persons in anonymous urban settings have little or no biographical information about one another; they are strangers to one another.

CITY LIFE AS A WORLD OF STRANGERS [1]

In seeking to discover the "hidden dimensions" of urban public life, one fact seems of unique importance. Anonymous public sectors are composed of persons who are strangers to one another. "Far from being constantly surrounded by persons who share his culture and have a stake in preserving his system of meaning and interactional rituals, the urbanite, whenever he ventures forth into the public sector of the city, is instead, plunged into a world peopled by many strange and alien

---

[1] Our thinking in this section has been heavily influenced by Lyn Lofland's (1973) penetrating study of the historical transformation of urban life. She argues that the basis for public order in preindustrial cities was persons' appearances. With the emergence of industrial cities, public order was determined by persons' geographical location rather than by appearances.

others" (Lofland, 1972: 97). The fact of urbanites' strangeness to one another would seem, on the face of it, to have profound implications for the way that public life is managed. Clearly, the way that we conduct ourselves in interaction is a function of the degree of intimacy that exists between ourselves and others.

We have already asserted, following our description of Goffman's dramaturgical model of interaction, that it is our unremitting task to appear proper in the eyes of others. Persons are concerned with presenting a "correct" self in any social encounter. In urban settings, the strategies employed by actors, the definitions of the situation they construct, the impressions of themselves offered to others, and the extent to which their activity is calculated are all inescapably related to their mutual status as strangers.

The status of stranger has long intrigued sociological theorists (Simmel, 1950; Schutz, 1960; Lyman and Scott, 1970; Milgram, 1972; Berger, 1970). In Georg Simmel's (1950) famous discussion, the relationship of the stranger to organized group life is stressed. Simmel is not so much concerned with one-to-one relations between persons as he is with the relationship between an individual and a larger social system (a group, a community, or an institution). The special quality of the stranger's status is the fact that while he or she may hold membership in a group, the individual nevertheless remains a peripheral or marginal member of the group. In Simmel's (1950: 404) words, the stranger is near and distant at the same time. "It is that synthesis of nearness and distance which constitutes the formal position of the stranger."

In another famous essay, titled "The Stranger," the philosopher Alfred Schutz (1964) also speaks of the status of the stranger in terms of the individual's relationship to some organized group life. In Schutz's case greatest stress is placed on the fact that the stranger simply is not knowledgeable about the "taken-for-granted" cultural pattern of the everyday life of the group to which he seeks admission. The stranger simply does not share the same relevancies of everyday life as the group members do. He is not sure exactly how to interpret social situations, social events, and social behaviors. The stranger, typified by the immigrant, is, at least initially, puzzled by the incoherence, lack of clarity, and seeming inconsistency of the group's cultural pattern. The stranger is forced to call into question those elements of group life that full-fledged members of the group utterly take for granted. In Schutz's own words, "the cultural pattern of the approached group is to the stranger not a shelter but a field of adventure, not a matter of course but a questionable topic of investigation, not an instrument for disentangling problematic situations but a problematic situation itself and one hard to master (1964: 104).

As insightful as they are, these conceptions of the stranger do not fully serve our purposes. In urban public settings individuals are rarely trying to relate to any specific group. More congenial to our purposes is Peter Berger's conception of "strangeness."

Berger (1970: 54) thinks about strangeness this way: "The strangeness lies in the fact that [persons] come from different face-to-face contexts ... they come from different areas of conversation. They do not have a shared past, although their pasts have a similar structure." By different areas of conversation, Berger means that persons possess different biographies, discrete experiences, and possibly, therefore, dissimilar definitions of the situation. In this regard we might suggest that it is the merging of separate biographies and the production of some kind of joint reality that transforms an anonymous, unanchored relationship between strangers into a relationship that has a career, a relationship that now has a past and the likelihood of a future.

A key, then, to understanding the relationship between strangers in public places lies in the fact that, by definition, they have little or no biographical information about one another. This lack of social information increases actors' conceptions of the potential risks that may be involved in public encounters.

INFORMATION AND RISK
IN STRANGER INTERACTION

All social interactions, even those between intimates, involve a degree of risk. The risk originates in the possibility that an information deficit will cause an actual or potential interaction to go awry. Risk is an inherent feature of interactions, as we can never be sure of the motives and intentions of those with whom we engage ourselves in interaction. We can never fully suspend doubt about the "true" motives of others. Our inability ever to suspend doubt fully is a constant feature of interaction and poses for us a problem that is never fully soluble. One paradox of interaction is that we must *doubt* and *trust* the other at the same time. While ordered interaction must proceed on the normative assumption that others' spoken words and actions reflect the actual nature of their interests, motives, and goals, we can never be sure that such an assumption is a safe one. We must, in short, run a course between complete trust on the one hand and paranoia on the other.

Encounters between strangers pose special problems. Strangers have little or no information about one another except that information which can be ascertained through immediate observation (dress, demeanor, and facial expression). Such readily accessible, although partial, information can be referred to as "face" information.

In some instances the potential risks are so clear that strangers will assiduously avoid even the slightest encounter. Here we refer to the case in which, on the basis of face information alone, it is easily apparent that either no meaningful interaction could take place or that any interaction might be improper. We are thinking, for example, of a badly dressed black man and a well-dressed white woman, or an old man and a little girl. Those who unwarily attempt to begin interactions, in anonymous public settings, even when these "face discrepancies" exist, do so at potentially great risk. The black man may possibly be suspected as a mugger, the old man as a "dirty old man," and so forth.

In short, we depend heavily on face information in determining which potential interactions are permissible and which impermissible because they involve too great a risk. We carry around with us fairly clear background expectancies concerning the appropriateness of social interactions. We know, for example, that when lost we ask only *certain* persons for directions. White cab drivers will sometimes pass by certain persons (blacks, those obviously drunk, those persons in particular areas of the city). And so on.

The point that we wish to make is that there are always risks to be run in engaging a stranger in interaction. There is the possibility of generating a set of obligations that one is not prepared for or is unwilling to pay off, the possibility of damage to one's presented self-image, attacks on one's identity, boredom, loss of time, and even the chance of physical danger. Just as the knowledgeable gambler understands that the one sure thing is that there is no such thing as a sure thing and works systematically to reduce the possibility of unforeseen contingencies in placing his bet, so should we expect all persons to attempt minimizing the odds of an unpleasant, risky interaction.

Beyond the fact that urbanites in anonymous situations are biographical strangers to one another, we must as well consider the sheer volume of potential interaction faced by persons in the midst of the large city. William H. Whyte (1974) has determined that on an average weekday some 38,000 persons pass between 57th and 58th streets on Lexington Avenue in New York—one short city block. The psychologist Stanley Milgram has recently considered the effect of this density and the unremitting nature of potential encounters in the city. He has stressed the need for adaptive mechanisms to deal with what he terms urban "overload."

A THEORY OF URBAN OVERLOAD

Like many others, Milgram (1970) begins his inquiry by making reference to Louis Wirth's (1938) essay on the city. He agrees at the outset that the criteria offered by Wirth adequately define the city. The city is large, dense, and heterogeneous. Milgram goes on to argue, however, that these demographic characteristics have not been used in producing an adequate enough social psychology of the city. As a psychologist he argues that we need an idea that "links the individual's experience to these demographic circumstances of urban life." The theoretical link proposed by Milgram stresses the idea of "stimulus overload." His argument, very simply, is that urbanites in their daily lives are bombarded with far more stimuli than they can successfully handle. The human organism simply cannot process and act upon all the stimuli that it necessarily confronts daily. "City life, as we experience it, constitutes a continuous set of encounters with overload, and of resultant adaptations." In his article titled "The Experience of Living in Cities," Milgram (1970) tries to outline some of the adaptations that urban persons are forced to make in the face of this stimulus overload.

It should be noted that the theory which Milgram here seeks to make explicit is to be found in rudimentary form in earlier works. Georg Simmel, as we noted in Chapter 2, indicated that urbanites must somehow come to grips with the multiple experiences of city life. Simmel suggests that the urbanite must maintain ever more superficial and anonymous relations with his fellow urbanites in order to maintain his "psychic life." The link between density, heterogeneity, and the psychology of the individual is made in the following statement from Simmel's article:

> With each crossing of the street, with the tempo and multiplicity of economic, occupational and social life, the city sets up a deep contrast with small town and rural life with reference to the sensory foundations of psychic life. The metropolis exacts from man

as a discriminating creature a different amount of consciousness than does rural life. Here the rhythm of life and sensory mental imagery flows more slowly, more habitually and more evenly. Precisely in this connection the sophisticated character of metropolitan psychic life becomes more understandable as over against small town life which rests more upon deeply felt and emotional relationships. (1950: 410)

The genius of Milgram's work lies in his ability to find "quasi-experimental" methods for testing the effects of stimulus overload and hence for detailing the various adaptations that urbanites must make in the city to maintain their "psychic lives."

The first effect that he notes is the need for the urbanites to set priorities regarding the phenomena in their everyday lives that they are willing to take into account. Principles of selectivity must be established in order to evaluate how much time and energy will be devoted to various inputs. In this regard, for example, the failure of urbanites to help drunks or those down-and-out on the city street becomes understandable. Such daily events must be given low priority because, were we to attend to every such street occurrence, we would soon find ourselves doing nothing but helping drunks on the street. The frequency of that situation is simply too great for us to deal with it in any kind of continuous fashion. The anonymity of the city and the relative indifference paid to others in public places becomes meaningful as a necessary response to the overstimulation of the city. It is in this regard that the lessening of *social responsibility* can be made sense of.

Milgram argues that the urbanite must generate quite specific norms of "noninvolvement." The failure of the urbanite to help others in trouble can be understood in terms of a norm of noninvolvement. Urbanites are less willing to assist and aid strangers than their rural counterparts are. Milgram's students demonstrated this by comparing the number of persons in urban and "town" areas who were willing to allow strangers into their homes. Investigators claimed to have lost the address of a friend living nearby and asked if it was possible to use the phone of the persons approached. The question that Milgram sought to answer was whether these persons would gain more entries in towns than in cities. He reports (1970: 1463) that "in all cases there was a sharp increase in the proportion of entries achieved by an experimenter when he moved from the city to the small town."

Part of this general norm of noninvolvement is that "the traditional courtesies" or civilities of social life are less apparent in the city. Persons bumping into one another seldom stop to offer their apologies. Indeed, the norms of noninvolvement are so strong in the city that "men are actually embarrassed to give up a seat on a subway to an old woman" (Milgram, 1970: 1464). All these instances of noninvolvement, in their totality, constitute, for Milgram, the essence of urban anonymity. Milgram is quick to point out that the kind of anonymity he describes is not all bad. It is because of this anonymity that persons with various eccentricities are tolerated in the city. Because of norms of noninvolvement, stigmatized persons generally find greater acceptance within urban contexts. The general idea raised by Milgram is that the city offers many "protective benefits" not offered in the small town.

Milgram's analysis raises another important point. It seems clear from his writing that theories postulating a distinctive "urban personality type" may be substantially in error. Rather, we must see that the behavior of urbanites is "situationally defined." In Milgram's (1970: 1465) own words, "contrasts between city and rural behavior probably reflect the responses of *similar people to very different situations,* rather than intrinsic differences in the personalities of rural and city dwellers. The city is a situation to which individuals respond adaptively." (Emphasis is ours.)

While Milgram's theory is intriguing, it does not adequately enough explain how the norm of noninvolvement is maintained. It is to that issue that we now turn.

A MINI-MAX HYPOTHESIS OF URBAN LIFE

To this point our characterization of urbanites' public encounters still seems hazy and elusive. Urbanites seem to shun encounters with one another, minimizing their involvement whenever possible. They are constrained to generate a norm of noninvolvement because of the social risks that are tied to stranger interaction and because of the inability to cope with the sheer volume and complexity of potential encounters in the city. At the same time we have asserted, following Goffman, that persons have an investment in appearing "correct" in front of others —even strangers—so as to preserve their self-images. Persons seek to pick up information about others; this information on the one hand may facilitate interaction and on the other may be used successfully to avoid interaction. There seems to be a constant dialectic between indifference and involvement. A paradox of public urban interaction is that persons must systematically take one another into account in order to avoid unwanted encounters successfully.

The sociologist Lyn Lofland has suggested (1971) that public ordered life between strangers is possible because urbanites have successfully created a workable social contract, a kind of public social bargain. Indeed, she says that "all social life may be viewed as a kind of social bargain, a whispered enjoinder to let us all protect each other so that we can carry on the business of living" (1971: 226). Persons in public settings are expected to exert some effort in preserving both their own *and others'* public identities. The effort expended in this type of mutual protection is evident in one of Lofland's examples. She cites the case of an older man sitting in a restaurant booth carrying on an active conversation with an imaginary other. The conversation was quite complete as the man animatedly made a statement and then listened intently as the "other" made his or her reply. As the waitress approached to take the order, the man happened to be in the midst of a rather lengthy reply to a point made by the other. The waitress waited patiently until a "break" in the conversation and only then asked if he was ready to order. During this whole time the waitress showed no evidence that anything extraordinary was occurring. Unless persons pose some type of direct threat, urbanites are willing to tolerate, and to treat as "normal," quite eccentric public behaviors.

In urban contexts this social bargain seems to demand that persons cooperate with one another enough to insure some intelligibility and order in their everyday lives while seeking simultaneously to keep at a minimum their involvement with one another. We are asserting, then, a kind of mini-max description of urban encounters. Urbanites seek to *minimize involvement* and to *maximize social order*. Persons must act in concert. Persons must take one another into account. At the same time persons must protect their personal privacy, a commodity hard to come by in urban settings. Urbanites must, in other words, create a kind of "public privacy." They are required to strike a balance between involvement, indifference, and cooperation with one another.

These descriptions of city interaction may seem strange, if not contradictory—intimate anonymity, public privacy, involved indifference; yet these subtle combinations of apparently opposite ideas do capture the quality of a good deal of city life. They suggest that, while urban persons may spend relatively little time engaged in direct verbal interactions with one another, they are nevertheless deliberately acting in awareness of, and adjusting their own behaviors to, the possible response of others.

It is easy enough to say that city persons must consistently take one another into account in order to create the proper balance of indifference and involvement as they move through urban public places. If public encounters are to be carried off successfully, however, persons must share an enormous amount of social knowledge in common—must share a large number of meanings about city life in common. There must be some degree of consensus among persons relative to the meanings that they attribute to both their own and others' behaviors. Persons must share some notion of what constitutes appropriate involvement with others in public settings. As a continuing step in our analysis, we must specify the knowledge that persons acquire and use in anonymous situations.

SOCIAL KNOWLEDGE AND
MEANING ATTRIBUTION

The problem of how individuals attribute meaning to each others' acts is a long-standing one in sociology. The famous sociologist Max Weber (1947) emphasized in his early discussion of "social action" the need to understand the subjective meaning of the actor. He saw the goal of social science as understanding social action, an understanding that was possible only by grasping the subjectively intended meanings of social actors. Weber, in other words, directly and seriously concerned himself with the problems of attributing meaning to social action. In one of his famous works titled *Economy and Society,* Weber defined the methodological boundaries of sociology this way:

> Sociology is a science which attempts the interpretive understanding of social action in order to thereby arrive at a causal explanation of its course and effects. (1947: 88)

Later he defined social action as follows:

> Action is social in so far as, by virtue of the subjective meaning attached to it by the acting individual, it takes account of the behavior of others and is thereby oriented in its course. (1947: 88)

Despite Weber's delineation of the issue, much discussion of social interaction proceeds on the assumption that the meaning of social acts is unproblematic. Symbolic interactionists, on the other hand, have been influential in demonstrating the faulty nature of the sociologist's assumption that he simply knows the meaning of the social action that he happens to be observing.

There is now growing agreement that the same concrete act will be interpreted differently by different observers of the act; that there exists, in short, not one reality, but "multiple realities." According to this view, "the same events or objects can have different meanings for different people, and the degree of difference will produce comparable differences in behavior" (McHugh, 1968: 8).

On the face of it, the view that multiple realities exist seems inimicable to, or inconsistent with, the empirical observation of order in a society. If there are, indeed, multiple meanings attributed to concretely identical behaviors, how are we to explain persons acting in concert?

Peter Berger and Thomas Luckman (1967) provide an answer by arguing that, despite slight variations in meaning attributed to acts or events, society does provide us all with a *baseline of knowledge* in the form or rules or norms. They are suggesting that because actors consensually share a body of social knowledge, they are able to construct a working reality in common. They write:

> I know, of course, that others have a perspective on this common world that is not identical with mine. My "here" is their "there." My "now" does not overlap with theirs .... All the same, I know that I live with them in a common world. Most importantly, I know that there is an ongoing correspondence between my meanings and their meanings of the world, that we share a common sense about its reality. (1967: 23)

While the world, in one sense, is a subjective entity, the extent of our knowledge shared in common allows us to treat the world as though it were an objective reality. Without this commonsense sharing of knowledge, social order would be impossible. Such social knowledge is extremely far-reaching, encompassing literally thousands of social conventions. Before we describe some of the social conventions governing public urban behavior, an important caveat is necessary.

Social knowledge does not have a universal, unchanging character. It is an essential premise of symbolic interaction that the meaning of any social act, verbal or nonverbal, is situationally specific. The baseline of knowledge that Berger and Luckman suggest exists is just that

—a baseline. Our knowledge must be continually reevaluated as we move from one setting to another. It is a body of knowledge continually open to reinterpretation and amendment. Having made this caveat, let us examine some of the normative regularities operative in anonymous urban contexts—normative regularities that allow persons to insure the "public privacy" about which we spoke earlier.

THE CONSTRUCTION OF PUBLIC PRIVACY:
A LOOK AT SOME LITERATURE

To this point our discussion has been on a fairly abstract level. The time has come to be more concrete, and in this section we shall detail some of the categories of norms within which everyday life is carried out. Our question is simply this: What are the types of normative conventions followed by city persons that maximize intelligibility and predictability in their relations with others while simultaneously maximizing their own sense of privacy in public? With the aid of research done by others, it is possible to describe some of the constraints typically imposed on persons as they face others within the city.

Two researchers, particularly Robert Sommer (1969) and Edward Hall (1969), have demonstrated the importance of spacial regulations in ordinary everyday behaviors (a field of study that has been labeled *proxemics*). Sommer (1969) has maintained, in a book titled *Personal Space*, that we all have a kind of invisible circle drawn around us that marks off our personal territory. It is a personal territory that, with few exceptions, we do not allow others to violate. Spacial conventions are evident in our simplest daily encounters. In American society, for example, normal conversational distance is about two feet; we become increasingly uncomfortable if persons come any closer to us. Imagine, if you will, how you might react should a relative or total stranger converse with you only inches from your face.

Spacial norms often work in conjunction with the way that we use our eyes. Next time the reader is in a public elevator, he or she ought to notice the way that persons carefully avoid eye contact by looking either at the floor or at the numbers over the door. A plausible explanation may be that eye contact is an invitation to verbal contact, and we do not wish to make verbal contact in a situation in which our personal space might be violated.

With regard to the use of social space, Edward Hall's work is particularly instructive in that he offers a variety of cross-cultural comparisons.

In his book *The Hidden Dimension,* Hall (1969), who formally considers himself an anthropologist, examines "man's use of space in public and private." A good part of this book is spent in detailing cultural variations in the use of, and response to, space. He describes, for example, variations in distance maintained by persons in different cultures under differing conditions. He is able to show that sense of private territory, conversational distances, and public distances maintained by Americans, Germans, Frenchmen, and Arabs are very different.

Given such cultural differences in the experience of space, it follows that there are variations between cultures in persons' felt need for privacy, the degree of population density and crowding that is tolerable, and the like. In comparing Americans with Arabs, for example, Hall notes that olfaction (the sense of smell) is an important distance-setting mechanism for Arabs. Arabs directly breathe on one another while talking. Arabs find it pleasant and desirable to experience each other's body odors. Arabs, it follows, typically maintain a closer conversation distance than do Americans. While Germans seem to have a strong need for the kind of privacy produced by closed-in walls and doors, Arabs hate to be similarly "hemmed in." In terms of territory and ownership of space, Arabs have no real conception of boundaries. In the United States "ownership" of some public territory (a seat in a public place, for example) is determined by the party who first occupies that space. For Arabs, the ownership of space is determined, alternatively, by which person first began to *move toward* the unoccupied space, regardless of who arrives there first. While Hall's book is filled with examples similar to those cited above, it is important to keep from getting caught up in the examples while losing sight of the general point. Hall sees the importance of his particular brand of cultural anthropology of space (which he terms proxemics) this way:

> Proxemic patterns differ. By examining them it is possible to reveal hidden cultural frames that determine the structure of a given people's perceptual world. Perceiving the world differently leads to differential definitions of what constitutes crowded living, different interpersonal relations, and a different approach to both local and international politics. There are in addition wide discrepancies in the degree to which culture structures involvement, which means that planners should begin to think in terms of different kinds of

cities, cities which are consistent with the proxemic patterns of the people who live in them. (1969: 164)

In an earlier section of his book, Hall examined studies that reported on the effects of overcrowding in animal populations. The result of overcrowding among colonies of rats, for example, was the development of a variety of pathological behaviors—rats killed each other off, there were substantial changes in the biological structure of the rats, and the like. This combination of pathologies engendered by overcrowding has been termed a "behavioral sink." In a pessimistic fashion, Hall (1969: 172) predicts that, unless planners and architects begin fully to take into account the spacial needs of human beings and the way those needs vary from culture to culture, there will develop an "urban sink" with its own distinctive human pathologies. "The degree to which peoples are sensorially involved with each other, and how they use time, determine not only at what point they are crowded but the methods for relieving the crowding as well" (1969: 172).

As evidence that "urban sinks" may occur if we do not adequately consider the effects of crowding, Hall notes that rates of crime and illness are highest in the most crowded areas of the city. We must, however, be careful not to leap to any conclusions from these data. Is it crowding that is creating the pathology, as Hall suggests, or might it be that crowding is merely another symptom of conditions brought about by poverty? Might it not be that poverty is the "real" cause of some of the behaviors mentioned by Hall? While we may argue endlessly about the specific effects of different spacial configurations, one thing is clear. There is a direct relationship between the use of space and the nature of human interaction possible. Hall's conclusion that architects must design cities with an eye to the spacial needs of persons seems unassailable.

Some of the most influential and far-ranging work on city life has been accomplished by researchers utilizing experimental and quasi-experimental methods. Very frequently in this kind of work the strategy is somehow to disrupt the normal, natural processes of everyday life. If researchers are correct in understanding how everyday urban life is normally conducted, they should, then, be able to predict how persons will behave once these "normal" routines have been disrupted. Put more directly, if the researcher believes that certain norms are important in guiding some aspect of social life, the best way to establish the norm's existence is to transgress that "alleged" norm and to note the reaction of persons to the transgression. A combination of close, careful, naturalistic observation and the purposive manipulation of social settings can reveal a great deal about how "everyday" urban life is constructed, ordered, and typically carried off. This is nicely demonstrated, for example, in Wolff's (1973) work on "pedestrian behavior." His work amply illustrates that persons in "anonymous" urban street situations are very much taking each other into account.

He notes correctly at the beginning of his study that "one of the most striking and yet routine aspects of city life is the movement of large numbers of people into, around, and out of the mid-town business district each day" (1973: 35). In this study, conducted on 42nd Street in New York City, the author sought to discover how pedestrian behavior was coordinated. What were the "cultural prescriptions" that ordered this commonplace behavior? The author had one male and one female experimenter approach subjects on a direct "collision course." This was done under two conditions—one was a low-density condition (where there were five–fifteen people in the immediate geographical area of encounter) and the other designated as a high-density condition (between sixteen and thirty persons in the area). Of primary interest here was to discover the "yield" distance under varying conditions. (Yield distance refers to the distance at which the subjects altered their course in order to avoid the approaching collision with the experimenter.) Would the yield distance vary with the sex of the experimenter and the density of the situation? The researchers found that there were very significant constancies in the behavior of subjects approached. Under low-density conditions, subjects consistently yielded at a distance of about seven feet. In high-density conditions, there was again great uniformity—in this case persons yielded at about five feet. Wolff also showed that when the experimenter was the same sex as the approaching subject, the yield distance was at a slightly shorter distance than when the sex of subject and experimenter were different. Another variation of this experiment was to place a stationary object on the sidewalk around which persons would have to make a detour. In this situation the subjects began to alter their course and prepare to get around the object at a considerably greater distance—sixteen and one-half feet.

Of equal interest was the analysis of video-tape pictures made of persons walking on the street. The experimenters set up a camera on an adjoining building so that they could later analyze in great detail the patterns of pedestrian behavior. Analysis of these tapes indicate that "the most outstanding characteristic of pedestrian behavior that has emerged is the amount and degree of *cooperation* between persons on the streets of the city" (1973: 48). The researchers were able to show that there are a number of consistent patterns of "accommodation" made by persons on the street. Among these were the following:

1. *Step-and-slide pattern.* The researchers describe a constant pattern of behavior that they label the *step-and-slide*. As persons pass one another, there is not a total avoidance of physical contact. There is a "slight angling of the body, a turning of the shoulder and an almost imperceptible side step—a sort of step and slide. While pedestrians do not make a totally "clean pass," they cooperate with one another by pulling their hands inward and twisting their bodies so as to minimize the amount of physical contact. It is worth noting, as a test of the operation of the step and slide that when the experimenters purposively did not cooperate, the response of persons were of the following sort: "Watsa madder? Ya blind? Whyn't ya look whea ya goin? Ya crazy?"

2. *The head-over-the-shoulder pattern.* When walking behind a person fewer than five feet away, a pedestrian strives to maintain a "head-over-the-shoulder" relationship with the person or persons in front. This accommodation serves two purposes. It allows the individual to clearly see what is occurring in front of him and makes it less likely that he will stumble into the feet of the person in front.

3. *The spread effect.* In order to maximize efficiency on the street, persons walking in one direction on a sidewalk distribute themselves to the fullest width that the natural boundaries will allow.

4. *Detouring.* A person forced to detour around an object or person attempts to retain his/her original path once the detour has been accomplished.

5. *Avoiding perceptual objects.* People tend to treat perceptually distinct parts of the pavement, such as grating, as obstructions to be avoided or circumnavigated when possible.

6. *Monitoring.* Persons are continually monitoring the environment in order to avoid collisions as well as to evaluate the potential behaviors of others. Especially interesting here is the observation that persons scan the faces of persons approaching them on the street. "If the oncoming pedestrians appear to be fixating in the same direction and, more importantly, are expressing surprise, fear, or general excitement, this is taken to be a cue to make a full-head turn, stop

for a full check-out, or both. In this sense, pedestrians use other pedestrians as a "rear-view" mirror.

These observations demonstrate that a set of behaviors which we wholly take for granted as urbanites is really well organized and dependent upon a distinctive "normative cooperation" among actors.

In another context, J. Levine et al. (1973) have done systematic observations of subways and have shown how persons indicate that they do not wish to be communicated with. Persons in this face-to-face situation place a high premium on avoiding unnecessary encounters. As in many other public contexts, individuals engage in what Erving Goffman has described as "civil inattention"—persons are forced to recognize each other's presence while trying to minimize the possibility of a "focused" interaction with them. Persons, in other words, work to minimize the interactional claims that others might make on them. This interactional work is, of course, reciprocal, as all the actors in the setting are doing the same. Subway riders will always choose a seat that maximizes their distance from fellow travelers; they will limit their visual attention to props that they may have with them (books, magazines, newspapers) or to advertising over the windows. They will take great pains to avoid physical contact, will keep their hands very visible to defeat any possible charge of a sexual impropriety once the subway car begins to get crowded, and the like. These regulations, shared and known about by all participants in the setting, are designed to "protect unacquainted individuals from accessibility to one another" (1973: 216).

Frequently the order of public life is best seen in those situations in which persons' moral identities are most potentially called into question. Karp (1973) studied the behaviors of persons in Times Square pornographic bookstores and movie theatres. Times Square was a useful context for investigation because it epitomizes the anonymous inner-city area. As such, it was a good testing ground for a number of assumptions found in the urban literature about urban interpersonal relations. His Times Square data show that persons engaging in unconventional behaviors in a typically anonymous sector of the city are concerned with being defined as "social" or "proper," even by total strangers. Despite the fact that persons were not engaged in direct verbal interaction, they were very much taking one another into account in this setting. Karp describes a number of maneuvers engaged in by persons while involved in these settings.

He reports that persons frequenting bookstores have available and use a number of devices for hiding, shielding, or obscuring the nature of their "deviant" involvement from "outsiders" (nonparticipants in bookstore pornography) as well as from persons similarly involved in buying or using pornographic materials. In order to insure that the nature of their dominant involvement (that is, buying or using pornographic materials) will be hidden from those around them, persons utilize a kind of "waiting" behavior. Before entering a store, persons spend a long time looking in the window or generally hanging around outside the store. In doing so, they hope to communicate to those around them that they are "merely curious" or "idly curious" about the contents of the store. Such "stalling" behavior also serves the purpose of checking out the environment before entering the store.

Once in the store, persons maintain a strict impersonality toward one another. There is a conscious avoidance of any overt, focused interaction. Under no circumstances in these stores do customers make physical or verbal contact with one another. The normative structure appears to demand a silence and a careful avoidance of either eye or physical contact. The workers in the store complement these behaviors by quickly ejecting any individual who interferes with the *privacy* of other customers.

There are, as well, regular behaviors engaged in by persons when purchasing pornographic materials. Persons adopt techniques that allow them to complete purchases as quickly and unobtrusively as possible. That customers are best left alone in terms of buying potential is illustrated by a datum from Karp's work. In speaking to a store manager he was told the following:

> "You couldn't have noticed this because you haven't spent enough time in the store. There are guys who come into the store who just look at the highline but don't touch anything."
> "The highline?"
> "The highline is the long table in the middle of the room that has the most current, most expensive items. These guys make a circle around the table, never touching anything. Then they go to the back of the store and spend a little time there. They aren't really interested in what's in the back. On their way out they make their selections . . . 1, 2, 3, 4, 5. You can't say a word to these guys or you will lose a sale." (1973: 442)

The attempt clearly is to minimize the amount of time that one must spend in making the purchase and thereby to appear as disinterested as possible.

The import of the data suggests that persons in this semipublic urban setting are involved in a highly structured social situation in which privacy norms are highly standardized and readily understood. The system works so that each person's bid for privacy is complemented by the behavior of other persons in the store. We must, then, see that even in highly anonymous public places such as Times Square, persons are very much constrained in the production of their behavior. Despite the ability of cities to support a diversity of simultaneous activities that, in the flow of daily life, are likely to go generally unnoticed, despite the impersonality and anonymity of city life, and despite the fact that the overwhelming bulk of our actions in the public domain is performed in front of strangers, it is still our task to be perpetually engaged in the business of impression management. In short, when it comes to maintaining a proper image of ourselves, *everyone* counts.

In a book titled *Tearoom Trade* (1970), Laud Humphreys analyzes the behaviors of homosexuals meeting in public bathrooms (known as "tearooms") for sexual encounters. A major concern of this work is also to show how persons engaging in this kind of behavior maintain a distinctive public privacy. Humphreys describes these tearooms as well-organized places where persons strictly abide by the rules. He demonstrates that the activities of approaching the tearoom, positioning oneself inside the tearoom, signaling one's availability, contracting for the nature of the sexual exchange, completing the sexual act, coping with intrusions, and finally leaving the situation are well-patterned activities. Moreover, nearly all this activity occurs with virtually no verbal interaction between the participants.

We must be careful to assess the meaning of works like Humphreys' in the proper light. The importance of the study goes far beyond the description of behaviors in a limited social context. Obviously it is a very small percentage of urban persons who engage in the behaviors described by Humphreys. The fact, however, that the kinds of behaviors can be accomplished at all serves to make a broader commentary on the nature of urban life, and for our purposes, the orderliness of "everyday" public activities. In Humphreys' words:

> Analysis of the highly structured patterns that arise in this particular situation increases our understanding of the more general

rules of interaction by which people in routine encounters of all kinds manage their identities, create impressions, move towards their goals, and control information about themselves, minimizing the costs and risks in concentrated action with others. (1970: 9)

We suggest that the mechanisms used by persons in these rather "unique" urban social settings designed to protect personal identities, to minimize social risk, and to let participants appear "proper" are not unlike the mechanisms used by urban strangers in more usual settings. That the same or similar kinds of "self-management" mechanisms are used by strangers in routine public encounters is demonstrated in the work of Lyn Lofland.

In an article appropriately titled "Self-Management in Public Settings," Lofland (1972) describes the various mechanisms and devices used by persons to protect their self-esteem when in the presence of strangers in public places. Lofland agrees with one of our earlier assertions when she (1972: 95) states: "If a person is to exist as a social being, as an organism with a self, there must be some minimal guarantees that in interaction with others he will receive the affirmation and confirmation of himself as 'right.' " The danger in confronting strangers in public places may be the inability of certain persons to provide this needed confirmation. At the extreme there is the ever-present possibility that persons may provide disconfirmation of one's "rightness." Remember that the problem of strangers' interacting in public stems from their relative lack of knowledge about one another. Lofland is concerned with the way that public actors compensate for this uncertainty and inherent risk imposed by the urban public place. Her observations are, we think, confirmed by our own everyday experiences.

Although suggesting that there are many strategies used by strangers in public to insure their self-images under the scrutiny of others, she names the following major techniques or maneuvers:

1. *Checking for readiness.* Actors prepare themselves before entering a potential encounter situation by checking their appearance, making sure that hair is in place, that zippers are zipped, and so on.
2. *Taking a reading.* Here the person essentially stops to take stock of the social setting. Persons may briefly delay entering a room until they have had a chance to scan it with their eyes, noting the placement of furniture, and the like in that setting.
3. *Reaching a position.* The final step in this sequence is to reach a stopping point. Persons seek to enter the situation as inconspicu-

ously as possible—to minimize the time during which they are under the social spotlight. Once having decided the spot or territory that they wish to occupy, persons may make a no-nonsense direct "beeline" approach to the spot, or approach the chosen position slowly and by degrees, stopping briefly at various points until the destination is reached.

It is worth noting that the tactics described by Lofland in routine settings are not unlike the "waiting" or "stalling" behaviors described by Karp in the relatively unique situation of the pornographic bookstore. Again we are forced to see that there are clear uniformities, crosscutting a number of urban settings, in the way that persons present themselves to others.

In a follow-up article, Lofland (1972) goes on to describe the self-management styles of persons once they have positioned themselves in some context. Among the styles mentioned, persons may posture themselves in such a way as to close off interaction with others completely (refusing to make eye contact, making little movement from the spot chosen in the setting, and the like); persons may "nest" in a particular spot by spreading their belongings (props) around in such a way to mark off their territorial boundaries; persons may "investigate" the setting by moving around while nevertheless remaining careful not to offer any invitations to others for social interaction.

We have been speaking primarily about the ways in which persons minimize the interactional claims that others may make on them. Bibb Latané and John Darley (1970) have recently investigated one dramatic instance of urbanites' noninvolvement, those cases where persons fail to intervene when others appear to be in trouble. In a book titled *The Unresponsive Bystander,* these investigators provide demonstrable evidence that the failure of urbanites to intervene in "trouble" situations is not a function of gross alienation, indifference, or apathy singularly produced by cities and city life.

In a number of ingeniously conceived studies, Latané and Darley offer strong support for the nonobvious hypothesis that the more bystanders to an emergency, the less likely, or more slowly, any one bystander will intervene to provide aid. Their argument is that the failure of persons to intervene derives from what they call a "diffusion of responsibility." Each person, aware that others are witnessing the event, assumes that one or more of these others will take the responsibility to intervene. The result of this "pluralistic ignorance" is that no one steps forward to intervene. Their work amply illustrates that we must not stop our analysis of the city with the simple description of events. To do that is to make us susceptible to the beliefs about city life that it is our task to question.

Latané and Darley have succeeded in uncovering features of social life that cast doubt on the description of urbanites as apathetic. Their findings cause us to reevaluate the assertion frequently made that there exists a *distinctive urban personality*. Our attention is called once again to the *situational basis of urban behavior*.

SEEING ANONYMITY

The data discussed above show that although persons in cities are typically operating in highly anonymous situations, their behaviors are not without "social" character; that is, anonymity does not preclude the existence of patterned, highly structured, predictable social relationships. Quite to the contrary, the studies reviewed allow us to argue, somewhat paradoxically, that anonymity demands social relationships. Persons must "work" to maintain anonymity, and that work is of a highly social nature.

Anonymity cannot be considered a "given," existing spontaneously and wholly independently of social action. Anonymity is, rather, *produced* by actors. Instead of defining a situation in which there are no interpersonal relations, as it would seem to do by definition, anonymity can obtain only because there *are* interacting agents. Contrary to some images of urban life, anonymity does not define a situation of enormously decreased social control. Although anonymity does increase the potential for personal freedom of action, we must at the same time recognize that *in those situations characterized as anonymous, anonymity itself constitutes a norm to be maintained*. There are rules for preserving anonymity, which, like all other rules if broken, cause the transgressor to be subject to negative sanctions. Breaking the rules of anonymity, where they apply, constitutes the basis for being defined as improper or "nonsocial."

What this leads us to say, by way of summary to this point, is that an error of the urban sociologists who advocated the relationship between anonymity and the absence of social controls, as well as the absence of social relations, is their too simple equation between anonymity and normlessness. These writers were misled in their view of urban life by their failure to "look behind" the concrete signs of anonymity. One can never see the social character of relations in an anonymous situation simply by describing what an anonymous situation "looks like." In other words, it is the very special characteristic of anonymity that it is the *result* of a *normatively guided social production* giving the appearance of normlessness and the absence of social character. To see the social character of anonymity, therefore, one must see how anonymity is *produced.*

Our intent here is not to suggest that the city is a highly "personal" place. We do, however, believe that the equation between anonymity and normlessness found in a good deal of the urban literature misses an important point. An important quality of the city has been missed by the failure of the "urbanologist" to view interaction in the urban setting on a microsociological level. Such an analysis reveals that anonymity is socially produced in accordance with a system of rules that constrain individuals. An examination of "face-to-face" behavior in the midst of large cities indicates that urban persons are not in a state of detached normlessness. That actors will strive to preserve their image as proper persons in front of total strangers is a strong statement on urbanites' relations with one another.

BALANCING THE PICTURE: DIVERSITY AND ACTIVITY IN THE CITY

So far in this chapter, we have stressed the ways in which urbanites "protect" themselves in public places from the intrusions of others. Among other things we discussed the importance of maintaining a distinctive "public privacy," and we suggested that there is an "anonymous intimacy" of sorts in public places. We agreed with Goffman that persons maintain a social distance through the operation of what he calls "civil inattention." We characterized urban social relations as constituting a combination of involvement and indifference.

Overall, we have argued that while urban persons spend relatively little time engaged in direct verbal interactions with one another, they are nevertheless quite deliberately and consistently taking one another into account in public settings. We have tried to outline the methods through which actors cooperatively and consensually maintain a social/moral "public bargain." There is an unwritten "social contract" that governs a good deal of everyday urban life. While we have stressed to this point the mechanisms through which urbanites maintain this fine balance between indifference, silent cooperation, and involvement, we must not overlook the vibrant, active, public street life in cities.

Cities seem to vary in their capacity to support direct interactions among strangers. Part of this has undoubtedly to do with differences in city tone, tempo, and mood (Milgram, for example, has noted that walking rates vary from city to city); differences in architectural layouts of cities (the shape of cities, the patterning of streets, the placement of public parks); and finally differences in the historically developed images that residents of various cities hold. Goffman makes this observation in comparing the "tightness" of city street life in different settings:

> The same kind of social setting in different communities will be differently defined as regards tightness. Thus, public streets in Paris seem to be more loosely defined than those in Britain or America. On many Parisian streets one can eat from a loaf of bread while walking to and from work, become heatedly involved in a peripatetic conversation . . . etc. (1963: 200)

As an extension of Goffman's observations, we may note that not only do cities appear to vary in the degree to which persons feel the need to maintain a norm on noninvolvement but also that there are differences within cities as well. In any city there seem to be areas known about by all city residents (and frequently known to outsiders as well) as places teeming with a diversity of activities—Boston's North End, Greenwich Village in New York, or North Beach in San Francisco. It is precisely the street life in such areas that draws persons to them.

At this point the reader will recall our discussion in Chapter 3 of Jane Jacobs' recommendations for the maintenance of viable urban communities. To repeat a point made earlier, we emphasize again Jacobs' (1961: 59) statement that "a good city street achieves a marvel of balance between its people's determination to have essential privacy and their simultaneous wishes for differing degrees of contact, enjoyment or help from people around."

Much the same view about these issues is expressed about New York in a recent article by William H. Whyte (1974). Whyte and his students recently completed a four-year study of street life in that city. Rather than concentrating their efforts on selected areas of the city that traditionally have a good deal of street action, such as Greenwich Village or Brooklyn Heights, they concentrated their observational efforts specifically on the downtown and midtown areas. In the article they state their findings this way: "schmoozing, smootching, noshing, ogling are getting better all the time. The central city is alive and well!"

Whyte's (1974: 30) observations call into question the image of the city as a center of insensate crowding, a place of "squeezed-up masses of anonymous faces, harried, neurotic, dulled . . . persons." Actually, having looked at interaction in these areas over a four-year period, he is able to show that more persons are using the city's open spaces, more persons are conversing in parks, the number of street entertainers has increased, more persons are eating outdoors, and there are more impromptu street conferences. There is, in other words, a viable street life in New York. Once again, Whyte (1974: 31) argues that part of the reason for this activity is the high density and heterogeneity of the city of New York. "As a pedestrian environment, New York already has fundamentals that other cities are desperately trying to achieve. It has a tightly knit core, with great concentrations of activities within easy walking distance."

Beyond making the observation, like the observations made by Jacobs, that one key to an active, interesting street life is the creation of *diversity,* he goes on to make practical suggestions for the use of city space. Like Jacobs, he argues that providing space alone will not create greater interaction among strangers in the city. It is the use of space, the way that space is laid out, and how it is managed that is most important. He notes that in New York some plazas and parks seem to generate a good deal of activity whereas others do not. Such a comparison is useful to the extent that it calls attention to how space is differently used to create more or less activity. He notes that the widely used plazas are those that have considerable seating (in some instances movable seats)—places where the seats are strategically placed so that those using them can easily view any activity occurring. Widely used plazas or parks allow food vendors to ply their trade, and they are places with pleasing greenery. In general, Whyte advocates widening sidewalks to create more pedestrian space, putting in more street benches in those areas of highest activity, and the like.

We have much to learn from the layout of such cities as Paris, Florence, and Venice. These are cities that stimulate the pedestrian and so stimulate interaction between persons. These are cities made for people. Spaces are designed in such a way that persons are not insulated from human contact. Speaking of Paris, Hall says:

Paris is known as a city in which the outdoors has been made attractive to people and where it is not only possible but pleasurable to stretch one's legs, breathe, sniff the air, and take in the people and the city. The sidewalks along the Champs-Elysees engender a wonderful expansive feeling associated with a hundred foot separation of one's self from the traffic. It is noteworthy that the little streets and alleys too narrow to accept most vehicles not only provide variety but are a constant reminder that Paris is for people. (1969: 175)

CONCLUSION

We have tried to suggest in this last section that *too much emphasis* can be placed on strangers' lack of direct interaction with one another in urban settings. Urban life is a well-controlled blend of indifference and involvement. While we still subscribe to the idea that most urban relations are characterized by a need for privacy and an attempt to preserve and maintain the protection of urban anonymity, it is still possible for urban persons to have much to do with one another in a direct way. There are occasions when persons come together and do begin to construct ongoing interactions in public places. There are situations wherein persons can begin to dissolve the strangeness that exists between them. In some situations the normal considerations of "public risk" becomes minimized, and interaction between urbanites assumes a much more intimate tone. There are conditions where urbanites need not engage in their usual practice of extensive "civil inattention." There are conditions where needs for privacy and anonymity seem to diminish somewhat. There are situations where urban strangers are able to become more familiar with one another. There are conditions where anonymity seems to become more intimate.

The city can be a humane, personal place. If we agree upon the value of creating even more humane cities, we must understand the normative demands of public interaction. We must understand the limits and potentialities of public city life. To do that, we must not casually take at face value the readily accessible and commonly expressed images of city life promoted by the mass media and frequently sustained by our most distinguished literary and philosophical figures. If our conceptualizations of the urban environment become too rigid, we severely restrict the range of possible experiences that urban residents may undergo.

We have meant to show in this and the last chapter that one function of an urban social psychology is to call to our attention how some of our images of the city may too severely restrict our conception of the ways in which urbanites can and do relate to one another.

REFERENCES

Berger, Peter. "The Social Construction of Marriage." Pp. 51–61 in Hans Peter Dreitzel (ed.), *Recent Sociology*. Toronto: Collier Macmillan, 1970.

Berger, Peter, and Thomas Luckman. *The Social Construction of Reality*. Garden City, New York: Anchor Books, 1967.

Douglas, Jack. *Understanding Everyday Life*. Chicago: Aldine, 1970.

Goffman, Erving. *Asylums*. Garden City, N.Y.: Doubleday, 1961.

Goffman, Erving. *Behavior in Public Places*. New York: The Free Press, 1963.

Goffman, Erving. *Frame Analysis*. New York: Harper and Row, 1974.

Goffman, Erving. *The Presentation of Self in Everyday Life*. Garden City, N.Y.: Doubleday, 1959.

Goffman, Erving. *Relations in Public*. New York: Basic Books, 1971.

Goffman, Erving. *Stigma*. Englewood Cliffs, N.J.: Prentice-Hall, 1963.

Hall, Edward T. *The Hidden Dimension*. Garden City, N.Y.: Doubleday, 1969.

Humphreys, Laud. *Tearoom Trade*. Chicago: Aldine, 1970.

Jacobs, Jane. *The Death and Life of Great American Cities*. New York: Random House, 1961.

Karp, David A. "Hiding in Pornographic Bookstores: A Reconsideration of the Nature of Urban Anonymity." *Urban Life and Culture*, 4 (January 1973): 427–51.

Latané, Bibb, and John Darley. *The Unresponsive Bystander: Why Doesn't He Help?* New York: Appleton-Century-Crofts, 1970.

Levine, Janey, Ann Vinson, and Deborah Wood. "Subway Behavior." Pp. 208–16 in Arnold Birenbaum and Edward Sagarin (eds.), *People in Places: The Sociology of the Familiar*. New York: Praeger, 1973.

Lofland, Lyn. "Self-Management in Public Settings, Part I." *Urban Life and Culture*, 1 (April 1971): 93–117.

Lofland, Lyn. "Self-Management in Public Settings, Part II." *Urban Life and Culture*, 2 (July 1971): 217–31.

Lofland Lyn. *A World of Strangers*. New York: Basic Books, 1973.

Lyman, Stanford, and Marvin Scott. *A Sociology of the Absurd*. New York: Appleton-Century-Crofts, 1970.

McHugh, Peter. *Defining the Situation*. New York: The Bobbs-Merrill Co., 1968.

Milgram, Stanley. "The Experience of Living in Cities." *Science*, 167 (March 1970): 1461–68.

Milgram, Stanley. "The Familiar Stranger: An Aspect of Urban Anonymity." *Division 8 Newsletter* (July 1972): 1.

Schutz, Alfred. "The Stranger: An Essay in Social Psychology." Pp. 91–105 in A. Broderson (ed.), *Collected Papers: Studies in Social Theory, II.* The Hague: Martinus Nijhoff, 1960.

Simmel, Georg. "The Stranger." Pp. 402–8 in K. Wolff (ed.), *The Sociology of Georg Simmel.* New York: The Free Press, 1950.

Sommer, Robert. *Personal Space.* Englewood Cliffs, N.J.: Prentice-Hall, 1969.

Weber, Max. *The Theory of Social and Economic Organization.* Translated by A. M. Henderson and Talcott Parsons. New York: Oxford University Press, 1947.

Whyte, William H. "The Best Street Life in the World." *New York Magazine,* 15 (July 1974), 26–33.

Wilson, Thomas P. "Conceptions of Interaction and Forms of Sociological Explanation." *American Sociological Review,* 35 (August, 1970), 697–710.

Wirth, Louis. "Urbanism as a Way of Life." *American Journal of Sociology* 44 (July 1938): 1–24.

Wolff, Michael. "Notes on the Behavior of Pedestrians." Pp. 35–48 in Arnold Birenbaum and Edward Sagarin (eds.), *People in Places: The Sociology of the Familiar.* New York: Praeger, 1973.

5

Life-Style Diversity
and Urban Tolerance

In New York City there is an individual, affectionately called Moondog, who can be found almost daily on an uptown Manhattan street dressed in full Viking regalia. Moondog has become a permanent part of the New York street scene. He is one of many "city characters"; he is, indeed, a tourist attraction, a city asset. In Boston, Sidewalk Sam creates chalk drawings of famous paintings as hundreds of passersby stop to admire and applaud his efforts. Every large city has its own characters who may put on impromptu song and dance acts, helpfully direct traffic, preach religious or political "truths," warn us about the imminent end of the world, or stop us on the street asking for change so that "I might get my Rolls Royce out of hock." In some areas of the city we are likely to be stopped by those who will "give us a great deal on a genuine diamond-studded watch." If we choose to, we can watch wide-brimmed-white-hat-wearing pimps lounging on their purple Cadillac "hogs." There are also those who want us to read their hand-bills, those who tout customers for massage parlors, or those who chant "Hare Krishna" for themselves and for anyone who stops to listen. In addition, there are those characters who can be slightly annoying, distasteful, or "pleasantly deranged": down-and-outs, persons animatedly talking to themselves in public places, and the like.

One of the hallmarks of a great city is that it fosters a tolerance for differences in behavior and group life style. Urbanites learn to cope with, adapt to, and often enjoy life-style differences; they seem to have developed a sophistication about life-style diversity. In this chapter we want to explore the basis for this sophistication and tolerance. To disregard the varieties of culture that flourish within cities would be to miss one of the important essences of the city itself. The city is large, dense, and composed of groups with heterogeneous life styles. Each of these diverse city groups undoubtedly interprets the nature of the city differently; for each, the city, in its various aspects, is likely to carry a different meaning. The city is, to use Anselm Strauss's (1975) term, made up of a series of distinctive yet interdependent "social worlds." Everett Hughes put it nicely when he said:

> The city is a place of crises for many persons. There may be enough people who share one peculiarity to allow them to join together to make a cult of it. Esoteric cults burgeon. But so do organizations of alcoholics, of parents of retarded children, of fatties who plan on getting thin. Older people form Golden Years clubs, which become matrimonial bureaus. The reorganization of life in the city proceeds in part by the rise of peculiar institutions which resolve personal crises. (1969: 146)

In trying to account for the extent of tolerance and freedom provided "ultra-life style" groups in the city, we pick up on a theme consistently found in some of the writing reviewed in earlier chapters. Recall that classical thinkers and early observers of city life recognized the greater potential for freedom of action in cities than in small towns. Simmel, despite his distaste for what he saw as the rationalized, intellectualized, anonymous character of metropolitan relations, certainly did allow that the city, precisely because of these characteristics, made possible a degree of freedom that could not be found in the small town. The indifference, anonymity, intellectualization, and cosmopolitanism of urban life provided an independence of action and thought that the "pettiness and prejudices" of small town life precluded.

In Chapter 3 we reviewed the theoretical and empirical researches of Robert Park and his students and colleagues at the University of Chicago. They, too, were concerned with documenting and understanding the tolerance for diversity in large cities. At base they tried to understand the connection between the ecological characteristics of the city and the social psychology of urban persons. A consistent argument in the writings of Park and Louis Wirth claimed that the growth of secondary, and the weakening of primary, relations in cities permitted a greater diversity of individual expression than could be found in the small town. Park (1925: 41) commented: "The small community often tolerates eccentricity. The city, on the contrary, rewards it. Neither the criminal, the defective, nor the genius has the same opportunity to develop his innate disposition in a small town that he invariably finds in a great city." The city was seen as supporting a variety of groups, each with its distinctive behaviors, attitudes, and life styles; groups that ecologically segregated themselves into their own "moral region." Persons with characteristics in common—color, ethnicity, social status, and life-style preferences—find each other in cities, are drawn together, and create their own living space together.

Evidence that the city is composed of a number of distinctive social worlds—a mosaic of separate cultures that stand in sharp contrast to each other—was provided in the ethnographies of Park's students. Studies of "hobohemia," the rooming-house districts, the inhabitants of both the "Gold Coast" and the slum, the world of the immigrant, and various ethnic enclaves substantiated the existence of distinctive urban worlds. Each of these worlds generated its own distinctive values and life styles in response to the particular contingencies confronting persons in the urban environment. We should note, however, as discussed in Chapter 3, that "social areas" (Bell, 1969) need not be composed of contiguous geographic areas.

More recent research has followed the tradition of documenting the inner life of distinctive urban subcultures. Researchers have, for example, produced ethnographies describing in detail the urban worlds of black pimps (Milner and Milner, 1972), pool hustlers (Polsky, 1967),

Indians (Guillemin, 1975), secret societies (Cohen, 1971), and delinquent gangs (Schwitzgebel, 1965). In addition, we documented in earlier chapters the research of those who analyzed the internal dynamics of the homogeneous ethnic communities found in all large cities (Whyte, 1943; Gans, 1962; Suttles, 1968; Jacobs, 1961). All this research contains, if only implicitly, the same message as the ethnographies of Park's students do. It is, again, that cities provide persons—whatever their idiosyncratic tastes, needs, values, or life styles—the opportunity to find others who share the same tastes, needs, values, or life styles. Moreover, the city provides individuals a degree of freedom and tolerance to engage in their preferred life styles that would not exist in a small community.

Before continuing, it is important to say a few words about terms used in this chapter. The reader should note that we have chosen to speak of tolerance for "ultra-life style" groups rather than for "deviant" groups. This choice is dictated by the belief that the term *deviance* has been much abused, if only unwittingly. Despite sociologists' efforts to make clear that theirs is a morally neutral position when they speak of deviance, the term has come to have a distinctly pejorative, negative connotation. While a simple change of labels will not fully solve the problem, we shall adopt the term "ultra-life style" to signal our interest in any group with "different" or "distinctive" life styles. Certainly we are interested in the way in which groups that transgress laws are dealt with in cities. We are, however, also interested in the treatment of groups whose behaviors may be questionably "moral" rather than illegal. Finally, we intend the term *ultra-life style* to encompass groups expressing values and ideologies that may be contrary to dominant values or ideologies. Any explanation of city tolerance must extend to all these groups regardless of whether the term *deviance* can appropriately be attached to their behaviors. Our interest must go beyond tolerance for deviance to tolerance for diversity more generally.

Having made this point, we now present the questions that will guide our analysis in this chapter. Among other questions, we want to ask: What is it about the structure of the city that makes tolerance for ultra-life style groups possible? What is it about urbanites' social psychology that leads to greater tolerance than would likely exist in less citified, more homogeneous areas? Are there degrees of tolerance? Does the nature of tolerance vary for different types of groups? How is tolerance related to political processes in cities? Very importantly, what are the conditions under which tolerance for ultra-life style groups breaks down? Our focus, then, will be on the processes through which tolerance is gained and lost.

IS THE CITY A CULTURE OF CIVILITY?

The general tone of our discussion has been to say that there is a direct relationship between urbanism and tolerance; that, as a generalization, the level of tolerance for ultra-life style groups is greater in highly urbanized areas than in noncity places. Such a position can, of course, be overstated. It is clear that there are many instances of intolerance in cities. Political groups are harassed, prostitutes are routinely arrested for soliciting, and racial conflicts are not uncommon. Around particular issues, whether in rural or urban areas, it is difficult for groups to sustain a temperate attitude toward other groups defined as adversaries. This is especially so if groups' direct economic interests are involved. Economic inequities are so basic to persons' daily life conditions that a degree of hostility between certain city groups becomes nearly inevitable. This is most obviously a frequently dominating factor in the animosity between city ethnic and racial groups. Lower-class whites may become fearful when they see blacks climbing the social/economic ladder. They become afraid that they will themselves be deprived of jobs and other scarce resources.

The recent history of school busing in Boston and Louisville reveals just how tenuous and fragile are the relationships between racial groups in cities. A degree of tolerance, or at least nonintervention, is maintained as long as minority groups do not "invade" particular, homogeneous ethnic communities. There are, to use Suttles' (1972) term, "defended neighborhoods" within cities whose boundaries are not to be trespassed by alien groups. Suttles notes:

> Cities inevitably bring together populations that are too large and composed of too many conflicting elements for their residents to find cultural solutions to the problems of social control. The result seems to be a partitioning of the city into several village-like areas where the actual groupings of people are of more manageable proportions. (1972: 21)

In a recent study, Claude Fischer (1971) examined the extent of racial and ethnic tolerance in cities. Through his research Fischer wanted to determine whether there is, in fact, a *direct* relationship between urbanism and tolerance (as suggested in the writings of Louis Wirth and others) or whether the extent of city tolerance was more a function of the particular demographic characteristics of persons living in large urban areas. Would he find, as claimed by Wirth, that the extent to which a place was urban would be related to the degree of freedom and tolerance experienced by ethnic and racial minorities? Following Wirth, Fischer set out two hypotheses he wished to test. They were the following:

1. The more urban a person's place of residence (defined in terms of selected demographic variables), the more likely are persons to be tolerant of racial and ethnic differences.
2. Community size will be directly related to tolerance of racial and ethnic groups.

To test these hypotheses, Fischer made use of available data from five Gallup polls conducted between September 1958 and July 1965. These polls contained data on 7714 persons who responded to the question: "Would you vote for a Negro, Jew, or Catholic for President?" His data indicate that, while there is a general increase of tolerance as areas become larger and more urban, this relationship may have less to do with *urbanism* and more to do with the *social characteristics* of persons who inhabit larger, more urban communities.

Once Fischer takes into account these social or demographic population variables, he is able to report that "after an initial rise (in tolerance) the trend is for a definite decrease in the association between city size and the combined tolerance scale" (Fischer, 1971: 85). Tolerance tends to increase as the percentage of non-Southerners, non-Protestants, and higher economic status persons in an area increases. Fischer goes on to explain that the relatively greater tolerance in cities for racial and ethnic groups is a function of the fact that cities draw to them persons with certain social characteristics. There is, he goes on, a kind of contextual effect. If persons are surrounded by others who are tolerant, they are themselves likely to become more tolerant. He claims, therefore—contrary to the theorizing of Wirth and others—that we cannot impute a *direct* relationship between urbanism and tolerance. He concludes that "while urbanites are less likely to be prejudiced than rural residents, the implications of Wirth's theory that urban life directly leads to 'universalistic' attitudes is not supported" (Fischer, 1971: 855). In other words, Fischer argues that were noncity areas inhabited predominantly by high-status non-Protestant and non-Southern persons, they would be just as tolerant of ethnic and racial minorities as city areas with similar populations.

We might question whether the choice to study racial tolerance was the most reasonable one to assess city tolerance. We should not assume that, because there is no direct association between urbanism and racial tolerance, such a linkage does not exist with reference to other diverse groups and issues. Fischer's data may simply serve to remind us that tolerant attitudes do not develop equally for all ultra-life style or minority groups in a city.

At this point, we can provide some evidence that it is possible for a "culture of civility" to develop in cities. To do that, we turn to the recent writings of Howard Becker and Irving Louis Horowitz (1972), who try to account for the unusual tolerance shown for "deviance" in San Francisco. These writers specify at the outset that San Francisco's civility is uncommon in other American cities. However, examination of an extreme case may profitably alert us to the general potentialities and limits of tolerance in cities. They begin their article with some examples of the expanded limits of toleration in San Francisco:

> Walking in the Tenderloin on a summer evening, a block from the Hilton, you hear a black whore cursing at a policeman: "I wasn't either blocking the sidewalk! Why don't you motherfucking fuzz mind your own goddamn business!" The visiting New Yorker expects to see her arrested, if not shot, but the cop smiles good naturedly and moves on, having got her back in the doorway where she is supposed to be.
>
> . . .
>
> You enter one of the famous rock ballrooms and, as you stand getting used to the noise and lights, someone puts a lit joint of marijuana in your hand. The tourist looks for someplace to hide, not wishing to be caught in the mass arrests he expects to follow. No need to worry. The police will not come in, knowing that if they do they will have to arrest people and create disorder.
>
> . . .
>
> The media report (tongue in cheek) the annual Halloween Drag Ball, for which hundreds of homosexuals turn out at one of the city's major hotels in full regalia, unharassed by the police. (Becker and Horowitz, 1972: 4)

Becker and Horowitz argue that city tolerance in San Francisco is based on a specific type of interaction between members of ultra-life style groups and members of the larger community. Members of quite diverse groups, they suggest, strike a silent unwritten bargain, a kind of social contract. The essence of this bargain is that members of the minority life-style group moderate their behaviors in certain ways so as to be acceptable to the groups around them. There are, in other words, implicitly agreed upon boundaries—social behavioral boundaries—beyond which the several groups "promise" not to go. In effect, Becker and Horowitz present us a modified "exchange" theory (Homans, 1961; Blau, 1967). They speak of a reciprocity between various city groups.

Each group, they suggest, seeks to maximize its opportunities for a peaceful, free, ordered life. In order to accomplish this end, members of different groups learn to keep their moral and value judgments to themselves; they learn not to impose their own behavior standards and values onto each other. It is a true reciprocity, as each group is willing to give something up to maximize order. The police will not break up congregated groups on street corners as might be the normal practice elsewhere. In turn, members of the congregated group will police themselves so as not to engage in behaviors that may be interpreted as "troublesome." In short, an accommodation has been developed between the police and community "straights" on the one hand and members of marginal groups on the other. All concerned benefit. "Straights" do not become outraged by "freaks," and the latter are provided a greater freedom for engaging in their preferred life style than would otherwise be possible in the absence of the "live and let live" bargain.

There is a self-fulfilling prophecy quality to the social bargain described. As different groups abide by the social bargain, they simultaneously begin to recognize that the stereotypes and images that they may previously have held of each other are incorrect. In this socialization process, members of the conventional community come, for example, to understand that gay persons are not child molesters or that hippies are not drug addicts. This further increases their civility toward such groups. The city consequently becomes known for its civility —as a desirable place to live if one wishes to maximize freedom for an ultra-life style existence. It follows that such persons gravitate toward the city to live and settle down. Finally, once these persons find a place to live where they are relatively unharassed, they become less likely to engage in "erratic" or "undesirable" behaviors. The result of this process is a spiraling of tolerance.

The natural question to ask is "why San Francisco?" Here the authors are forced to speculate about the demographic and historical factors in the city's growth that may have contributed to the development of a culture of civility. They indicate three historical antecedents that might have been instrumental. First, San Francisco has always been a major seaport, catering from the beginning to the "vices" traditionally engaged in by sailors. Second, a history of trade unionism has left the city with a "left wing, honest base which gives the city a working-class democracy and even eccentricity, rather than the customary pattern of authoritarianism" (Becker and Horowitz, 1972: 10.) Finally, San Francisco has an unusually high proportion of single persons, who need not worry about what effects the unusual activities of ultra-life style groups may have on their children.

This last point leads us to suggest an hypothesis about urban tolerance worthy of future empirical investigation. We might argue that in addition to the kinds of socioeconomic variables (for example, education, occupation, and income) studied by Fischer, it is equally important to take into account the age and family-life cycle characteristics of urbanites. We suspect that those urban areas marked by high percentages of young, single persons and young married couples without children are the most likely places for high degrees of tolerance to be sustained.

Despite their generally optimistic image of this one city, Becker and Horowitz are careful to point out that there are situations in which the parties involved are unable to create a set of negotiated accommodations. As mentioned earlier, these most likely involve economic inequities. Moreover, in some situations it is extremely difficult to work out a bargain whereby both sides give up equal amounts and gain equal amounts. In some conflict situations between city groups, in other words, it is difficult to create a fully reciprocal arrangement of costs and rewards. Often these situations—in which equitable arrangements are difficult to create—involve the relationship between minority racial groups and majority groups. Becker and Horowitz offer these examples:

> It may be possible to improve the education of poor black children, for instance, only by taking away some of the privileges of white teachers. It may be possible to give black youths a chance at apprenticeships in skilled trades only by removing the privileged access to those positions of the sons of present white union mem-

bers. When whites lose these privileges, they may feel strongly enough to fracture the consensus of civility. (1972: 15)

Although San Francisco presents a somewhat unique case, we can learn several things from Becker and Horowitz's discussion that will facilitate our own analysis. We may presume that in all cities members of different groups have some notions about acceptable boundaries of ultra-life style behaviors. If we learn the general dimensions of those boundaries or regulative norms, we may better understand the conditions under which tolerance is most likely to exist. If only implicitly, Becker and Horowitz indicate the necessity for analyzing the role of *political* processes in the development or hindrance of tolerant attitudes. Finally, although it is beyond the province of this chapter, their study indicates the need to investigate the distinctive histories of cities to understand why they support higher or lower levels of tolerance.

Despite the insight provided in the analysis we have described, there are a number of points in Becker's and Horowitz's discussion that we believe may be misleading. Becker and Horowitz have implied too rigid a notion of tolerance. They have only, it appears, a *positive* notion. They imply that tolerance exists only because the different groups involved consciously value it. While this is undeniably often so, it may equally be the case that tolerance in cities is a byproduct of avoidance. This is to say (as we noted in the previous chapter) that persons develop social procedures to minimize the probability of their coming into intimate contact with those whom they do not find particularly congenial. In still other cases, tolerance may be the unintended consequence of persons not even knowing of the presence of ultra-life style groups. These authors also fail to describe when the relationship between groups is an obligatory one.

More important still, Becker and Horowitz appear to have a rather static view of the bargains created between groups. One gets the impression that once the bargain is understood by all parties, it remains indefinitely the basis for interactions between groups. What happens, we might ask, when groups come to feel that the bargain is no longer equitable; when ultra-life style groups develop the collective idea that others' definitions of them and their behaviors are inappropriate? What are the processes, in other words, through which accommodations are renegotiated? What happens when ultra-life style groups begin to test the limits of a community's tolerance? Becker and Horowitz do not extend their analysis to the elements responsible for the disintegration of tolerance.

In the next section of this chapter, we amplify on some of the ideas provided us by Becker and Horowitz. We shall consider more extensively some of the structural and social psychological factors providing opportunities for tolerance in cities that do not exist in noncity areas.

CREATING AND MAINTAINING TOLERANCE

In previous pages we have briefly described two apparently contradictory interpretations of the basis of city tolerance. We remarked that social ecologists provide a picture of the city in which different groups are segregated and isolated from each other and consequently have little contact with one another. There are, according to this view, clear territorial groupings composed of persons with similar characteristics who largely restrict their activities to those well-defined territories. Suttles (1972: 21) describes the "defended neighborhood" as a "residential group which seals itself off through the efforts of delinquent gangs, by restrictive covenants, by sharp boundaries, or by a forbidding reputation." The defended neighborhood, by providing rules governing spacial movement, helps to preserve order by segregating groups that might otherwise come into conflict. And Louis Wirth made explicit the relationship between ecological segregation and the production of tolerance for the quite diverse groups drawn to cities:

> The voluntary segregation of Jews in ghettoes had much in common with the segregation of Negroes and immigrants in modern cities, and was identical in many respects with the development of Bohemian and Hobohemian quarters in the urban community of today. The tolerance that strange ways of living find in immigrant colonies, in Latin Quarters, in vice districts and in other localities is a powerful factor in the sifting of the population and its allocation in separate cultural areas where one obtains freedom from hostile criticism and the backing of a group of kindred spirits. (1969: 20)

The literature stressing ecological segregation of groups seems to imply that tolerance is possible in cities because groups are isolated from one other; because groups have little or no contact with one another. Yet we have seen that Becker and Horowitz offer a quite dif-

ferent explanation for tolerance. They have suggested to us that tolerance is produced and maintained through a special type of *interaction;*
that different life-style groups do indeed come into contact with each
other but must learn to moderate their behaviors in each others' presence. Is this an insoluble theoretical dilemma? Must we choose between
the two alternative explanations—one stressing isolation and the other
stressing interaction? We shall argue that ecological segregation of ultra-
life style groups does exist and operates to produce a *controlled contact* between these different city groups.

Spacial Segregation and Controlled Contact

Very appropriate to our present interests is Lyn Lofland's (1973) recent
book, *A World of Strangers.* In that book Lofland tries to answer these
questions: What is the basis for public social order in cities? How is
the potentially chaotic world of strangers transformed into a system of
predictable social relationships? The central thesis of her historical
research is that the way urban order is achieved in modern cities is
different from that in preindustrial and early industrial cities. The
transition has been from a primarily *appearential* order in these latter
cities to a *spacial* order in present-day cities. "In the pre-industrial
city, space was chaotic, appearances were ordered. In the pre-industrial
city a man was what he wore. In the modern city a man is where he
stands" (Lofland, 1973: 82).

Before we think about the nature of this spacial ordering and how
it functions, we might briefly raise a methodological question. Why,
we ask, did she choose to frame her analysis of modern cities in historical terms? Why not simply present data on modern cities and
leave it at that? Lofland does not directly answer that question in her
book; but, were this question put to her, she would probably respond
by saying that the historical comparison helps us better to see how
our own lives are unique. Because we tend to take for granted how
our lives are organized, we need the "shock" provided by history to
recognize this uniqueness. We have continually argued in this book
that persons are capable of transforming the social world—the urban
world—as their changing needs dictate. Lofland's book is about the
value that persons place on order and intelligibility in their lives. It is
through the historical comparison given us by Lofland that we most
clearly see how urban persons have transformed the urban place to
produce this order.

There is, then, a spacial ordering to city activities. If we are properly socialized urbanites, we know that certain types of persons—persons engaging in certain behaviors and practicing distinctive life styles —will be found in certain areas of the city. Lofland (1973: 69) defines what she calls *locational socialization* as the process by which the urbanite continually "learns about the meaning of locations, about what is expected to go on where and who is expected to be doing it." The ecological segregation and concomitant locational socialization is important because it gives urbanites knowledge. They may choose to be in areas of the city that put them in contact with different life-style groups or they can choose to avoid such contact. Urbanites have, in other words, a certain autonomy over the contact that they will have with various life-style or marginal groups. Such contact is a controlled contact.

If, for example, one wants to avoid contact with homosexuals or hippies or prostitutes or those selling pornography, one simply avoids those areas of the city that such persons are likely to frequent. Tolerance is contingent on this controlled contact. Spacial segregation is a primary requisite for tolerance, as we must be able to choose how, when, and where groups different from our own will touch our lives. Spacial segregation of groups and activities, then, provides a comforting predictability relative to the encounters that we shall have with cultural strangers. In this regard, it follows that tolerance will likely begin to break down when the conditions for controlled contact are not met. It frequently happens that a public clamor is raised when members of ultra-life style groups begin to appear in city areas where they "don't belong." In several cities, for example, a certain section of the downtown area is informally designated as an "adult entertainment area." While there has been some dispute about whether such an area should exist and while theatre managers are occasionally arrested for showing hard-core pornography, those who earn their living by supplying sexual services are pretty much left alone as long as they restrict their activities to the informally designated area.

We noted earlier that urbanites do not always wish to avoid contact with those whom they perceive as having unusual life styles. We agree with Becker and Horowitz that the opportunity to observe, and even on occasion to participate in, the behaviors of such persons is part of the life and character of a city. Every city has its areas to which persons may go for their observations: their urban sightseeing. Certain public parks normally come to serve this function. In such places persons may stroll and watch the "antics" of those with whom they would otherwise have no contact. In these places persons representing a fairly large range of life styles may come into moderate contact. Like the anthropologist who ventures into different societies to observe the "strange" cultural patterns of the natives, urban persons know where they may learn about culturally diverse city natives. Unlike the anthropologist, however, urban observers do not have to gain the acceptance of the natives by meeting, as far as possible, their cultural standards.

In a recent study, Love (1973) analyzed the reasons why persons used a particular park in Portland, Oregon, that attracted a wide diversity of persons. Her interviews indicate that watching other people was a central reason for visiting the park. Fifty-three percent of first goers, 50 percent of occasional park visitors, and 59 percent of frequent visitors spontaneously mentioned "people watching" as their main motivation for visiting the park. She notes that even within the park itself there is an ecological segregation of persons and activities, with most of the "ultra-life style" groups congregating around the fountains. The author makes this conclusion:

> Tolerance of diversity was at evidence at the fountains judging by the pleasure many respondents took in the people around them. Only 9 (6%) expressed distaste for the hippies, the old people, or the white collar visitors at the fountains. Neutral territory, such as central city parks, then, might function as places where people can become familiar with diverse social types. (1973: 205)

In sum, it is the spacial ordering of activities in cities that allows persons to "distance" themselves from certain levels of intimacy with ultra-life style groups. "The distinctive feature of distancing as against territoriality seems to be that it does not simply divide individuals or groups into mutually exclusive affiliations, but defines their associations at discrete points along a continuum" (Suttles, 1972: 176). Another way to speak of controlled contact, then, is contact that allows persons to determine carefully the degree of the intimacy of that contact—that allows them a degree of autonomy over the depth of their involvement with others. By being able to control the place and timing of contact with ultra-life style groups and by knowing what kinds of behaviors to expect of persons in different city spaces, urbanites simultaneously can monitor the extent of their involvement with persons from culturally different groups.

In our discussion so far of ecological ordering of city activities, we have discussed city spaces in rather "objective" terms. The reader has likely pictured the city as broken up into clearly delineated and bounded city spaces, each of which supports a different set of persons and activities. To view city space as made up of a number of neat self-contained areal packages somewhat simplifies urbanites' sense of space, however. We want to carry our analysis of the relationship between the spacial ordering of behavior and the maintenance of life-style freedom one additional step. We propose, following the writing particularly of Kevin Lynch (1960, 1972), that for many urban persons, the areas of the city inhabited by different groups are, in fact, not even considered part of what they define as the "real city." Lynch and others have suggested that the city environment is conceived differently by different groups; that persons carry around in their heads images of what the city is. For some, the areas of the city inhabited by ultra-life style groups may not even appear on these "cognitive maps" of the city. One cannot feel particularly threatened by "down-and-outers" on skid row, for example, if that area of the city is not even part of one's consciousness. To expand on this idea, we must consider just how urbanites do conceive of city space. Here we shall argue that tolerance is maintained not because of specific forms of contact with ultra-life style groups but through what we might term a "spacial myopia" that may, for some, make ultra-life style groups essentially invisible, or at least blur their existence.

Tolerance and Urbanites' Sense of Place

In his book *The Image of the City* (1960), Kevin Lynch created what he called a cognitive map of Boston by interviewing a sample of that city's residents. While nearly all persons interviewed mentioned certain common landmarks (such as Paul Revere's house and the Boston Common), the most salient finding of his effort was that the individual images of the city of each person interviewed were quite different. He also found that their sense of their own location in city space was quite different, and (most closely related to our interests here) that, for each person interviewed, vast areas of the city were simply unknown.

In a recent review of research on urban proxemics, the findings of a study with the same results as Lynch's was described. In this study (Hurst, 1975: 146) the urban images of two distinct class groups living in Vancouver, British Columbia, were compared. The groups compared were, on the one hand, professionals and businessmen living in the city's exclusive areas, and on the other, welfare recipients living in the nonexclusive East Side of the city. Again, while both groups mentioned a number of city landmarks in common, their overall images of the city were quite different. The professional group's image was bounded by the central business district, certain clubs, and their immediate exclusive areas of residence. The welfare group had an even more localized image of the city, centering on the rooming-house district and a few local bars, stores, and community facilities.

The research recently cited indicates that urban persons in communication with others define their own unique sense of city space. Certain locations come to be invested with particular meanings. The city is defined psychologically by the symbolically meaningful, familiar, and comfortable spaces within which one's daily round of activities is carried out. In addition, certain groups of persons are likely to share the same general cognitive map of the city. As Edward Hall (1966: 2) puts it, different persons and different groups "inhabit different sensory worlds."

There are a number of ways that urban sociologists might construct persons' and groups' mental maps of the city. One could, for example, sample a number of geographical points in any city and then ask persons to try identifying photos of these points. It would then be possible to create an index for each geographical area simply by counting the proportion of persons interviewed who correctly identified the point, object, or area (see Milgram, 1970). As an alternative method, one could stop persons on the street and ask directions to a particular point or area. What percentage will know how to get there? What consistencies will there be in the landmarks mentioned? How frequently was each landmark mentioned?

Toward the end of his article on the experience of city life, Stanley Milgram (1970) comments on the potential importance that such constructed maps could have in gaining insight into the very different conceptions held of the city by its different groups. Cognitive maps may be used to determine how persons' image of the city and sense of city space may be affected by age, ethnicity, social class, sex, and the like. Could it be, for example, as Milgram speculates, that ghettoization may hamper the expansion of black teenagers' sense of the city? While such research remains to be done, we can safely agree with Michael Hurst, an urban geographer, who writes:

Since there is a variety of life experiences in the city, there will be varieties of urban experiences that arise from the ways people sense different places in the urban environment. The Afro-American, Chinese or Indian's knowledge of the city, life experiences and sense of place will differ from those of the Anglo-American; the fortunate elite will differ from the working poor; teenagers will differ from adults.... Each will have highly individualized conceptions of what we commonly think of as the same urban world. (1975: 44)

We can further specify the nature of persons' cognitive maps—the way that they are constructed and how they will vary for different persons and different groups—by looking at the elements that are involved in the creation of a sense of place. Researchers interested in the social organization and perception of space have distinguished between *personal space, home or territorial space,* and *lived space.* A person's total sense of space is a function of these three elements, which we can briefly discuss in turn.

Edward Hall (1966) and Robert Sommer (1969) have both paid special attention in their research to the protective bubble of *personal space* that surrounds our immediate bodies. Here they suggest that in our daily encounters with others we carefully regulate the distances between ourselves and others. In American society, for example, normal conversational distance is at about two feet. If persons come any closer than that, we feel that our personal space has been violated. Personal space does not remain constant for persons but will vary in different social situations and different contexts. Sommer distinguishes personal space from "territory" in that personal space has no geographic reference points; it moves with the individual and, unlike territory, expands and contracts under varying circumstances.

In addition to one's sense of personal space, we may speak of a person's immediate *territorial space.* In cities this territorial space is made up of the person's home and immediate neighborhood. This is, of course, the space where the urban person spends most of his time and is the most familiar, comfortable space for the individual. The collective home bases (or territorial space) of groups may take the form of the small ethnic community or a "gang's turf." Relatively fixed and clearly delineated, the person's or group's territorial space does not expand and contract in different situations as will one's personal space.

Third, there is the urban person's *lived space.* Lived space is fairly elastic, created as it is by paths of interaction between home territories and the various city places where urbanites spend their time—work place, movie theatres, schools, parks, local stores, friends' homes, and the like. Urbanites' activities and interactional networks will dictate which city objects, areas, and elements will be invested with special symbolic significance. Depending upon activities and interactional networks, "parts of city reality are excluded, distorted, crushed, converged, elongated, and stretched out" (Hurst, 1975: 145).

To say that urbanites have their own distinctive lived sense of space is not to suggest that they are unaware of, ignorant of, or nonknowledgeable about city areas outside of this lived space. Typically, however, these "outside" areas are known only at second hand and are invested with slight symbolic significance. Middle-class whites certainly know about the predominantly black areas that likely exist in their cities. These areas are not, however, part of their cognitive maps of the city; they do not constitute part of what they know as the real city. "Unable to experience first-hand most of the built environment, we tend to rely on other people and the media to inform us about the large portion of the city that may not be directly accessible [to us]" (Hurst, 1975: 161). Our restricted mental images of the city are, in addition, reinforced by other features of the modern city, such as the automobile that engulfs its occupants in a "cocoon of privacy" as they move through the city. Persons may pass through certain areas and come to perceive those spaces "only in terms of city streets which are traversed by automobile and which provide access to the various little private and semi-private spaces that make up their world" (Hurst, 1975: 164).

In many cases persons who have lived in cities all their lives have never passed through certain areas. While teaching for a time in New York, one of the authors was somewhat surprised to learn that many of his students had never been to areas of New York other than those in which they were brought up and presently lived. Many students who lived in Queens, for example, had never been to Brooklyn, and still others had never been to Manhattan. These areas were not part of their conception of the city. Their lives were contained within a living space that did not extend beyond Queens itself. This pattern of spacial provincialism, we maintain, describes the experience and perception of the city of most urbanites.

The point of our description of a city person's sense of place is that marginal groups restricting their activities to specific city areas are effectively "invisible" in a psychological sense to large numbers of persons—to all those urbanites whose conception of the city does not include the areas where these groups are found. Urban persons, we suggest, normally become concerned only about those ultra-life style groups operating within the boundaries of *their* lived space. This has important consequences for tolerance. Only in rare instances will a large number of persons mobilize themselves to restrict the activities of any one group. Because of the wide variation in cognitive images of the city, relatively few persons will be moved to action against one or another group commonly defined as undesirable. Persons living in a particular city area may feel a distant antipathy toward homosexuals, prostitutes, or certain political groups; but they are unlikely to translate that dislike into action against these groups as long as they remain immediately unaffected by them.

To this point we have discussed the relationship between persons' sense of spacial or ecological reality in cities and the maintenance of tolerance for ultra-life style groups. We may extend the idea of urbanites' sense of reality in yet another direction. Before groups of persons will take action against other groups, these latter groups must somehow be seen as a threat to the first group's collective, shared version of reality—a threat to a view of the world that they share in common. We want to use the idea of "reality construction" to account more fully for the differences between urban and nonurban areas in the extent of freedom allowed ultra-life style groups.

Tolerance and the Diffusion of Social Reality

Recent discussions of "deviance" in sociological literature have emphasized the idea that conceptions of morality, respectability, and deviance are *social constructions* and that no behaviors are intrinsically immoral or deviant (Becker, 1963; Kitsuse, 1962; Erikson, 1962; Douglas, 1970). Morality is, according to this view, a relative notion. An individual's or group's behaviors are identified as wrong, evil, immoral, or threateningly different only in terms of the current, commonly held construction of reality of some dominant group in a given setting. Immoral behavior *is* immoral only because it has been so defined in terms of some prevailing notion of social reality. Moreover, as pointed out by Peter Berger and Thomas Luckman (1967) in their book *The Social Construction of Reality*, persons develop an investment, a commitment to their own idea of morality, propriety, or reality generally, and may in some cases take action against those individuals or groups representing an alternative or contrary version of reality. This is, of course, most likely to happen if the different or alternative reality is conceived as threatening to one's own. Berger and Luckman (1967: 108) comment that "the appearance of an alternative symbolic universe (version of reality) poses a threat because its very existence demonstrates empirically that one's own universe is less than inevitable."

We must now consider that ultra-life style groups are those composed of persons whose behaviors are motivated by beliefs, attitudes, ideologies, or values that are different from those of some majority group in a setting. Ultra-life style groups are those, in other words, whose members hold to a version of social reality that departs identifiably from some existing, more widely accepted definition of reality. In the case of homosexuals it is primarily a sexual reality that is different. In other cases, ultra-life style groups advocate political, economic, religious, or moral realities that depart significantly from prevailing standards.

The likelihood that persons in one or another setting will become intolerant of those practicing unconventional life styles is a function of a number of factors. First, it would seem, is the sheer *number* of such persons. A few persons engaging in unusual behaviors may not pose much of a threat. Should the number increase substantially, however, they might be seen as possibly "taking over." Second is the *visibility* of such groups. If they maintain a low enough profile, their activities are less likely to be called into question. We have already discussed the relationship between urbanites' sense of space in cities and the visibility of certain "different" groups.

We now ask, under what conditions is a high degree of consensus about proper values, beliefs, and life styles likely to develop? Or still more closely related to the direction of our analysis here: Is there a difference between city and noncity areas in the consistency, clarity, and rigidity of persons' ideas about what is right, proper, and moral, and therefore agreement about boundaries of acceptable behavior?

As Durkheim (1947) pointed out in his *Division of Labor in Society*, the basis for social solidarity and integration in small, relatively well contained communities is persons' *similarities*. You will recall from Chapter 1 that Durkheim referred to the social solidarity based on persons' similarity or likeness as *mechanical solidarity*. In a homogeneous, undifferentiated society, individuality is at a minimum. Here a single, coherent, well-defined *collective consciousness* guides, motivates, constrains, and controls persons' behaviors. Persons are guided by a rigid set of traditional criteria relative to proper behavior. In such a society of similarly socialized persons—and therefore, one of uniformity of moral beliefs and practices—deviation is easily observed, clearly visible to all, and stands in naked contrast to the otherwise profoundly regular standards of conformity. Because those whose behaviors mark them as different are so easily seen, repressive measures are swiftly taken against them. Views about the values, beliefs, and attitudes that one *ought* to have will be clearly delineated in the small homogeneous society or community. There will be a most obvious dominant, official version of reality that sets the mark that all must toe. One's behaviors in the well-contained, homogeneous community are subject to rigid, traditional controls.

The city, alternatively, as we have so frequently noted, is characterized by the *heterogeneity* of its population. One of the defining characteristics of the city is that it is made up of a diversity of ethnic, racial, age, class, and religious groups. While there is little to differentiate persons in the small community, the populations of cities are highly differentiated. Again, as noted by Durkheim, this demographic, structural, or morphological difference in the social organization of cities as against small towns had significant implications for changing bases of social control. He noted that, in contrast to the peasant community, the type of solidarity in urbanized areas—*organic solidarity*—was based on *differences* between persons: on the meshing of individual specializations that characterizes a complex division of labor.

Durkheim argued that, as individuals moved away from their place of origin to larger urbanized areas, the hold on them of traditional, rigid community values was weakened. In addition, the anonymity of large population aggregates in urbanized areas allowed for greater individual variation, with the effect that persons experienced a greater freedom from the traditional controls that had previously bounded their lives and dictated their behaviors. "Implicit throughout the *Division of Labor* is the notion that the performance of complex differentiated functions in a society with an advanced division of labor both requires and creates individual variation, initiative and innovation, whereas undifferentiated segmental societies do not" (Nisbet, 1965, 165).

The very same behaviors constituting an outrage in the small town may be seen as only slightly unusual in cities. In cities, groups must be more "way out" before they draw singular attention to themselves and become recognized as a threat to the collective consciousness of city dwellers. The same behaviors perceived as an affront to "our way of life" in small towns may be dismissed among sophisticated urbanites as merely one among the many sets of behaviors vaguely seen as "slightly different."

Our discussion of the basis for tolerance in cities would be incomplete if we did not add to the factors already mentioned some consideration of the *politics* of tolerance. When a concerted effort is made to arrest prostitutes for soliciting, does this merely reflect an attempt to enforce the law or might there be political motivations involved as well? Do politicians have something to gain by a dramatic indication that they are, indeed, doing something about crime and vice? Must the police occasionally "beef up" their rates of arrest to provide concrete evidence that they are maintaining law and order? Are there, to use Howard Becker's (1963) apt description, "moral entrepreneurs" who are continually on a crusade to create and enforce moral regulations? To what extent may tolerance or intolerance be understood in terms of the motivation of "professional enforcers" invested with the political or legal power to regulate the activities of ultra-life style groups? To what extent is tolerance for illegal or quasi-legal activities a function of political or economic interest? In short, to understand city tolerance fully, we must look beyond the social psychology of urban persons. We must consider, as well, the factors affecting the activities of those with the discretionary power to blind themselves to the activities of some groups and to stop the activities of others.

POWER, POLITICS, AND TOLERANCE

Questions of morality are inextricably related to questions of power and political influence. As an example, consider the fate of the President's Commission report on pornography, published in 1970. Many of the studies reported on in this volume seemed to provide evidence that pornography is not only harmless but potentially beneficial. One such study (Kupperstein and Wilson, 1970), for example, indicated that persons imprisoned for sexual offenses had much less exposure to pornography than did a comparative sample of "normal" persons. The decision to use the report was based less on the quality of its findings than on their ideological, political import. In this case, the president's disavowal of the report was largely a function of the political undesirability of its findings. It would have been politically disadvantageous for the president to declare, based on the findings of experts, that harassment of those selling pornography ought to stop immediately.

Around a different issue, Becker (1963: 150) reports that "it is sometimes rumored that Nevada gambling interests support the opposition to legalize gambling in California because it would cut so heavily into their business, which depends in substantial measure on the population of Southern California." In still other cases, it has been demonstrated that some persons have enormous autonomy and power to define right and wrong in a society. One such group of societal "experts," for example, are psychiatrists who have been granted that license and power to define mental illness and to make decisions about the fate of those so labeled (Szasz, 1961; Scheff, 1966; Daniels, 1970). Our examples are meant to suggest that decisions about the behaviors and activities that will be tolerated in any social system cannot be separated from questions of power and, in many cases, personal interest. We might ask who benefits when certain behaviors are allowed to continue or are stopped? This question has been posed by researchers who have examined tolerance for "crime."

Egon Bittner (1967) has shown, for example, that the police make it easier for themselves to maintain order in the city by keeping skid-row inhabitants confined within a geographically limited area. The police most successful at maintaining "order" have learned to disregard certain activities and to take action against others. In this context the police must use their intimate knowledge of the area and its inhabitants as the basis for *personal* rather than *purely legal* decisions about the maintenance of order and the distribution of justice. In a broader sense, however, the way that the police view their work and respond to the activities of certain persons and groups depends on the way that they are tied into a number of networks and institutions.

In his early and classic observational study of the North End of Boston, William F. Whyte (1943) detailed the complex network of interrelations between the police, local community people, politicians, and local businessmen. He indicated how gambling enterprises in that city area continued through a well-established, institutionalized, and wellelaborated system of "payoffs." In a more recent study, William Chambliss (1974: 169) concluded, after the presentation of convincing evidence, that "the people who run the organizations which supply the vices in American cities are members of the business, political and law enforcement communities—not simply members of criminal society."

To demonstrate that political and economic arrangements may influence the freedom allowed certain ultra-life style groups to continue their activities, we can briefly consider one specific case. It has been reconstructed from events that occurred in a city on the East coast. Within the last two years there has developed a controversy about the continued operation of two gay bars in a semiresidential area of the city. The case received wide coverage in city newspapers primarily because of the many political charges and countercharges involving relatively high level city government officials. In presenting this case—an instance of the breakdown of tolerance—our intent is not to establish which parties were right and wrong. Rather, our concern is twofold: (1) to show the possible connections between various persons who did become involved in this very political case, and (2) to show how different groups (police, politicians, bar owners, community persons, and the homosexuals themselves) perceive the politics involved and the reasons for the deepening intolerance.

THE BREAKDOWN OF TOLERANCE:
A CASE STUDY

The elements of the case described here in a shorthand fashion and the networks of persons involved in it have been constructed through a content analysis of all the newspaper reports (both city dailies and underground papers) from the time that the continued operation of the two bars became a city issue. To understand the complexities of the case, the reader must first know the places, the regulatory boards, and the persons playing major roles in the case.[1] They are as follows:

The places	*Burt's Place* and *The Blue Jay* are the two gay bars that had been operating in the area since the early 1960s.
The regulatory agencies	The city's Liquor Licensing Board and The Alcoholic Beverage Control Commission (ABCC)
The persons	James Lane, owner of *Burt's Place* and *The Blue Jay*
	Robert Lane, James' brother
	Steven Brown, chairman of the Liquor Licensing Board up to 1972
	Steven Brown, Jr., Steven Brown's son
	Paul Sullens, James Lane's lawyer; also Steven Brown's lawyer
	Mark Bush, adviser to James Lane
	Deputy superintendent of police
	Deputy mayor of city
	Mayor of city

[1] In the following account the names of the bars and the central participants in the case have been changed.

The two bars—*Burt's Place* and *The Blue Jay*—have been in operation since the early 1960s. Early in 1971 the Liquor Licensing Board and the ABCC began to receive complaints from community residents about late night noise around the bar. They claimed that the bars' existence was contributing to the general deterioration of the neighborhood. The complaints continued sporadically through 1973 without any action taken against either of the two bars. In the next two years, however, and primarily in 1975, the sentiment against the continued operation of the bars heated up considerably. After five weeks of hearings, beginning in February 1975, during which the licensing board evaluated some twenty-seven alleged violations committed by bar owners and patrons (for example, serving minors, drug use, vandalism, traffic problems), the decision was made to force the bars to relocate by the year's end. That ruling was subsequently reversed by the Alcoholic Beverage Control Commission on the grounds that there was insufficient evidence of wrongdoing to warrant the revocation of the bars' liquor license and their forced relocation. The debate continues as of this writing. Community members and opponents of the bar are presently asking higher authorities in the state to decide whether the ABCC has the legitimate authority to overrule the earlier decision of the Liquor Licensing Board. As a complement to this very quick overview and to fill in some of the gaps in the story, we can reconstruct chronologically some of the major events, benchmarks, or turning points in the development of this public issue. Significant events, as constructed from newspaper accounts, were as follows:

Sometime in 1972	Steven Brown is replaced as chairman of the Liquor Licensing Board.
May 9, 1973	Licensing Board meets to hear complaints against *Burt's Place* and *The Blue Jay* by community residents.
November 8, 1974	Three youths leaving the bar are accosted by armed pair —a man and a woman. One youth is shot in the leg.
January 1, 1975	A black man is attacked by six or seven youths within 200 feet of the bars.
January 4, 1975	City mayor, little-city-hall managers, and deputy mayor visit the bars.
February 7, 1975	Puerto Rican male murdered near the two bars at 2 A.M.
February 16, 1975	Bar manager discovers the police videotaping activity outside the bars.

February 18, 1975	Licensing Board opens hearings on bars.
February 19, 1975	Police and political officials offer testimony about noise and drug abuse in and around the bars.
February 21, 1975	Paul Sullens (lawyer for bar owner) testifies and claims that racial, ethnic, and social prejudices lie behind attempts to close the bars.
February 25, 1975	City mayor orders that the bars must close by 11 P.M.
March 6, 1975	Mayor urges Liquor Licensing Board to close down the bars. Urges the police to enforce the laws against other bars with equal vigor.
March 18, 1975	Mark Bush, adviser to James Lane, testifies under oath that on January 4, 1975, the deputy mayor attempted extortion by demanding that James Lane pay $50,000 to the mayor's reelection campaign. The deputy mayor allegedly promised Bush that once the contribution was made, the harassment of the bar by police would end.
March 18, 1975	James Lane testifies that a number of persons are out to get him, particularly that local politicians want to punish him for not previously supporting their campaigns for office.
March 18, 1975	Bush presents evidence to Liquor Licensing Board indicating that the crime rate in the areas of the bars is no different from and in many cases lower than, other city areas.
March 21, 1975	State Attorney General exonerates deputy mayor of any wrongdoing.
March 24, 1975	Deputy mayor changes jobs. He is given another high-ranking post in the city government.
March 25, 1975	Licensing Board refuses to hear testimony of five witnesses to deputy mayor's alleged extortion attempt.
March 26, 1975	Paul Sullens claims that James Lane is on a city hall enemy list.
May 27, 1975	Licensing Board orders that *Burt's Place* and *The Blue Jay* relocate by December 31, 1975.
August 16, 1975	The ABCC overturns the Licensing Board decision, indicating that the evidence against the bars was not sufficient to warrant the demanded relocation of the bars.

Public interest in the gay-bars controversy and its generally newsworthiness were heightened as some careful investigation by news reporters revealed the nature of the personal, economic, and political linkages existing among some of the central figures in the case. Consider, for example, the relationships that some of the figures already named have with one another. Paul Sullens, James Lane's lawyer, is also the lawyer for Steven Brown. As the previous chronology of events indicates, Steven Brown was replaced as chairman of the Liquor Licensing Board some time in 1972; and, beginning in early May 1973 with a new chairman, the Licensing Board met to hear complaints against the two bars by community residents. James Lane is also the board chairman of a multi-million dollar amusement park in a nearby state. His brother Robert and Robert's wife hold substantial stock in this amusement park. Steven Brown's son, Steven, Jr., is a major shareholder in this venture. Paul Sullens' wife and his law partners also own stock in the amusement park. The interrelationships between persons just described is a matter of public record. The persons named clearly shared economic interests in common. In other instances, the possible linkages among persons cannot be definitively ascertained, and one must infer them. As an example, the newspapers made a point of reporting that the lawyer representing the two bars had previously been involved in an unsuccessful attempt to prosecute the deputy superintendent of police on charges of illegal wiretapping. One possible inference to be drawn from this historical fact is that the deputy superintendent is possibly using the bar issue to satisfy a long-standing vendetta against this lawyer. Investigative reporters also indicated that James Lane had given considerable financial support in recent elections to the opponent of the district's present representative. The present representative opposes the continued operation of bars in the area. In such newspaper reports the intimation is strongly made that the vigorous opposition to the bars of a number of powerful persons might be as much a function of political motives as a dispassionate assessment of violations committed in and around bars.

Of particular interest in this case is the fact that the official authorities at the lower levels—police and licensing boards—were unable to prevent the issue from literally "spilling over" and engulfing the deputy mayor of the city, then the mayor, and, subsequently, higher officials in the state.

It will be helpful, finally, to hear the words of some of the persons involved in the controversy. Many persons have been quoted in the newspapers, and we can only give a small sampling of the statements representing different definitions of the situation held by police, representatives of the bars, politicians, community persons, and bar patrons.

With regard to the use of drugs in and around the bar, one detective assigned to the case had this view of homosexuals:

> Ninety-nine percent of the ones [gays] I have known or seen use drugs to more or less justify their existence. It puts them in another world and helps them to forget what they are doing.

And the police lawyer warned the Liquor Licensing Board that:

> If these bars are allowed to continue as a haven for those who dwell upon [sic] homosexuals; for those who use and abuse drugs; for those who vandalize homes for kicks, you [the board] will have to live with it. The people of the area have had to suffer too long. The bars attract a certain element of our society which we might not be proud of but which nevertheless exists.

The residents of the area who have been vocal in the case maintain that they bear no ill feelings toward homosexuals because they are homosexuals but are concerned about noise, vandalism, parking problems, and incidents of violence that contribute to the deterioration of their neighborhood. The following is a sampling of community residents' opinions:

> *Burt's Place* was just a quiet neighborhood bar when we moved in thirteen years ago. *The Blue Jay* was a nice respectable restaurant.
>
> They accuse us (the residents) of being anti-gay but the truth is that the bar managers let their gay customers be exploited.
>
> When I go to a neighbor's house. I do it on a dead run. I'm not against prostitution, but I don't care for it particularly at my back door or at the end of my street.
>
> The noise gets bad after midnight and exceedingly bad between 2 A.M. and 3 A.M., especially in the summer. I personally feel vulnerable if I happen to be out at night.

The politicians also claim in their public statements that they are concerned only with protecting the rights of the area's residents. On many occasions they felt the need to indicate that they bore no personal animosity against either the bar owner or the homosexuals. In response to news reporters' questions, the local representative made statements of the following sort:

> The bars have been singled out, not because of any prejudice, but because of noise and trouble. The establishments have been singled out for the simple reason that they cause more noise and

disruption than any others. There are many bars in my district and 80 percent of the complaints I get are from these places.

Yes, I do object to noisy fags and dykes at 2 A.M. when people are trying to sleep. I object to noisy monseigneurs at 2 A.M.

And the city mayor when asked his opinion responded at one point by saying "These are normal people here. I don't see any problem." Later he denied making this statement and was quoted as saying:

> Reports I have received from the city Police Department and residents, plus my own inspection of the area, convince me that these two bars are a menace to public safety. Over a number of years they have become symbols of disorder—cabarets for young thugs and hoodlums venturing into the area.

As noted earlier, those persons associated with the bars maintain that the attacks against them are politically motivated. They particularly maintain that the "unusual" police harassment stems from a desire of some to destroy James Lane personally. Although those representing the bars do not deny that there have been problems in the area associated with the bars, they assert that the magnitude of the problems does not warrant the action that has been taken against the bars (a position recently upheld by the Alcoholic Beverage Control Commission). Their perspective of the situation as having political overtones is evidenced in these statements made by Lane's lawyer, Paul Sullens:

> The crimes that occur in that neighborhood are much fewer than one would expect in a neighborhood of this kind. The area is no Vatican City and these two bars are not St. Peter's Basilica. I'm just saying that the neighborhood is relatively free of crime. Responsibility for the crimes has been willfully, falsely and I might say, corruptly been put on the two bars.

> The hearings have been an attempt simply to destroy James Lane and close his two bars. He has earned himself a place on City Hall's enemies list.

> The case has been merely fabricated or manufactured from nothing. Somebody in City Hall has said, "We're going to make it appear you're responsible." No one has ever been charged and convicted with selling drugs in the premises of either establishment.

James Lane, the bar owner, expresses much the same opinion:

> It's a personal attack. I've done nothing wrong, but I've been harassed and abused—personally abused. Why? Because I'm in a

very unpopular business. I've got a lot of respect for the police, don't misunderstand me. You can't be in this business without the police. The day-to-day police are excellent, and very sympathetic to the problems of the industry.

It's harassment by the Superintendent of Police and the licensing board. You know, they can pick and choose whoever they want to put in for a violation. There is so Goddamned little protection in this industry. Someday I'll leave this business, but when I do it will be by choice not force.

Finally, the homosexual patrons of the bars see the dispute as yet another instance of their victimization because of their different sexual preferences. They are angry that their own fate is tied up with the fate of James Lane. As indicated by their own words below, they see themselves caught in the middle between reactionary "straights" and, as they put it, "bourgeois" gays who do not frequent bars such as *Burt's Place* and *The Blue Jay*. At one point during the controversy, a reporter from one of the city's underground newspapers received a statement from a group referring to itself as "Black, Latino and poor white faggots." This statement spells out what they see as their marginal status:

> We are everybody's hated faggots. To straights we are loathsome queers while bourgeois gays reject us for not sharing their mania for reformism—get a job, get ahead, prove to the straights we're just like them and we'll all be free.

And, lamenting the possible closing of the bars, a spokesman for the patrons raised these questions:

> Where are we supposed to go when *Burt's Place* and *The Blue Jay* close? Who wants us? At what other bars are we welcome? What has the gay movement in the city to offer us and who has made our fate inseparable from that of Lane's? Are we . . . simply supposed to disappear?

The quotes from the various participants in this issue clearly dramatize an important theme of this book; namely that social realities are constructed in accordance with persons' particular locations in social structures. The social characteristics of the participants—be they owners, customers, police, or politicians—have certainly led to differing views of, and responses to, the "reality" of the situation.

In the situation described in the last few pages, public officials saw fit to take direct action against a group of persons whose behaviors, they claimed, had become intolerable. Of course, we might argue that the question of "intolerable for whom" is at the root of the issue. We cannot assert unequivocally from the data presented that personal, political, or economic interests largely motivated the action taken against the bars. Rather, the case described sensitizes us to the fact that such factors *may* have been operating; and if they were not operating in this case, they most certainly do in many. In all instances in which tolerance has broken down, however, it would be shortsighted to assign the cause of such a breakdown to any one set of factors. There is likely an intertwining of several factors involved in setting the stage for eventual action against one or another group. Some group of persons must have come to perceive the ultra-life style group's behaviors and continued presence as troublesome—as a *social problem*. Perhaps the members of the ultra-life style group have ventured into areas of the city where they are defined as "not belonging." Groups may behave in ways that contravene the implicit social bargain that had previously existed between themselves and members of the "conventional" community. It could be that just a few members of some group engage in behaviors that constitute an outrage to a community's collective consciousness. And so on. The breakdown of tolerance may then be hastened once selected persons recognize how it may be to their advantage to pursue the case further: to mobilize opposition against the group; to see that "justice" is done; to see that threats to morality, real or imagined, are done away with.

REFERENCES

Becker, Howard. *Outsiders: Studies in the Sociology of Deviance.* New York: Free Press, 1963.

Becker, Howard, and Irving Louis Horowitz. *Culture and Civility in San Francisco.* New Brunswick, N.J.: Transaction Books, 1972.

Bell, Wendell. "Urban Neighborhoods and Individual Behavior." Pp. 120–46 in Paul Meadows and Ephraim Mizruchi, eds., *Urbanism, Urbanization and Change: Comparative Perspectives.* Reading, Mass.: Addison-Wesley, 1969.

Berger, Peter, and Thomas Luckman. *The Social Construction of Reality.* Garden City, New York: Anchor Books, 1967.

Bittner, Egon. "The Police on Skid Row; A Study of Peace Keeping." *American Sociological Review,* 32 (October 1967): 699–715.

Blau, Peter. *Exchange and Power in Social Life.* New York: John Wiley, 1967.

Chambliss, William. "The Police and Organized Vice in a Western City." Pp. 153–70 in Lawrence W. Sherman, ed., *Police Corruption*. Garden City, N.Y.: Doubleday Anchor, 1974.

Cohen, A. "The Politics of Ritual Secrecy." *Man,* 6, No. 3 (1971): 427–49.

Daniels, Arlene Kaplan. "The Social Construction of Military Psychiatric Diagnoses." Pp. 182–205 in Hans Peter Dreitzel (ed.), *Recent Sociology No. 2*. New York: Macmillan, 1970.

Douglas, Jack (ed.). *Deviance and Respectability: The Social Construction of Moral Meanings*. New York: Basic Books, 1970.

Durkheim, Emile. *The Division of Labor in Society*. Glencoe, Ill.: The Free Press, 1947.

Erikson, Kai T. "Notes on the Sociology of Deviance." *Social Problems,* 9 (Spring 1962): 307–14.

Fischer, Claude. "A Research Note on Urbanism and Tolerance." *American Journal of Sociology,* 76 (March 1971): 847–56.

Gans, Herbert. *The Urban Villagers*. New York: The Free Press, 1962.

Guillemin, Jeanne. *Urban Renegades: The Cultural Strategy of American Indians*. New York: Columbia University Press, 1975.

Hall, Edward T. *The Hidden Dimension*. Garden City, N.Y.: Doubleday, 1966.

Homans, George. *Social Behavior: Its Elementary Forms*. New York: Harcourt, Brace and World, 1961.

Hughes, Everett C. "Institutions in Process." Pp. 236–47 in Alfred McClung Lee (ed.), *Principles of Sociology*. New York: Harper and Row, 1969.

Hurst, Michael. *I Came to the City*. Boston: Houghton Mifflin, 1975.

Jacobs, Jane. *The Death and Life of Great American Cities*. New York: Random House, 1961.

Kitsuse, John. "Societal Reaction to Deviant Behavior: Problems of Theory and Method." *Social Problems,* 9 (Winter 1962): 247–57.

Kupperstein, L., and W. C. Wilson. "Erotica and Anti-social Behavior: An Analysis of Selected Social Indicator Statistics." *Technical Reports of the Commission on Obscenity and Pornography*. Washington, D.C.: U.S. Government Printing Office, 1970.

Lofland, Lyn. *A World of Strangers*. New York: Basic Books, 1973.

Love, Ruth Leeds. "The Fountains of Urban Life." *Urban Life and Culture,* 2 (July 1973): 161–208.

Lynch, Kevin. *The Image of the City*. Cambridge, Mass.: M.I.T. Press, 1960.

Lynch, Kevin. *What Time Is This Place?* Cambridge, Mass.: M.I.T. Press, 1972.

Milgram, Stanley. "The Experience of Living in Cities." *Science,* 67 (March 1970): 1461–68.

Milner, Christina, and Richard Milner. *Black Players*. Boston: Little, Brown, 1972.

Nisbet, Robert. *Emile Durkheim*. Englewood Cliffs, N.J.: Prentice-Hall, 1965.

Park, Robert E. "The City: Suggestions for the Investigation of Human Behavior in the Urban Environment." Pp. 1–46 in Robert E. Park, et al. *The City*. Chicago: University of Chicago Press, 1925.

Polsky, Ned. *Hustlers, Beats and Others*. Chicago: Aldine, 1967.

President's Commission. *Report of the Commission on Obscenity and Pornography*. New York: Bantam Books, 1970.

Scheff, Thomas. *Being Mentally Ill: A Sociological Theory*. Chicago: Aldine, 1966.

Schwitzgebel, Ralph. *Streetcorner Research*. Cambridge, Mass.: Harvard University Press, 1965.

Sommer, Robert. *Personal Space*. Englewood Cliffs, N.J.: Prentice-Hall, 1969.

Strauss, Anselm. "Social Worlds." Paper presented at the annual meetings of the American Sociological Association, San Francisco, 1975.

Suttles, Gerald. "The Defended Neighborhood." Pp. 21–43 in Gerald Suttles, *The Social Construction of Communities*. Chicago: University of Chicago Press, 1972.

Suttles, Gerald. *The Social Order of the Slum*. Chicago: University of Chicago Press, 1968.

Szasz, Thomas. *The Myth of Mental Illness*. New York: Hoeber-Harper, 1961.

Whyte, William F. *Street Corner Society*. Chicago: University of Chicago Press, 1943.

Wirth, Louis. *The Ghetto*. Chicago: University of Chicago Press, 1969.

WE'VE CARRIED THE
RICH FOR 200 YEARS-
LET'S GET THEM
OFF OUR BACKS!

6

Stratification and Power
in the Urban Setting

In the last chapter we focused on the manner in which various groups
strive to achieve control over definitions of what may be thought of as
"conventional" or "unconventional" modes of behavior. Not all groups
in the city, of course, are in equally strategic locations to have their
definitions of morality translated into actuality. While, as interactionists, we argue that reality is socially and symbolically constructed, we
must also note that not all persons play an equal role in the construction of social worlds. The differential access of various groups to

165

decision-making processes is reflected in the social stratification arrangements that prevail in particular societies.

The general issue of social stratification, or the process by which individuals socially place and differentiate one another, has long been of concern to social scientists. The very term *social stratification* is itself revealing, calling to mind a conception of social ordering modeled on the "strata" found in geological studies. American sociologists studying the phenomenon of stratification have usually viewed it in terms of an hierarchical continuum in which persons are ranked from high to low on the basis of possessing a certain "amount" of things such as education, income, or occupational prestige. In this chapter we shall discuss some of the influential work in this area and evaluate it in terms of its relevance for a symbolic interactionist view of urban stratification.

CLASSIC CONCEPTIONS OF STRATIFICATION:
MARX AND WEBER

As noted in Chapter 1, the rapid development of industrial cities in nineteenth-century Western Europe exerted a profound influence on the thinkers whose writings contributed to the establishment of modern sociology. In this regard we call attention to the emergence of an urban-based conglomeration of people who formed the mass base for the manpower needs of the expanding factory system. Karl Marx, a German-born philosopher-sociologist who wrote in the latter part of the century, referred to this collection of propertyless workers as the "proletariat" class. His writings focused on both the previous historical development of this class and its potential for dynamically transforming and shaping the society of the future.

In Marx's model of society, two main classes—the bourgeoisie and the proletariat—emerged as a result of the development of capitalism. The origins of these classes are found in the historical process by which cities became the arenas within which the manufacturing industries (or the factory system) grew to prominence. The growth of cities was, for Marx, a result of a process of "expropriation":

> The expropriation of the agricultural producer, of the peasant, his separation from the soil, is the basis of the whole (capitalist) process. The history of this expropriation, in different countries,

assumes different aspects, and runs through its various phases in different orders of succession, and at different periods. (1956: 135)

Such a process was part of the larger transformation of feudal society and the medieval guild system brought about by the increasingly prominent role of middle-class merchants and financiers in the expansion of Western European economies.

The uprooted masses who congregated in the cities were bereft of property and wealth. In order to subsist, they were forced to sell their "labor-power" to those who owned the factories or, in Marx's terms, the "means of production." The bourgeoisie, who owned the means of production, acted in terms of their "interests," leading them to maximize profits and to minimize the wages paid the workers. The workers (proletariat), having little bargaining power in such a relationship, were forced to accept these subsistence-level conditions of employment, which, Marx believed, dehumanized the workers by robbing them of any possible identity with, and pride in, their work. For Marx, the "true interests" of the workers lay in the development of a collective "class consciousness," allowing them to transform the capitalist system to one in which the workers themselves controlled the means of production, thereby deciding among themselves the nature of their working conditions. Bertell Ollman has succinctly noted this:

> For Marx, rather than inhibiting understanding, the very extremity of the worker's situation, the very extent of his suffering, makes the task of calculating advantages relatively an easy one. All the facts stand out in stark relief, and the conclusions to be drawn from them cannot be missed. His needs (the worker's), too, urge recognition of the general means for their satisfaction, both those available within the system and those requiring the system's transformation. For the capitalist conditions alone cannot secure for workers, even extremely alienated workers, what they want. In this way, the worker's entire life is his education in becoming class conscious, of learning to accept the interests of his class as his conscious goals. (1971: 239)

The development of class consciousness among the workers, according to Marx, would be promoted by their participation in social organizations (such as labor unions and political parties) with the ultimate aim of bringing the working class into a position of dominance in society. Whether these organizations would come to power through nonviolent electoral politics was an issue that Marx thought would be determined by the nature of the specific sociohistorical situation.

In effect, then, Marx's notion of class involved both an "objective" and a "subjective" dimension. The objective class situation was a function of the person's relationship to the means of production—either one owned it or worked for those who did. In the societies that Marx wrote about in the middle to latter nineteenth century, work occupied a central place in the institutional order, and workers labored enormously long hours seven days a week. Therefore, having no say about one's working condition meant literally having little control over one's entire life. The objective class situation, then, was one in which those who controlled the means of production, to a large extent, controlled as well the waking hours of large numbers of people. The "subjective" aspect of class lay in the notion of class consciousness and the *collective* efforts on the part of the workers to seize control of their life situations.

Unlike many later students of stratification, Marx was very sensitive to the issues of history and *process*. His notion of the dialectic reveals an awareness of the manner in which various historical processes exert a mutually transforming influence on each other. Thus, the "inherent" conflict between the "forces of production" (such as technology) and the "relations of production" (such as private ownership of the technology) leads in Marx's model to a new form of society in which the collective ownership of the means of production by the workers themselves insures the production of goods that meet basic human needs.

While Marx's writings demonstrate an awareness of the existence of more than two classes in society,[1] his model of stratification is essentially an hierarchical one in which people are arranged along a single dimension—their ownership or lack thereof of the means of production. The behavior of persons is then explained by virtue of their location on this dimension. It is a pyramidical view of stratification consisting of two layers. The top layer consists of a small handful of people who have most of the wealth and power. Those in the bottom layer, the overwhelming majority of the population, have very little of either.

---

[1] For studies in which Marx demonstrates a keen awareness of the existence of more than two social classes, see Marx and Engels (1950). With reference to this issue, Zeitlin has noted:

> However, if Marx's focus on two classes is a function of his model, it is also due to his expectations about capitalist development. There can be little doubt that as he projected the trends of the capitalist system, its continuous development was supposed to eliminate, slowly but surely, all older and intermediate classes and strata and leave basically two classes. (1967: 87)

A possible alternative to, and extension of, the Marxian view of stratification was put forth by Max Weber, a German sociologist who wrote during the latter part of the nineteenth and early twentieth centuries. Weber, like Marx, was responding to the emergence of industrial cities and their significance in changing Western European society. He conceived of social stratification as composed of several distinct but interrelated social orders: the class (or economic order), the status (or prestige order), and the political (or power order). His work in the area of stratification was devoted to an analysis of the historical conditions under which specific orders achieved dominance.

In his well-known essay "Class, Status, Party," Weber (1958) argued for a multidimensional view of stratification. He acknowledged that the economic order is of critical importance to the stratification process, but he also argued that it is only one of several possible orders. He conceived of class in essentially Marxist terms as the process whereby persons' life-chances result from their relationship to the means of production.

The status order is conceived of as the arrangement of persons in terms of their conspicuous display of *respectable* symbols, that is to say, the respectability of their life styles. Status order arrangements center on the kinds and amounts of *deference* that particular life styles mobilize. What is important here is *consumption* because it is possible to buy symbols of respectability.

In addition to the orders of class and status, a third order, that of political power, is also noted by Weber. The dimension of political power is determined by control of the means of administration, that is, the bureaucracy. While Weber linked the notion of political power to the political party, he was also aware that there existed class power and status power. Thus, the ownership of the means of production could be thought of as the power to determine the nature of persons' working lives; a group that mobilized a great deal of deference from others could be seen as having the power to define life styles.

While in actuality these three dimensions of social stratification always exist simultaneously, the dominance of any particular dimension depends on the nature of the historical epoch. In other words, Weber calls attention to the *historical boundedness* of stratification arrangements, a point that has been overlooked by many sociologists in their positing of stratification as a *static,* thing-like entity. Of particular interest here is the switch back and forth between the predominance of class and status. For Weber, the class order predominates in periods of relative economic instability. During such periods there is often violence between social classes because here the classes are related precisely in terms of an "objective" conflict of interest. Conflicts between the workers and owners rise to prominence in these periods because it is not in the interests of heads of industry to take into account the conditions of the workers, while it is certainly in the interests of workers to take into account such issues as working conditions, shorter hours, and wages.

In periods of economic stability the status order becomes dominant. Here the "status groups"—groups characterized by common life styles —relate to one another through the phenomena of *emulation upward* and *exclusion downward*. This is to say, lower-ranking status groups try to copy the life styles of the groups above them, while simultaneously upper-status groups deny nongroup members the possibility of marrying into their circle and thereby entering into relations of intimacy.

In contrast to status groups, Weber notes that social classes, as defined previously, are not necessarily communities; that is, collectivities. He takes issue here with Marx in noting that there is nothing about one's class (economic) position that will automatically lead one to realize that he has something in common with others in his class.[2] In opposition to this, status groups are viewed by Weber as ordinarily comprising communities. Members of similar status groups intermarry, visit one another's homes, eat at the same table, and possess a highly stylized inventory of symbols.

While Weber's work on stratification displayed a keen awareness of, and sensitivity to, the multiple forms of stratification, ensuing students of the area have tended to blur many of the distinctions put forth by Weber. They have promoted a view of stratification in which the concepts of class and status are merged into a single concept—socioeconomic status—which is then conceived of in terms of a single hierarchical continuum. Persons are then ranked from high to low on this continuum. In addition, both Marx's and Weber's emphases on the processual or historical dimension of stratification have also been obscured by the kinds of methodologies utilized by sociologists that often simply focus on a person's attributes at one point in time. An important influence in generating a research tradition based on the socio-

---

[2] For a penetrating discussion of the diversity of responses that workers may make to the phenomenon of industrialization, see Blumer (1960).

economic status notion was a series of studies conducted by the social anthropologist W. Lloyd Warner and his colleagues.

W. LLOYD WARNER AND THE MEASUREMENT
OF SOCIAL STRATIFICATION

Warner and his collaborators' first study was based on data collected during the 1930s in Newburyport, Massachusetts, a small New England town. Ensuing studies by Davis (1941) et al. (members of the Warner research group) dealt with Natchez, Mississippi, and Morris, Illinois (Warner, 1949).

Throughout their studies Warner and his colleagues were concerned with the life styles that corresponded to the various social strata in the community. To probe this issue, Warner developed two techniques for measuring what he called "social class." These techniques and the underlying image of stratification from which they were derived were to exert a profound influence on future studies in this area. The first of these techniques—the method of Evaluated Participation (E.P.)—derived from the assumption that the members of any community are capable of evaluating and ranking other community members. An individual's social class position on the E.P. rating was arrived at by Warner on the basis of information given in interviews with townspeople. When the townspeople rated each other by Evaluated Participation, Warner found that they considered such issues as these:

> Is the person included in the membership of a particular family, clique, association, or church, or is he excluded? Is the status of an individual superior, inferior, or equal to the status of some other individual or family whose status has been previously established? Is the person (or family) identified with well-known (and easily used) symbols of superiority or inferiority (so that the attachment of the symbol to the individual places him in a particular social class)? (1960: 38–39)

The second technique employed by Warner in his investigation of social class—the Index of Status Characteristics—derived from the assumption that "economic and other prestige factors are highly important and closely correlated with social class" (1960: 39). To obtain a person's score on the I.S.C., Warner constructed an index composed of four factors: occupation, source of income, house type, and dwelling area. Each item was scored from 1 (high) to 7 (low) and then given a weight that was multiplied by the score on each factor. For example, persons who scored the lowest possible score (7) on each item would have the following weighted total:

Status Characteristic	Rating		Weight		Weighted Rating
Occupation	7	×	4	=	28
Source of income	7	×	3	=	21
House type	7	×	·3	=	21
Dwelling area	7	×	2	=	14
		Weighted Total			84

According to Warner (1960: 43), the use of these two procedures helped the social scientist to achieve a "clear understanding of social class in a community and the place of any individual or family in this status structure."

Warner's work is significant not so much in terms of the actual procedures used for studying social stratification as in the impetus given future generations of sociologists to conceive of social stratification as a single hierarchical continuum. Warner speaks as if stratification were entirely a matter of what Weber (1958) referred to as *status*—or the deference accorded persons—and he ignores the consequences of *class* position; that is, one's relationship to the means of production. A major exception to his emphasis on status can be found in the fourth volume (1947) of his series (called the *Yankee City* series), but even here he does not really reverse his unidimensional view of stratification.

Warner's technique of Evaluated Participation is particularly questionable in its utility for stratification studies of urban areas, as a number of sociologists have noted (see particularly Pfautz and Duncan, 1950). The technique assumes that everybody in the community knows everyone else, thereby making possible a kind of collective gossip. Such a procedure could only be used with the greatest difficulty in any large urban setting; there persons simply cannot know all of the other people in the city space.

Warner's E.P. also assumes that everybody in the community is evaluating the performance of every other member of the community; that everybody is caught up in the *status* world and engaged in making invidious comparisons of every other member of the community. Studies by Form and Stone (1953, 1957) and Chinoy (1952) raise serious questions about this assumption of pervasive status concern. Form and Stone's (1957) work indicates that blue-collar workers, for example, are not concerned with this sort of thing. Chinoy's (1952) study of automobile workers also demonstrates that rather than a concern with status, blue-collar workers are primarily concerned with the conditions of employment (is the job a steady one?) and the monetary returns from the job (does it pay well?). Such views are in marked contrast to those of white-collar employees, who evidenced concern with the status or *respectability* of the position.

The work of Warner and his colleagues stimulated an enormous amount of research that was instrumental in directing sociologists' attention to the centrality of the prestige or status order in stratification. In fact, studies in stratification came to be viewed as synonymous with studies of the prestige order. It is important to note that Warner discovered the significance of the status dimension primarily as a result of his studies in Newburyport, Massachusetts, and Natchez, Mississippi —settings in which Warner (1941: 5) claimed that "social organization ... had developed over a long period of time under the domination of a single group with a coherent tradition." [3]

As a result of Warner's work, a number of studies were undertaken in the 1940s and 1950s by researchers who continued the focus on the prestige order (see, for example, Hollingshead, 1949; Lenski, 1952; and Cuber and Kenkel, 1954). Warner's work and the studies following it must be viewed within the context of the larger social setting in the United States during the 1940s. Sociologists began to discover the prestige order of American society at a time when the country was on an economic upswing after the Great Depression in the 1930s, which left more than 25 percent of the labor force unemployed. Studies conducted earlier in the 1930s, by the Lynds (1937), for example, which had emphasized the importance of occupational variables in defining the way that class order was organized, never achieved the significance later accorded the Warner studies largely because of their ideological implications for a country organized in terms of "free enterprise."

Despite the sophisticated methodological developments in the area of social stratification (see, for example, Laumann, 1970), contemporary studies still conceive of stratification in the urban setting as having a unidimensional character. C. Wright Mills' critique of Warner's work,

---

[3] An important critique of Warner's approach from the perspective of the historian can be seen in Thernstrom (1965).

first published in 1942, is still worthy of consideration. In reviewing Warner and Lunt's (1941) *The Social Life of a Modern Community,* Mills wrote:

> Class, as defined and used throughout the book indiscriminately absorbs at least three items (class, status and power) which, when considering "stratifications," it is very important to separate analytically.... From the insistence upon merely *one* vertical dimension and the consequent absorbing of these three analytically separable dimensions into the one sponge word "class" flow the chief confusions of interpretation and the empirical inadequacies which characterize this study. (1963: 41)

Our critique of Warner's work provides us with the basic elements for reflecting about alternative views of stratification. We now turn to this issue.

AN INTERACTIONIST VIEW OF STRATIFICATION

The concept of stratification developed in the works of Marx and Warner involves an implicit assumption that a person's place on the socioeconomic status or class continuum almost automatically dictates a particular kind of behavior. By contrast, Weber's work, as well as that of Blumer (1960), contains an awareness of the fact that there is nothing inherent in one's position in a social stratum that mechanically predisposes persons to realize that they have something in common with others in that category. Weber and Blumer, then, suggest that the manner in which both persons themselves, as well as others, define their status is of great significance in the study of social stratification.

In a more recent work, Gregory P. Stone (1970) makes a useful distinction between the concepts of "circumstance" and "situation." He notes that "status is a *circumstantial* fact for some people, a network of life fate, but, for others, status is a *situational* phenomenon, eminently capable of manipulation and established by one's self or one's social circle by the artful staging of appearances" (1970: 250). Here again we are presented with a basic assumption of the interactionist perspective: persons are *active* participants in the creation of social worlds, although, of course, the degree of participation certainly varies by virtue of the differential power wielded by specific groups. As students of stratification, then, we must remain sensitive to the manner in which people respond to their status, to the meanings that they, in communication with others, confer on their status.

While much of present-day research in stratification emphasizes the "circumstantial" aspects of status, we do well to acknowledge that "it is the very situational character that status has for some people that enables them to 'escape' the limits of status 'objectively' imposed upon them" (Stone, 1970: 259).

With these thoughts in mind, we shall now discuss the findings from a number of studies in the stratification literature that have much relevance for the development of an interactionist view of urban stratification. Our aim is to synthesize the findings from these studies in the effort to formulate a broad theoretical statement. The studies to be examined will be dealt with in terms of the following headings: (a) the issue of instabilities in status arrangements; (b) the issue of localism-cosmopolitanism as salient dimensions of stratification; (c) the significance of status symbolism in the urban setting. These issues have been selected because of their implications for an alternative to the uni-dimensional approach to urban stratification.

Instabilities in Status Arrangements

Figure 6–1 presents the typical image of stratification that was discussed earlier in connection with our analysis of Warner's work. Pyramidical

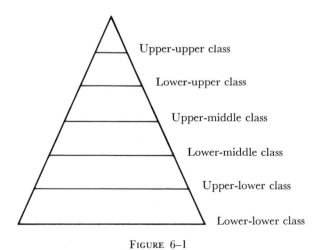

FIGURE 6–1

in form, it conveys an image of society as essentially organized into layers of varying socioeconomic status, ranging from high to low.

In the 1950s Stone and Form (1953) conducted an empirical study in a community that they called Vansburg (located in Michigan), which was similar in size to the communities studied by Warner and his associates. As a result of the difficulties encountered in trying to implement Warner's approach to the study of community stratification, Stone and Form were led to the conceptualization of various forms of status arrangements that involved instabilities in status hierarchies. The arrangements presented in Figure 6–2 derive from the issues discussed by Stone and Form and present an interesting contrast to that noted in Figure 6–1.

Columns 1 and 2 of Figure 6–2 portray what Stone and Form (1953: 156) have described as situations involving "status opposition." In these instances "two or more status groupings are engaged in an indecisive contest for status." Column 1 portrays a "status contest" occurring at the upper status levels. In the Vansburg study, the data revealed a conflict between the members of two high-ranking status groups, the "old families" and the "cosmopolites." The old families had a "localite" orientation in that the local community was the focal point for their identities and social relationships. The cosmopolites were newcomers to the town, who tended to concern themselves with issues transcending the immediate local community. The stage for such a status contest had been set when certain national manufacturers singled out Vansburg for the location of decentralized assembly plants and warehouses. Managerial personnel were brought in from the larger cities. In addition, Vansburg was a county seat, and various state agencies had opened offices there. The top-level personnel of these organizations thus constituted an educated "elite" who moved into Vansburg from the surrounding metropolitan centers. These persons were referred to as cosmopolites by Stone and Form.

The cosmopolites in Vansburg sought out one another and succeeded in establishing a community whose members were oriented to the "sophisticated, blasé, and busy life of the metropolis" (1953: 155). Their life styles called into question the claims of the old families in the town, the members of which constituted an indigenous upper class.

Warner had claimed that status groups gain in status by emulating the life styles of the groups above them. In Vansburg, however, the cosmopolites, rather than emulate the old families, proceeded to establish their own life styles and managed to impose their own symbols

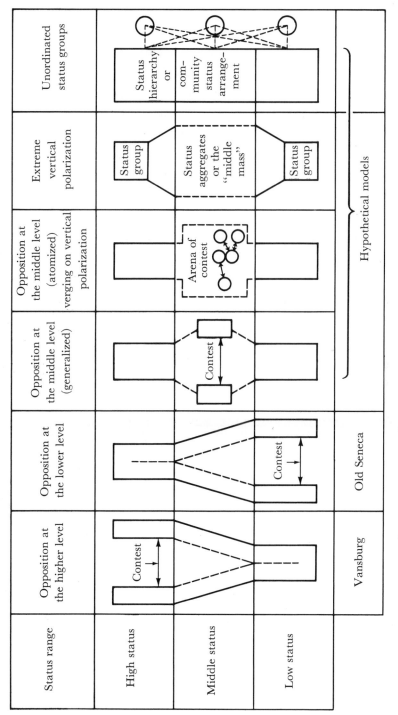

FIGURE 6–2 Varieties of community status arrangements

on the larger community. The cosmopolites exhibited their life styles in numerous ways, all of which clashed with the images of "respectability" cherished by members of the old families. The cosmopolites

> appeared publicly in casual sport clothes, exploited images of "bigness" in their conversations with established local businessmen, retired late, and slept late. With all the aspects of a *coup,* they "took over" the clubs and associations of the "old families." The Country Club, for example, has undergone a complete alteration of character. Once the scene of relatively staid dinners, polite drinking, and occasional dignified balls, the Country Club is now the setting for the "businessman's lunch," intimate drinking, and frequent parties where the former standards of moral propriety are often somewhat relaxed for the evening. Most "old families" have let their memberships in the club lapse. Moreover, in the attempt to consolidate their appropriated status, a group of the cosmopolite set has purchased a large section of land just outside the city and reserved it for restricted housing. (1953: 155)

The V shape of the middle range of the status order in column 1 calls attention to the fact that the status contest at the upper levels had the effect of splitting, along age lines, the allegiances (or "deferences" in Weber's terms) of status groups in the middle range. Thus, the younger middle-class members of the community tended to align themselves with the cosmopolites, while the older members of the middle class retained their allegiances to the old families.

In a classic work written shortly before the Stone and Form study, C. Wright Mills had noted a similar status contest resulting from the movement of "big business" into local communities:

> Local men begin to realize that their social standing depends upon association with the leading officials of the absentee firm: they struggle to follow the officials' style of living, to move into their suburbs, to be invited to their social affairs, and to marry their own children into these circles. (1956: 48)

While Stone and Form found no evidence in Vansburg of a status contest occurring at the lowest levels of the status order, their data suggest that this kind of contest can break out at any level of the status order. Column 2 in Figure 6–2 presents an example of a status contest at the lower status levels suggested by data presented in Havighurst and Morgan's (1951) study of a community that they referred to as Old Seneca. This study indicates that little conflict developed between status groups at the upper levels of the status order. In this community, however, a conflict did develop between lower status "newcomers" and those persons of similar status who were long-term members of the community. Such a status contest extended up through the middle levels of the status order.

Column 3 refers to a status contest in the middle levels of the status order, which may be occurring in the arenas of the larger society. This may be the situation referred to both by Mills and by Riesman (1950) as involving a "characterological struggle" between the "old" and the "new" middle class. As Riesman has noted:

> It seems possible that the open class struggle is characteristic of societies in a state of transitional growth—this is the period that Marx lived in and observed in Western Europe—while in these same societies in the state of incipient decline the social struggle goes on primarily among people of nominally identical class and status positions, that is, among the vastly increased and differentiated middle class. (1950: 34)

The Vansburg study also gave rise to Stone and Form's conceptualization of a phenomenon that they termed "vertical polarization." In comparison with column 3 of Figure 6–2 (where there is total opposition between two competing status groups), column 4 illustrates a possible series of "atomized status contests among diverse social and economic groups vying for social honor" (1953: 157). Stone and Form call attention to the fact that the power of organized labor has played an important role in making possible the movement of lower-ranking status groups in the middle class. Such moves will likely result in opposition from those groups within the middle class who feel their own statuses threatened by the encroachment of newcomers.

Column 5 illustrates a situation of extreme vertical polarization. This is significant for students of urban stratification because of what it suggests about the concept of the "middle class." Rather than being a status group characterized by a similarity of life styles, it is, according to Stone and Form, a medley:

> The "middle class" represents a veritable medley of social positions certainly not characterized by easily specified shared symbols or by consensually integrated roles, and certainly not by tight social closure. . . . If it has no other attribute, it serves as a locus of status achievement and contest which makes the extremes (of the status order) more stable and visible. (1963: 41)

The size and heterogeneity of the middle class led Stone and Form to suggest that it might be more fruitful for sociologists to view it as a "middle mass." Wilensky's (1961) study of careers and social participation also supports the saliency of the notion of the middle mass. He presents these conclusions:

> With advancing industrialization and urbanism, traditional indicators of social class—present income and occupational category of self or father—no longer discriminate among styles of leisure and degrees of integration for a growing middle mass. As determinants of social relations, media exposure, and consumption, these "class" variables are becoming less important than career pattern, mobility orientation, and work milieu. (1961: 539)

Gerstl's (1961) study of three upper-middle-class professions—advertising, dentistry, and college teaching—also called attention to the proliferation of heterogeneous life styles within occupational levels of similar prestige or status. Like Wilensky's study, Gerstl's also makes problematic the ability of traditional indicators of social class to predict personal behavior. Berger's (1968) study of a suburban working-class community sensitizes us to the fact that stratification arrangements are manifested in the symbolic meanings conferred on persons' life styles: "The function of stratification symbols is to maintain viable distinctions among different categories of people, and when criteria which formerly distinguished rank no longer do so because they have become widely available, it is not too much to expect a restructuring of the symbolic aspects of stratification—if, that is, their distinction-maintaining function is to remain viable" (1968: 93).

In addition to the concepts of status opposition and vertical polarization, Stone and Form also referred to the phenomenon of "unranked status groups." Contrary to Warner's notion that all groups in the community could be ranked on a single socioeconomic status continuum, Stone and Form's data revealed the presence of groups that were unranked because community residents were unable to achieve consensus on their status location within the community.

> The unranked status group is always a group, but it is unique because its members have rejected in greater or lesser degree the values, symbols, and norms of the larger social order, supplanting them with values, symbols, and norms of their own. (1953: 159)

In the case of the Vansburg study, for example, the members of the community had great difficulty in evaluating a group called the "tramps," composed of people who had a marginal relationship to the community. In more urban settings, to lump such types as intellectuals, artists, and revolutionaries into a middle-class category not only fails to specify the function of these groups in the larger status order, but also blurs their role in the processes of social change.

As the dotted lines in column 6 of Figure 6–2 indicate, any status level of the community may supply recruits for unranked status groups. The way that members of unranked status groups see themselves is often at variance with the way that those in the community see them. The most significant aspect of the phenomenon of unranked status groups lies in the fact that members of such groups are not dependent on the definitions of nongroup members for their sense of social solidarity. As a result of such autonomy, the members of unranked status groups, as Speier (1936: 202) noted, may engage in a process of "revaluating" existing social arrangements. Such a revaluation, made possible by their marginality, may lead to new stratification arrangements.

The concepts of status opposition, vertical polarization, and unranked status groups were treated at length in view of their significance for suggesting stratification schemes in the urban setting that depart considerably from the traditional hierarchical one. These concepts call our attention to the fact that the stratification arrangements emerging in any community are a function of the *meanings conferred on salient symbols by members of diverse groups.* When little consensus exists over the "respectability" of various symbols, we may expect to find competition over the right to control the definition of respectability. Such competition is most likely to occur when persons' orientations to the community are fundamentally different. One way to describe persons' orientations to the community is to distinguish between "localites" and "cosmopolites." In the following section we examine how these orientations bear upon the issue of urban stratification.

Localism-Cosmopolitanism as Dimensions of Stratification

The terms *localite* and *cosmopolite* are important for an interactionist view of urban stratification in that they call our attention again to the fact (as noted in Chapter 3) that the "community" is a *symbolic* and not necessarily a physical thing; that is to say, people may be oriented to communities, as in the case of cosmopolites, that far transcend the immediate physical setting in which they live their lives. Indeed, to be a member of a scientific community, for example, involves the person in an internationally organized network of communications. This is not to deny, however, that orientations to one's immediate physical situation, as in the case of the localite, are not possible; rather, we note, even the person's orientation to the local community is a function of the meanings that the community has for the person.

The ideas of localite and cosmopolite first achieved prominence in sociological literature as a result of the writings of Robert K. Merton (1968: 441–74). In a study of a small community on the Eastern seaboard, Merton was led to this important observation: *"In short, it is the pattern of utilizing social status and not the formal contours of the status itself which is decisive"* (1968: 456). From an interactionist view, then, the crucial issue concerns the interpretation that *both* the bearer of a status and his audience make of one's status.

While Merton's work does not refer to the Vansburg study conducted earlier by Stone and Form (1953), one of his final suggestions clearly supports their position as well as that of Wilensky and Gerstl cited earlier. Merton states:

> This preliminary inquiry strongly suggests . . . that formal criteria such as education, income, participation in voluntary organizations, number of references in the local newspaper and the like, do not provide adequate indicators of those individuals who exert a significant measure of interpersonal influence. Systematic interviewing supplemented by direct observations are required. Otherwise put, location within various social hierarchies of wealth, power, and class does not predetermine location within a local structure of interpersonal influence. (1968: 469)

A number of empirical studies have appeared in the years following Stone and Form's and Merton's work, all of which show the importance of the localism-cosmopolitanism distinction for an interactionist view of stratification. Gouldner's (1957, 1958) study of academicians at a small liberal arts college in Ohio indicated the saliency of this dimension for differentiating the life styles and scholarly productivity of college faculty members. Glaser (1964) utilized a similar conceptualization to probe the orientations of research scientists. In more recent studies, Roof (1972, 1974) demonstrated the salience of what he termed "breadth of perspective" as a factor in prejudice. Emphasizing the distinction between localite and cosmopolite orientations, Roof (1974:

661) found that "localistic reference orientations are consistently related to anti-Semitic, anti-black, and anti-Catholic prejudice ... [sug-
gesting] that a more generalized world view, or ideology, may be
operating."

Thielbar's (1970) study of academicians drawn from four liberal arts
colleges and one large public university in the Minneapolis area revealed that variations in localism-cosmopolitanism are not limited just
to orientations of individuals. It is also possible for *places* or *situations*
to vary in the extent to which they promote localism and cosmopolitanism. Stone and Farberman (1970: 211) present a diagram (Figure 6–3)
that nicely illustrates possible variations in both persons and places
with regard to this issue.

Institution	Community			
	Local		Cosmopolitan	
	Personal local	*Personal cosmopolitan*	*Personal local*	*Personal cosmopolitan*
Local				
Cosmopolitan				

FIGURE 6–3   Personal and contextual combinations of localism-
cosmopolitanism*

As the diagram indicates, communities may be thought of as local
or cosmopolitan in nature, as can institutions within the community
and individual persons. Persons can be localites in cosmopolitan settings as well as cosmopolites in localite settings. Indeed, Figure 6–3
calls attention to the fact that it is possible for people in cities, let us
say, like New York and San Francisco, to identify these cities as literally "the world" to such an extent that they never develop an interest
in more distant events and places. In that sense, then, one can certainly
be a localite in a very cosmopolitan setting.

---

* Source: Gregory P. Stone and Harvey A. Farberman (eds.), *Social Psychology
Through Symbolic Interaction* (Waltham, Mass.: Ginn-Blaisdell, 1970), p. 211. Reprinted by permission of John Wiley and Sons, Inc.

In contrast to the view that stratification should be thought of as hierarchical in nature, Thielbar's research points to the importance of communication networks in the creation and maintenance of stratification arrangements:

> Status stratification occurs within social orders or interactive networks. Interactive networks which give rise to status stratification are multiple, and boundaries are not always clear. . . . In this complex situation, some persons limit their participation to microcosmic status orders (localities) and others extend their social participation beyond them to larger social spheres (cosmopolites). (1970: 274)

The ultimate significance of localism-cosmopolitanism as dimensions of stratification lies in the fact that the nature of contemporary urban society (viz., the middle-mass notion) makes it increasingly difficult to predict a person's behavior solely by his or her quantitative score on an index of socioeconomic status.

Status Symbolism in the Urban Setting

In the previous section we reviewed a number of studies bearing upon the issue of life styles. The works examined all suggest that what persons subjectively "take into account" (that is, their orientations to the "world") is a crucial question for stratification researchers. Our previous discussion alerts us again to the existence of "multiple realities" and the "socially constructed" nature of stratification arrangements. Since varied orientations and life styles exist in the urban milieu, it is of special importance for the sociologist to examine the kinds of criteria that various segments of the population are using to evaluate the status of others. This is particularly so, since the previous research suggests that members of the community may be using criteria that differ widely from those employed by sociologists. We turn now to some empirical studies of "status symbolism" in the urban setting.

The technique of Evaluated Participation developed by Warner derived from a social setting in which it could be reasonably assumed that practically everyone in the community was capable of evaluating the participation of everyone else. The proliferation of anonymous relations in the urban setting, however, which we noted in Chapter 4, makes such an assumption problematic. In the absence of personal knowledge of all the "others" comprising their daily milieus, urbanites, unlike small-town dwellers, develop a sensitivity to the symbols of status presented by anonymous others. Such symbols are of great saliency as strangers are trying to place and to appraise one another. The contrast between the situation of the small town and the city centers on the difference between a reliance upon highly visible symbols of appearance and manner in the latter, while in the former the status appraisal derives from personal knowledge about others' social positions in the community.

A few years after the Vansburg study, Form and Stone (1957) conducted a series of interviews in Lansing, Michigan, in an effort to examine empirically Hans Speier's (1936: 76) insight that "for honor to arise it is essential that there be bearers, bestowers, and observers of status." They asked their respondents how they would recognize members of four social categories ("high society," "middle-class," "working class," and "down and outers"). The question was posed with reference to meeting members of these categories in either the central business district or in a department store. Their results indicated that there was much ambiguity evidenced by their respondents in the placement of persons into these four categories. Their respondents were most uncertain in evaluating the middle-class category. This finding is similar to the result reported in the earlier Vansburg study; there was consensus among the raters on the very high and very low occupations in the community, but considerable disagreement over the middle range of occupations.

Respondents in the Lansing study were also asked to evaluate several measures that are frequently employed in stratification studies. They were asked to indicate whether they believed such measures as income, education, and occupation to be "important," "irrelevant," or "unimportant," as indices that they themselves would use in judging and appraising others. The data revealed that "fewer upper stratum and more lower stratum respondents than would be expected by chance judged these indexes (education and occupation) to be unimportant or irrelevant for their appraisals of others" (1957: 514).

The meaning of such differences must be subjected to further empirical investigation, since at least two contrary hypotheses are suggested by Form and Stone's data: (1) because of their reliance on the measures of education and occupation as indicators of social status, sociologists may be mirroring the definitions of status held by higher status groups and sociological studies are thereby "ideologically based"; (2) if indeed, upper status groups are *the* bestowers of status in any given community, then the use of criteria defined as relevant by members of these groups is an accurate way of studying status bestowal.

In the period since the publication of Form and Stone's work, very little empirical data have been brought to bear on the issue of status symbolism. Fortunately, a recent study by Reichert (1975) was conducted in Minneapolis in an effort to replicate the Lansing study of Form and Stone. Reichert's (1975: 227) study was undertaken with the hypothesis in mind "that the extent of consensus over rank symbolism (the symbolism employed to place people in various statuses) would decrease as the population becomes more diverse and urban in character—that the consensus over specified symbols would be greater in Lansing than in Minneapolis." His findings, however, revealed: "So little consensus over symbolism was found in either Lansing or Minneapolis that it became a comparison of 'very little' versus 'hardly any'" (1975: 227).

Like Form and Stone's work, Reichert's also indicates that the greatest degree of uncertainty and ambiguity occurred in reference to the placing and appraisal of persons in the social category called middle class. In effect, then, the vertical ranking of respondents along the single dimension of lower to middle to upper socioeconomic groups often obscures the rich complexity of life styles and behaviors occurring within these categories: behaviors that do not readily lend themselves to hierarchical gradations, as our treatment of localism-cosmopolitanism suggested.

At this point in our discussion, let us pause briefly to highlight the points that we have developed. We discussed some classical approaches to stratification and the particular influence of Warner's work in promoting a view of stratification as hierarchical in nature. We then suggested that the nature of urban life is such that a number of alternative stratification arrangements are indeed possible. In this regard we elaborated on the notions of "status opposition," "vertical polarization," and "unranked status groups." These concepts sensitize us to persons' ability to transform the social setting in terms of the meanings which they, in interaction with others, confer on the setting.

We then discussed some additional aspects of a multi-dimensional view of urban stratification. Here we called attention to the issues of localism-cosmopolitanism and status symbolism. Such phenomena point to the continually ongoing nature of the social constructions that urbanites engage in during their daily interactions in the city. Every definition of status, as Blumer (1969) reminds us, must ultimately be mutually reaffirmed by the acting participants in their daily communications. Society is indeed a symbolically negotiated phenomenon in which (if we may use a haberdashery metaphor) persons are constantly refashioning the social fabric. Wendell Bell cogently alerts us to this issue:

> Some persons, unlike rats in a maze, view the social structure as tentative and approximate. They proceed more like the psychologist himself, experimentally testing to learn which parts of the system are subject to manipulation. At the extreme, such persons may decide that the social structure, the maze itself, is subject to some extent to their will and may decide to shape it, as best they can, to suit themselves. To do this, moving through either social or geographical space may be unnecessary, for it is not the person who moves *spacially* into a different structure but the structure itself that is changed. Usually in cooperation with others, some people try to manipulate the real world to conform more closely to their images of the future: push out some walls, add some new openings, widen the passage-ways, create some new opportunities. (1968: 163)

In the remainder of this chapter we shall investigate the processes that affect the ability of various persons in the urban setting to, as Bell says, "manipulate the real world to conform more closely to their images of the future."

THE STUDY OF COMMUNITY POWER

While we have placed great stress on the existence of nonhierarchical status arrangements, it would be very naïve indeed to argue that hierarchical stratification arrangements do not exist. We suggest instead, along with Stone and Form (1953: 152), that "status arrangements will tend over time to take on the aspect of hierarchical structures. It is in this sense, and in this sense only, that the *essential* nature of status arrangements may be said to be hierarchical."

Weber (1958), as we noted earlier, also called attention to the significance of what he termed "guarantees of status stratification." By restricting interactions and intimacy (as in the selection of marital partners), high-ranking status groups are able simultaneously to reaffirm their "superiority" while calling attention to the "inferiority" of nongroup members.

On the broader, societal level Robert Michels, a German political sociologist, noted the operation of what he termed the "iron law of oligarchy." Michels (1962) argued that no matter how democratic an organization or social movement may be in its initial stages, it ultimately tends toward an organizational structure in which a great deal of power becomes more and more concentrated in the hands of a few high-ranking persons. The debate over community power that has long occupied social scientists (see, for example, Dahl, 1961; Hunter, 1953; Mills, 1959; and Polsby, 1963) may be seen as testimony to the significance of Michels' argument. On one side of the issue are those who see community power in "pluralist" terms, wherein a variety of local groups compete with each other on various issues, and no one group has dominance on every issue. On the other side are those who see community power in terms of "elites," wherein small, strategically located groups exercise major say on issues deemed of importance to their "interests." The elitist conception of community power tends toward a view of stratification as essentially hierarchical, while the pluralist is more conducive to a multidimensional view of stratification. Our aim in the following discussion is to specify the community processes that contribute to either hierarchical or pluralist power arrangements.

Processes Promoting Hierarchical Power Arrangements

Our previous discussions should have sensitized us to the notion that the social arrangements characterizing any locale are themselves products of a negotiated symbolic order, which is evidenced by a "complex network of competing groups and individuals acting to control, maintain, or improve their social conditions as defined by their *self* interests" (Hall, 1973: 45). The conditions under which such symbolic negotiations take place, however, are themselves functions of the power at the disposal of the groups involved. In short, the participants in various social worlds have differential access to the production and distribution of scarce and highly valued resources. The definition of what constitutes such highly valued "resources" is itself an outcome of a negotiated process, with the "winners" laying claim to a monopoly on "legitimate" definitions of "reality." In contemporary American society, access to the institutions influential in the production and distribution of property is a crucial factor in the ability of persons to establish dominant constructions of reality. Let us now examine some of the literature bearing on this issue.

In recent years social scientists have evidenced an increased interest in the distribution of wealth in the United States. The work of writers such as E. Digby Baltzell (1964, 1966), G. William Domhoff (1970), Ferdinand Lundberg (1968), and C. Wright Mills (1956, 1959) have all made significant contributions to the analysis of this problem insofar as they theorize about the political implications of the concentration of wealth in the hands of a relative few. Table 6–1 from the United States Bureau of the Census (1971: 28) nicely summarizes some of the relevant data.

Table 6–1. Income Distribution in the United States, 1950–1970
(in percent)

| Year | Share of total income received by each fifth of families | | | | |
	lowest fifth	second fifth	middle fifth	fourth fifth	highest fifth
1950	4.5	11.9	17.3	23.5	42.8
1955	4.8	12.2	17.7	23.4	41.8
1960	4.9	12.0	17.7	23.4	42.1
1965	5.3	12.1	17.7	23.7	41.3
1970	5.5	12.0	17.4	23.5	41.6

Source: Bureau of the Census, "*Current Population Reports,*" Series P-60, No. 80 (October 1971), p. 28.

As Table 6–1 indicates, in the period from 1950 to 1970 very little change occurred in the concentration of wealth in the United States. The highest fifth of the population in income accounted for 42.8 percent of the nation's total income in 1950, compared to 41.6 percent in 1970. The corresponding figures for the lowest fifth are 4.5 percent and 5.5 percent. Data from Lampman (1962) indicate that one-half of 1 percent of the adult American population accounted for 29.8 percent of all national wealth holdings in 1922 and for 25 percent of all national wealth holdings in 1956. More recent data, noted by Parker (1972: 120), indicate that "the top one percent of the American population (in 1968) received in one year more money than the poorest 50 million Americans." Table 6–2 succinctly specifies the distribution of types of personal wealth in the United States as of 1962.

Table 6–1 and 6–2 describe the nature of wealth distribution for the nation as a whole. How, then, do such figures relate to the nature of urban America? In his highly influential work *The Power Elite,*

Table 6–2. Distribution of Various Types of Personal Wealth, 1962

	Wealthiest 20% of the Population	Top 5% of the Population	Top 1% of the Population
Total wealth	76%	50%	31%
Corporate stock	96%	83%	61%
Businesses and professions	89%	62%	39%
Homes	52%	19%	6%

Source: Richard Parker, *The Myth of the Middle Class* (New York: Liveright Publishing Corporation, 1972), p. 212, based on materials originally presented in Frank Ackerman et al., *Income Distribution in the United States* (Cambridge, Mass.: Union of Radical Political Economists, mimeo: 1970). Reprinted by permission of Liveright Publishing Corporation.

C. Wright Mills (1959) called attention to the existence in major metropolitan areas of a compact and recognizable upper social class. The members of such an upper class achieved their "certification" through inclusion in a book known as the *Social Register,* which publishes listings only for the following cities: Baltimore, Boston, Buffalo, Chicago, Cincinnati, Cleveland, Philadelphia, Pittsburgh, San Francisco, St. Louis, New York, and Washington, D.C. As Mills noted:

> In each of the 12 chosen metropolitan areas of the nation, there is an upper social class whose members were born into families which have been registered since the *Social Register* began. This registered social class, as well as newly registered and unregistered classes in other big cities, is composed of groups of ancient families who for two or three or four generations have been prominent and wealthy. They are set apart from the rest of the community by their manner of origin, appearance and conduct. (1959: 57)

The members of this metropolitan upper class maintain their exclusivity by participating in social clubs and associations that rigorously exclude nonclass members. These clubs provide an important vehicle for the symbolic affirmation of upper-class consciousness. Such clubs exist at both the college and post-college levels, thereby providing an important source of continuity in class consciousness. Mills observes that the members of the metropolitan upper class

> belong to the same associations at the same set of Ivy League colleges, and they remain in social and business touch by means of the

big-city network of metropolitan clubs. In each of the nation's leading cities, they recognize one another, if not strictly as peers, as
people with much in common. (1969: 68)

E. Digby Baltzell's works also describe the existence of an upper-
class world in metropolitan America. Baltzell (1966) examined the
relationship between the following categories of persons: (1) those individuals whose occupational achievements had earned them high
status and inclusion in *Who's Who in America* (1940); (2) those individuals whose ascribed status, by virtue of family backgrounds, made
them eligible for inclusion in the *Social Register* (1940). Like Mills,
Baltzell also indicated that the schooling of the upper class, both prep
school and college, "serve to create and preserve an upper class inter-
city solidarity." Baltzell's data (1966: 273, Table 2) reveal a large concentration of elite members in the twelve metropolitan areas (listed
earlier) for which *Social Registers* have been issued. While these twelve
cities accounted for

> only approximately 20% of the total population of the U.S. (in
> 1940), 40% of all those listed in *Who's Who* in the country reside
> in these twelve metropolitan areas. Furthermore, it is certainly
> plausible to assume that the elite members in these cities have a
> more pervasive influence on the American social structure as a
> whole than the 60% who are listed in *Who's Who* from the rest of
> the country. (1966: 273)

Baltzell concludes his article by presenting some detailed evidence
on the nature of the upper class in Philadelphia. He characterizes it as
a "business and financial aristocracy" with a large concentration of
members in (1) the directorates of the six largest banking establishments in the city, (2) the six leading law firms in the city, (3) the directorates of the industrial institutions (1966: 274). In a study of Wall
Street lawyers in New York City, Smigel (1964: 39) also noted the significance of family lineage as a prerequisite for employment by one of
the prestigious New York law firms. Smigel (1964: 39) found that "30
percent of these 468 partners [in the twenty large New York firms
which had fifty or more lawyers] are listed in the *Social Register*." Recent work by Domhoff (1967, 1970) similarly documents the extent of
upper-class involvement in the social worlds of banking and corporate
law.

Up until very recently, the power of the metropolitan upper class
has largely been concentrated in the cities of the Northeastern United

States. Recent work by Kirkpatrick Sale (1974), however, suggests that the fulcrum of regional power in America is shifting from the Northeast to "America's Southern rim, the 'sunbelt' that runs from Southern California through Arizona and Texas, down to the Florida keys" (1974: 197). Within the higher echelons of power in American society a rivalry appears to be developing between the "cowboys" and the "yankees." The cowboys are those sunbelt *"nouveau-riche"* who have made large amounts of money in the "postwar decades, mostly in new industries such as aerospace and defense contracting, in oil, natural gas, allied businesses, usually domestic rather than international, and in real-estate operations, during the postwar sunbelt population boom" (1974: 197). These "self made" men and women are now jockeying for power with the "aristocracy" of the Eastern seaboard, who trace their fortunes and lineage back to earlier days in American history.

Sales (1974) notes that as a result of the reelection of Nixon in 1968, the cowboys "were firmly installed in the bedrooms of political power in Washington" (1974: 199). Nixon's establishment, while in office, of White Houses "at the two extremes of the Southern rim, San Clemente and Key Biscayne" is seen by Sale as symbolic of the cowboys' political ascendancy.

In terms of our earlier discussion, then, concerning stratification arrangements, Sale's (1974) work on the status contest between the cowboys and the yankees calls attention to the changing character of regional stratification patterns.

While the studies referred to in this section are certainly not conclusive on the subject of the upper class, they do at least provide some empirical evidence concerning the possible power and influence of this class in both urban and national affairs. At this point in our analysis we simply want to emphasize the importance of the upper class' access to, and involvement in, the major institutional bulwarks of the present property arrangements in the United States—the social worlds of finance and corporate law. Their relationship to these institutions provides upper-class members with an important lever for influencing the political process in the urban areas of America. Whether they utilize such a "lever" is, of course, an empirical question and one to be answered only by data from specific cities.

Having briefly sketched some of the broader contours of upper-class life in the United States, we now want to examine a number of studies that bear upon the relationship between socioeconomic status and participation in the political process. Such an examination will help to demonstrate that the process promoting hierarchical power arrangement is linked to the differential participation in public affairs of members of particular socioeconomic levels. In brief, our argument is as follows:

1. There is a documented relationship between high socioeconomic status (however it is measured) and participation in voluntary associations of various kinds.
2. Participation in voluntary associations is associated with the extent of one's political awareness and interest in politics.
3. The extent of political awareness among upper-class persons leads them to an involvement in the financing of election campaigns, and this may have an influence on the selection of political candidates.
4. Candidates who receive upper-class financing are more likely to be elected because of their exposure to the public through the mass media, which requires large amounts of money. The fact that persons of higher socioeconomic status are more likely than others to vote also increases the election chances of such candidates.
5. Once elected to office, incumbents are very likely to be reelected.

In effect, then, the political arrangements in the United States, from the local to the national level, have a self-reinforcing character that reaffirms the positions of those who are already powerful and makes the election of "reformers" a difficult affair.

For purposes of illustration we present the above model in the form of a diagram, Figure 6–4.

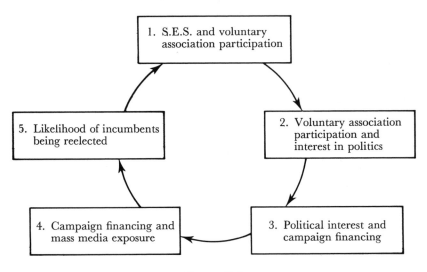

FIGURE 6–4

We shall now examine literature bearing on each of the five propositions.

Proposition 1. In an early empirical study of social participation in urban areas, Komarovsky (1946) found that the rate of participation in voluntary associations increased as the socioeconomic status of the respondent increased. More than two-thirds of the unskilled male workers interviewed in her study belonged to no associations at all, while the participation of professional men was exceedingly high. Also of importance were the different kinds of associations in which persons from various socioeconomic levels participated. Men and women in the professional category were more likely than others to belong to economic, political, and civic associations. Both skilled and unskilled workers, on the other hand, participated more frequently in fraternal associations.

A study by Bell and Force (1956) of four census tracts in San Francisco investigated the relationship between urban neighborhood types and participation in formal associations. They found that "within each of the neighborhoods (high or low economic status neighborhoods) persons of higher economic status, as indicated by their own individual educational level, income, and occupation, generally have a greater amount of associational participation than do individuals of lower economic status" (1956: 33). Bell and Force also called attention to the influence of the *neighborhood's* socioeconomic status on the participation of persons. They suggest that "the economic character of the neighborhood population as a unit may be an important indicator of the economic reference group for those living in the neighborhood, and may define a set of general societal expectations with respect to associational behavior of the residents" (1956: 33). This recalls our earlier discussion about the possible effects of the setting on localite or cosmopolite orientations.

In recent years a number of studies conducted in a wide variety of milieus have appeared that empirically examine the relationship between socio-economic status and voluntary association participation. Studies by Smith and Rawls (1965) and by Curtis (1971) found direct relationships between educational level and associational participation. Evaluating survey data from 1962, Hyman and Wright (1971: 205) also found support for this relationship. The data in Table 6–3 nicely illustrate the differential involvement in voluntary associations evidenced by persons of different socioeconomic status.

As the data indicate, members of the professional and business category making more than $7000 are more than twice as likely (36 percent

Table 6–3. Percent Belonging to Voluntary Associations by Occupation
and Income, 1962

| | Number of Associations Belonged to | | | |
Income Level	0	1	2+	N
Professional and business				
Above $7000	47%	17%	36%	143
Below $7000	53%	25%	22%	111
Labor[1]				
Above $7000	59%	24%	17%	191
Below $7000	72%	19%	9%	342

Source: H. Hyman and C. Wright, "Trends in Voluntary Association Membership of American Adults: Replication Based on Secondary Analysis of National Sample Surveys," *American Sociological Review,* 36 (April 1971), Table 6 on p. 202.

[1] Skilled, semiskilled, and unskilled.

compared to 17 percent) as laborers making more than $7000 to belong to two or more voluntary associations. In sum, then, a substantial body of studies exist that document the relationship between socioeconomic status and participation in voluntary associations.

Proposition 2. In an article reviewing a large number of studies dealing with the relationship between participation in politics and participation in voluntary associations, Erbe stated that such studies demonstrated that

> individuals who are involved in voluntary associations tend to participate more (in political activities) than those who are not, and that persons who are highly involved tend to participate more than those who are minimally involved. (1964: 199)

Erbe suggests that it is as a result of exposure to the "highly educated and outgoing people" who predominate in various voluntary associations that the individual's interest in politics, as well as other areas, may be stimulated. He also notes:

> Whether the specific measure used is income, education, occupation, home ownership, rent, race, some status hierarchy of religious affiliation, or some combination of any or all of these indices into a measure of "social class," the results are most uniform: the higher the social status, the more likely to register, to vote, to be interested in politics, to discuss politics, to belong to politically relevant organizations, and to attempt to influence the political views of others. (1964: 198)

In this regard, Table 6–4 dramatically illustrates the joint influence of socioeconomic status and organizational participation on political activity.

Table 6–4. Political Activity by Organizational Involvement and Social Status (in percent)

	Organization Involvement					
	High		Medium		Low	
	High Social Status	Low Social Status	High Social Status	Low Social Status	High Social Status	Low Social Status
Proportion who are politically active	75%	67%	41%	27%	32%	10%

Source: Data from Nie, Powell, and Prewitt (1969) and presented in Prewitt and Stone (1973: 218).

Looking at the "extremes" in the table, one is struck by the fact that high status persons with high organizational involvement are 7.5 times more likely than low status persons with low organizational involvement to be politically active (75 percent compared to 10 percent)! The latter persons, as Prewitt and Stone (1973: 218) remark, are "doubly penalized: first, by being without social and economic resources and second, by being without an organizational home."

A recent study by Olsen (1972) in the Indianapolis, Indiana, area also documents the relationship between social participation and interest in politics. According to Olsen, social participation

> tends to bring individuals into contact with political issues, actors, and affairs, and provides them with information and skills necessary for voting and other kinds of political participation. Partially as a result of this stimulation, the individual gives greater attention to political messages from the mass media, party workers, and other sources, and also develops stronger party identification and political interest. (1972: 331)

Reviewing a large number of studies of public leadership from varied locales in the United States, Bell, Hill, and Wright (1961) noted: "Formal leaders, reputational leaders, and active social participants are more likely to come from the upper strata than they are to be drawn from the 'working' or lower classes" (1961: 118).

We should note that the relationship examined here, particularly in the case of upper-class persons, may not be a simple one-way path from organizational involvement to political awareness, but rather one that is mutually reinforcing. Thus, their political awareness leads upper-class persons to join various kinds of voluntary associations; this awareness in turn is further developed as a result of such participation. Some evidence for this notion can be found in the treatments of the socialization of upper-class children and adolescents in the works of Domhoff (1970) and Baltzell (1964). Dawson and Prewitt also note:

> Higher status children have higher levels of interest and a greater sense of efficacy in the political world. Social status background is related to party preferences beginning by about grade five, and becomes increasingly pronounced in successively higher grades. (1969: 183)

The studies reviewed here, then, provide some degree of empirical support for proposition 2.

Proposition 3. With reference to the issue of campaign contributions, the dramatic concentration of large contributions in the hands of a small group of donors is clearly revealed by the fact that in the 1968 campaign eighty-nine persons together contributed more than $6.8 million (*New York Times,* November 14, 1971). Table 6–5 documents the relationship between wealth and campaign financing. As the data indicate, persons making $20,000 or more per year were more than 2.5 times as likely to contribute to political campaigns in 1968 and 1972 than were those making less than $10,000 per year. Data discussed in Alexander (1960: 25) for the 1952, 1956, and 1960 presidential elections also indicate that, for all three elections, those in the highest income bracket were far more likely to make a contribution than those in the lowest bracket.

Proposition 4. Domhoff (1972) has also noted that upper-class wealth makes it possible for such persons to loan large amounts to selected candidates that may be used for such purposes as travel and mailing expenses. They may also provide candidates with campaign workers who are employees of their own companies. The role of upper-class financing is particularly critical in the case of primaries at all levels of government since it is at this point that "the overly liberal candidates they (the upper class) oppose are usually eliminated from considera-

Table 6–5. Income and Educational Class Bias Among Campaign
Contributors

Income Group	Percentage Contributing 1968	1972	Education	Percentage Contributing 1968	1972
$ 0–$4,999	3.0	3.7	0–8 grade	4.8	5.4
5,000– 9,999	7.3	11.5	9–12 grade	5.5	9.6
10,000–14,999	8.4	11.7	Some college	10.0	17.8
15,000–19,999	14.3	19.8	College: 4 years		
20,000 or more	24.1	32.0	or more	18.6	28.4
All	7.6	12.4	All	7.6	12.4

Source: David W. Adamany and George E. Agree, *Political Money: A Strategy for Campaign Financing in America* (Baltimore: Johns Hopkins University Press, 1975), p. 30, Table 3–1. © The Twentieth Century Fund, Inc. The 1968 figures are retabulations of a University of Michigan Survey Research Center poll. The 1972 tabulations are based on the Twentieth Century Fund Survey discussed in Adamany and Agree.

tion" (1972: 14). Losing candidates who have received upper-class financing also benefit from special "discounts" such as the following:

> Hotels, airlines and telephone companies extend tens of thousands of dollars in credit to candidates of both parties, then settle with the loser at a cut-rate price—*with three cents on the dollar being a fairly typical figure.* (1972: 29) (Italics are ours.)

We noted earlier that "the higher the social status, the more likely to register, to vote." In addition, the previously cited Bell et al. (1961: 113) study of public leadership demonstrated that "studies of political behavior indicate that both interest in elections and voter turnout are more common among citizens of higher socio-economic and educational status." The relationship noted by Bell et al. becomes particularly important in view of the documented evidence that (a) sizeable percentages of those who are eligible to vote do not vote; (b) in many cities a very small percentage of voters can successfully elect a particular candidate.

In reference to voter participation, Banfield and Wilson present data in Table 6–6 pertaining to electoral turnouts in mayoralty and presidential elections in 1948 through 1952.

As the data reveal, in every one of the designated cities 48 percent or more of the eligible voters failed to vote in the mayoralty elections.

Table 6–6. Average Turnout[1] in Mayoralty and Presidential Elections
in Large Cities, 1948–1952

City	Mayoralty	Presidential	City	Mayoralty	Presidential
Chicago	51.5%	71.3%	New Orleans	40.5%	38.6%
Pittsburgh	50.5	61.3	Minneapolis	37.0	63.8
Philadelphia	49.8	63.5	Denver	36.7	66.1
Buffalo	49.1	64.2	Cleveland	34.8	53.0
Cincinnati	49.0	61.2	Detroit	33.8	58.0
Boston	47.0	62.6	Baltimore	31.5	46.2
San Francisco	46.3	60.6	Los Angeles	31.3	58.7
New York	42.3	57.7	St. Louis	30.4	59.2
Indianapolis	41.4	63.1	Kansas City	29.9	59.2

Source: Edward C. Banfield and James Q. Wilson, *City Politics* (Cambridge, Mass.: Harvard University Press and M.I.T. Press, 1963). © 1963 by The President and Fellows of Harvard College and The Massachusetts Institute of Technology. Reprinted by permission.

The above data presented by Banfield and Wilson are based on unpublished data gathered by Charles E. Gilbert and made available to those authors.

1 Turnout is here measured as the percentage of all persons of 21 years of age or over who vote in general elections. The figure for the presidential elections is the average of the 1948 and 1952 turnouts; that for the mayoralty elections is an average of the same period.

Also of note is the fact that in all these cities, with the exception of New Orleans, the participation in mayoralty (that is, local) elections is considerably less than the participation in the national presidential elections. Data from the Bureau of the Census presented in Table 6–7 indicate that in the elections of 1966 and 1968 only 46 percent and 56 percent respectively of those eligible to vote actually voted for candidates for the United States House of Representatives.

Proposition 5. A recent study by Kenneth Prewitt of cities in the San Francisco Bay area presents some important data on the *minimum* number of votes required for city councilmen in the cities studied to win a council seat. We present his data in Table 6–8. The vote has been averaged by Prewitt for five elections.

In a city of 71,000 people less than 10 percent of the total population was needed to elect a councilman. In discussing his findings, Prewitt noted:

> In a city of more than 13,000 residents, on the average as few as 810 voters elected a man to office. Such figures sharply question the

Table 6–7. Voter Participation in Presidential and House
of Representative Elections

In Millions. As of Nov. 1

Year	Estimated Civilian Population of voting age[1]	Vote Cast for President		Vote Cast for Representative	
		Total	% of civilians of voting age	Total	% of civilians of voting age
1940	84	50	59	47	56
1944[1]	81	45	56	45	50
1948	95	49	51	46	48
1952	98	62	63	58	59
1956[1]	103	62	60	58	57
1958	105	X	X	46	43
1960[1]	108	69	64	64	60
1962	110	X	X	51	47
1964	112	71	63	66	59
1966	114	X	X	53	46
1968	118	73	62	66	56
1970	121	X	X	NA	NA

Source: Bureau of the Census, *Pocket Data Book* (Washington, D.C., 1971), p. 105, Table 99.

[1] Population 21 years old and over except 18 and over in Georgia since 1944 and Kentucky since 1956; 19 and over in Alaska; and 20 and over in Hawaii since 1960. Includes aliens;
NA = Not Available; X = Not applicable.

Table 6–8. Minimum Number of Votes Needed to Win Office in Different Size Cities

City Population (1964 Estimate)	Average Total Vote of Lowest Winner— Five Elections[1] (1955–65)
71,000	5298
28,750	1931
13,450	810
6675	518
500	64

Source: Kenneth Prewitt, "Political Ambitions, Volunteerism, and Electoral Accountability," *American Political Science Review*, 64 (March 1970). Reprinted by permission of the American Political Science Association.

[1] To compute the average total vote of the lowest winner, Prewitt simply added the votes of lowest winner for five elections, there are never fewer than two winners for any council election.

validity of thinking that "mass electorates" hold elected officials accountable. For these councilmen, even if serving in relatively sizeable cities, there is no "mass electorate"; rather, there are the councilman's business associates, his friends at church, his acquaintances in the Rotary Club, and so forth, which provide him the electoral support he needs to gain office. (1970: 9)

Prewitt also calls our attention to the issue of reelection. His data (1970: 10, Table 4) reveal that, in 65 percent of the cities he studied, more than 50 percent of the councilmen who left office did so *voluntarily*, rather than through election defeats. He states:

Over the ten-year period, four out of five incumbent councilmen who stood for reelection were successful. This figure, though high, is even somewhat lower than one reported for members of the House of Representatives. During the years 1924–1956, 90 percent of the congressmen who sought reelection were returned by the voters. (1970: 9)

The data presented above, coupled with our discussions of propositions 1 through 5, illustrate the cumulative process by which upper-class power and involvement in political affairs contributes to the production of a self-affirming set of social arrangements in the United States. Our task now, however, is to specify the particular characteristics of urban communities that may be associated with pluralist power arrangements.

Processes Promoting Pluralist Power Arrangements

Previously we dealt at length with the role played by upper-class persons in the general political process. In large urban areas, however, a number of competing interests may vie with one another—all of which may be highly "organized." In such milieus, then, the question of upper-class dominance must be viewed within the context of other competing interests. What, we may ask, are the conditions that seem to promote the concentration or diffusion of power in a city? In a broad survey of the literature on community power, Aiken (1970) examined the conditions affecting the diffusion of power at the community level. His analysis revealed that the following interrelated factors were associated with pluralist power arrangements; that is, arrangements in which no single group had ultimate say on all issues:

1. Cities with heterogeneous populations—with many people of foreign descent. (1970: 514)
2. Cities with large municipal bureaucracies. (1970: 514)
3. Cities with a major-council form of government, with direct election of the mayor, large city councils, and elections by ward or district. (1970: 499)
4. Cities with weak executive power lodged in the office of Mayor. (1970: 499)
5. Cities with a high degree of absentee-owned businesses. (1970: 514)
6. Larger cities.[4] (1970: 514)
7. Older cities in the Northern United States. (1970: 495)

Items 1 and 2 are significant in that they at least provide an arena for the development of "interest blocs"—such as ethnic groups[5] and municipal employees—whose participation in the urban political process challenges the dominance of upper-class, business-related groups. Similarly, the lack of centralized power in the mayor's office (items 3 and 4) contributes to a competition among urban interest blocs for access to the formal channels of power.

Cities with a high degree of absentee-owned businesses tend to have diffused power arrangements, since the executives of these companies are likely to be cosmopolitan in orientation and sensitive to local affairs only when they directly bear upon the company's business. Such executives are oriented to *careers* in the organization rather than to success in the local community. This is not to deny, however, as Bachrach and Baratz's (1970) analysis of Dahl's work indicates, that such businesses do not possess great potential power should they define the situation as one requiring their involvement in the political process. In smaller cities with many absentee-owned businesses, the influx of new executives and company personnel into the community may result in what we described earlier as a status contest among the upper status groups in the community. These contests have the possible consequences of diffusing the previously concentrated power arrangements.

---

[4] Aiken's results on the question of city size, while not statistically significant, were in the expected positive direction for the total set of cities investigated. See Aiken (1970: 495).

[5] For an insightful view of the definitions of reality put forth by present-day "ethnics," see Michael Novak's (1973) *The Rise of the Unmeltable Ethnics.*

Finally the size of the city (item 6) and its age (item 7) are of relevance, since such cities were the locales in which the huge waves of immigrants to the United States first took up residence in the late nineteenth and early twentieth centuries. The history of such cities is thus linked to the proliferation of heterogeneous social groupings and their consequent interest blocs noted earlier.

The work of Theodore Lowi (1964, 1970), a distinguished political scientist at the University of Chicago, also contributes to a further specification of the social conditions under which hierarchical and pluralist power arrangements may be expected to occur. While the previous material dealt with characteristics of the community as a whole, Lowi's work[6] attempts a finer specification of the issue by treating specific "arenas of power" within the community itself. He makes the important observation that there are *numerous* political processes occurring in a given community—not just one process, as many theorists on both sides of the elitist-pluralist debate have assumed.

Lowi argues that those local agencies concerned with the issues of "Services and Welfare" are involved in matters of "redistribution" and, as such, are likely to be the arenas within which hierarchical arrangements predominate (1964: 139–143). Those city agencies concerned with "Regulation and Property Protection" (for example, Police and Fire Departments, License Department) are the arenas within which pluralist arrangements are generated since regulatory decisions "hit individual businessmen and citizens individually" (1964: 144). He also notes that pluralism in this arena is promoted by the access to regulatory decisions that various groups in the community may compete for.

The arena of "Governmental Inputs" (for example, Tax Department, Finance Department, Board of Assessors) is, like the Services and Welfare arena, one in which hierarchical arrangements prevail. He argues: "If there is a power elite in the city, it would include those who have perpetual influence over the thousands of individual assessments on individual pieces of property" (1964: 145).

Finally, the "overhead" arena (for example, Budget Bureau, Civil Service Commission) is the setting in which what Lowi calls "non-conflictual elites" coexist with one another. These elites are composed of the heads of various city agencies who have been appointed by the mayor and are believed to be personally loyal to him.

---

6 Our treatment of Lowi's work represents a synthesis of the various approaches contained in Lowi (1964, 1970).

Lowi's work is of great significance for an interactionist view of urban stratification, since he calls our attention to the numerous alternative definitions of "interests" made by various participants in the different arenas of power in urban locales. Such a position is fully congruent with our repeated emphasis on the notions of "multiple realities" and the socially constructed nature of stratification arrangements.

REFERENCES

Ackerman, Frank, et al. *Income Distribution in the United States*. Cambridge, Mass.: Union of Radical Political Economists, 1970.

Adamany, David W., and George E. Agree. *Political Money: A Strategy for Campaign Financing in America*. Baltimore: Johns Hopkins University Press, 1975.

Aiken, Michael T. "The Distribution of Community Power: Structural Bases and Social Consequences." Pp. 487–525 in M. Aiken and P. Mott (eds.), *The Structure of Community Power*. New York: Random House, 1970.

Alexander, Herbert, and Harold B. Meyers. "A Financial Landslide for the G.O.P." *Fortune,* March 1970.

Alexander, Herbert (ed.). *Studies in Money and Politics*. Princeton, N.J.: Citizens Research Foundation, 1960.

Bachrach, Peter, and Morton S. Baratz. *Power and Poverty: Theory and Practice*. New York: Oxford University Press, 1970.

Baltzell, E. Digby. *The Protestant Establishment*. New York: Random House, 1964.

Baltzell, E. Digby. " 'Who's Who in America' and 'The Social Register': Elite and Upper Class Indexes in Metropolitan America." Pp. 266–75 in R. Bendix and S. M. Lipset (eds.), *Class, Status, and Power*. New York: Free Press, 1966.

Banfield, Edward C., and James Q. Wilson. *City Politics*. Cambridge, Mass.: Harvard University Press and M.I.T. Press, 1963.

Bell, Wendell. "The City, the Suburb, and a Theory of Social Choice." Pp. 132–68 in Scott Greer et al. (eds.), *The New Urbanization*. New York: St. Martin's Press, 1968.

Bell, Wendell, and MaryAnn T. Force. "Urban Neighborhood Types and Participation in Formal Associations." *American Sociological Review,* 21 (1956), 25–34.

Bell, Wendell, Richard J. Hill, and Charles R. Wright. *Public Leadership*. San Francisco: Chandler Publishing Company, 1961.

Berger, Bennet M. *Working-Class Suburb: A Study of Auto Workers in Suburbia*. Berkeley, Calif.: University of California Press, 1968.

Bernstein, Victor H. "The High Cost of Campaigning." *The Nation,* June 27, 1966, 770–75.

Blumer, Herbert. "Early Industrialization and the Laboring Class." *Sociological Quarterly,* 1 (1960), 5–14.

Blumer, Herbert. *Symbolic Interactionism: Perspective and Method.* Englewood Cliffs, N.J.: Prentice-Hall, 1969.

Bureau of the Census. "Consumer Income." *Current Population Reports,* Series P-60, No. 80 (October 1971): 28.

Bureau of the Census. *Pocket Data Book.* Washington, D.C.: Bureau of the Census, 1971.

Chinoy, Eli. "The Tradition of Opportunity and the Aspirations of Automobile Workers." *American Journal of Sociology,* 57 (March 1952): 453–59.

Cuber, John F., and William F. Kenkel. *Social Stratification in the United States.* New York: Appleton-Century-Crofts, 1954.

Curtis, James. "Voluntary Association Joining: A Cross-National Comparative Note." *American Sociological Review,* 36 (1971): 872–81.

Dahl, Robert A. *Who Governs? Democracy and Power in an American City.* New Haven: Yale University Press, 1961.

Davis, Allison, Burleigh B. Gardner, and Mary R. Gardner. *Deep South: A Social-Anthropological Study of Caste and Class.* Chicago: University of Chicago Press, 1941.

Dawson, Richard E., and Kenneth Drewitt. *Political Socialization.* Boston: Little, Brown, 1969.

Domhoff, G. William. *Fat Cats and Democrats.* Englewood Cliffs, N.J.: Prentice-Hall, 1972.

Domhoff, G. William. *The Higher Circles.* New York: Random House, 1970.

Domhoff, G. William. *Who Rules America?* Englewood Cliffs, N.J.: Prentice-Hall, 1967.

Erbe, William. "Social Involvement and Political Activity." *American Sociological Review,* 29 (April 1964): 198–216.

Form, William H., and Gregory P. Stone. "Urbanism, Anonymity and Status Symbolism." *American Journal of Sociology,* 62 (March 1957): 504–14.

Gerstl, Joel. "Leisure, Taste, and Occupational Milieu." *Social Problems,* 9 (1961–62): 56–68.

Glaser, Barney G. *Organizational Scientists: Their Professional Careers.* Indianapolis: Bobbs-Merrill, 1964.

Gouldner, Alvin. "Cosmopolitans and Locals: Toward an Analysis of Latent Social Roles." *Administrative Science Quarterly* 2 (1957–58): 281–306, 444–48.

Hall, Peter. "A Symbolic Interactionist Analysis of Politics." Pp. 35–76 in A. Effrat (ed.), *Perspectives in Political Sociology.* Indianapolis: Bobbs-Merrill, 1973.

Harris, Richard. "Annals of Politics: A Fundamental Hoax." *New Yorker,* August 7, 1971, 37–64.

Havighurst, Robert J., and H. Gerthon Morgan. *The Social History of a War Boom Community.* New York: Longmans, Green and Company, 1951.

Hollingshead, August B. *Elmtown's Youth.* New York: John Wiley, 1949.

Hunter, Floyd. *Community Power Structure.* Chapel Hill: University of North Carolina Press, 1953.

Hyman, Herbert, and Charles Wright. "Trends in Voluntary Association Membership of American Adults: Replication Based on Secondary Analysis of National Sample Surveys." *American Sociological Review* 36 (April 1971): 191–206.

Komarovsky, Mirra. "The Voluntary Associations of Urban Dwellers." *American Sociological Review,* 11 (December 1946): 686–98.

Lampman, Robert J. *The Share of Top Wealth-Holders in National Wealth, 1922–1956.* Princeton, N.J.: Princeton University Press, 1962.

Laumann, Edward O. (ed.). *Stratification Theory and Research.* Sociological Inquiry 40 (Spring 1970): 1–258.

Lenski, Gerhard. "American Social Classes: Statistical Strata or Social Groups?" *American Journal of Sociology,* 58 (1952): 139–44.

Lowi, Theodore. *At the Pleasure of the Mayor.* New York: The Free Press, 1964.

Lowi, Theodore. "American Business, Public Policy, Case Studies, and Political Theory." *World Politics,* 16 (July 1964): 677–715.

Lundberg, Ferdinand. *The Rich and the Super-Rich.* New York: Bantam Books, 1958.

Lynd, Robert S., and Helen M. Lynd. *Middletown in Transition.* New York: Harcourt, Brace, 1937.

Marx, Karl. *Karl Marx: Selected Writings in Sociology and Social Philosophy.* Translated by T. B. Bottomore. New York: McGraw-Hill, 1956.

Marx, Karl, and Frederick Engels. "The Civil War in France." In Karl Marx and Frederick Engels, *Selected Works* (Vol. I). Moscow: Foreign Language Publishing House, 1950.

Marx, Karl, and Frederick Engels. "The Class Struggles in France." In Karl Marx and Frederick Engels, *Selected Works* (Vol. I). Moscow: Foreign Language Publishing House, 1950.

Merton, Robert K. "Patterns of Influence: Local and Cosmopolitan Influentials." Pp. 441–74 in Robert K. Merton, *Social Theory and Social Structure.* New York: Free Press, 1968.

Michels, Robert. *Political Parties.* Translated by Eden Paul and Cedar Paul. New York: Free Press, 1962.

Mills, C. Wright. *The Power Elite.* New York: Oxford University Press, 1959.

Mills, C. Wright. *Power, Politics, and People.* Edited by Irving Louis Horowitz. New York: Ballantine Books, 1963.

Mills, C. Wright. *White Collar.* New York: Oxford University Press, 1956.

Mintz, Morton, and Jerry S. Cohen. *America Inc.* New York: Dell, 1971.

Nie, Norman H., G. Bingham Powell, Jr., and Kenneth Prewitt. "Social Structure and Political Participation: Developmental Relationships. Part II." *American Political Science Review* 63 (September 1969): 808–32.

Novak, Michael. *The Rise of the Unmeltable Ethnics.* New York. Macmillan, 1973.

Ollman, Bertell. *Alienation: Marx's Conception of Man in Capitalist Society.* Cambridge, England: Cambridge University Press, 1971.

Olsen, Marvin E. "Social Participation and Voting Turnout: A Multivariate Analysis." *American Sociological Review,* 37 (June 1972): 317–32.

Parker, Richard. *The Myth of the Middle Class.* New York: Liveright, 1972.

Pfautz, Harold W. and Otis Dudley Duncan. "A Critical Evaluation of Warner's Work in Community Stratification." *American Sociological Review,* 15 (April 1950): 205–15.

Polsby, Nelson. *Community Power and Political Theory.* New Haven: Yale University Press, 1963.

Prewitt, Kenneth. "Political Ambitions, Volunteerism, and Electoral Accountability." *American Political Science Review,* 64 (March 1970): 5–16.

Prewitt, Kenneth, and Alan Stone. *The Ruling Elites: Elite Theory, Power and American Democracy.* New York: Harper and Row, 1973.

Reichert, Loren. *Social Rankings in Metropolitan Settings.* Unpublished Ph.D. dissertation, University of Minnesota, 1975.

Riesman, David. *The Lonely Crowd.* New Haven: Yale University Press, 1950.

Roof, W. Clark. "The Local-Cosmopolitan Orientation and Traditional Religious Commitment." *Sociological Analysis,* 33 (Spring 1972): 1–15.

Roof, W. Clark. "Religious Orthodoxy and Minority Prejudice: Causal Relationship or Reflection of World View?" *American Journal of Sociology,* 80 (November 1974): 643–64.

Sale, Kirkpatrick. "The World Behind Watergate." Pp. 197–210 in David C. Saffell (ed.), *Watergate: Its Effects on the American Political System.* Cambridge, Mass.: Winthrop Publishers, 1974. Originally published in the *New York Review of Books,* May 3, 1973, 9–13.

Smigel, Erwin. *The Wall Street Lawyer.* New York: The Free Press, 1964.

Smith, Joel, and H. D. Rawls. "Standardization of an Educational Variable: The Need and Its Consequences." *Social Forces,* 44 (September 1965): 57–66.

Speier, Hans. "Social Stratification in the Urban Community." *American Sociological Review,* 1 (April 1936): 193–202.

Stone, Gregory P. "The Circumstance and Situation of Social Status." Pp. 250–59 in Gregory P. Stone and Harvey A. Farberman (eds.), *Social Psychology Through Symbolic Interaction.* Waltham, Mass.: Ginn-Blaisdell, 1970.

Stone, Gregory P., and Harvey A. Farberman (eds.), *Social Psychology Through Symbolic Interaction.* Waltham, Mass.: Ginn-Blaisdell, 1970.

Stone, Gregory P., and William Form. "Instabilities in Status: The Problem of Hierarchy in the Community Study of Status Arrangements." *American Sociological Review,* 18 (April 1953): 149–62.

Thernstrom, Stephan. " 'Yankee City' Revisited: The Perils of Historical Naivete." *American Sociological Review,* 30 (April 1965): 234–42.

Thielbar, Gerald. "On Locals and Cosmopolitans." Pp. 259–75 in Gregory P. Stone and Harvey A. Farberman (eds.), *Social Psychology Through Symbolic Interaction.* Waltham, Mass.: Ginn-Blaisdell, 1970.

Warner, W. Lloyd, et al. *Democracy in Jonesville.* New York: Harper and Row, 1949.

Warner, W. Lloyd, et al. *Social Class in America.* New York: Harper and Row, 1960.

Warner, W. Lloyd, and J. O. Low. *The Social System of the Modern Factory.* New Haven: Yale University Press, 1947.

Warner, W. Lloyd, and Paul S. Lunt. *The Social Life of a Modern Community.* New Haven: Yale University Press, 1941.

Weber, Max. "Class, Status, Party." Pp. 180–96 in H. H. Gerth and C. Wright Mills (trans. and ed.), *From Max Weber.* New York: Oxford University Press, Galaxy Book, 1958.

Wilensky, Harold L. "Orderly Careers and Social Participation: The Impact of Work History on Social Integration in the Middle Mass." *American Sociological Review,* 26 (August 1961), 521–40.

Wirth, Louis. "Urbanism as a Way of Life." *American Journal of Sociology,* 44 (July 1938): 1–24.

Zeitlin, Irving M. *Marxism: A Re-examination.* New York: Van Nostrand Reinhold Company, 1967.

7

Looking Ahead

Much of our effort in this book has been directed at carefully examining some of the central images that have dominated social scientists' view of the city—images often created by social scientists themselves. Throughout we have sustained the notion that persons are not mere victims of their environments, as many sociologists would have it. Instead we have advocated the symbolic interactionist position that persons are capable of transforming their worlds; they are capable of transforming the city itself. This premise led us to examine how urbanites create identity-sustaining relationships in those situations in which impersonal ties seem to predominate. We disagreed with those who maintain that the fate of most urban persons must be isolation, alienation, and anomie resulting from the disappearance of *Gemeinschaft*-like communities. In another chapter we showed how the public life of urbanites is ordered and maintained through the cooperative production of anonymity. Later our focus shifted from the primarily individual level of analysis to inquire into group relations in the city. Here our concern was to describe how the city is able to support higher levels of tolerance for "ultra-life style" groups than is possible in more homogeneous communities. We also considered the conditions under which tolerance is likely to break down. In the previous chapter we indicated how the usual hierarchical conception of stratification systems may limit our understanding of urban class, status, and power arrangements.

It must be clear that our intention has not been to claim current understandings of the city to be wholly incorrect. We have not sought to reject the theoretical conceptions traditionally guiding social scientists' analysis of city life. Our goal has been the more modest one of amendment and specification of existing theoretical explanation. We began our analysis with a simple assumption; namely, that the questions asked about phenomena or processes are contingent upon scientists' views of the world. The theoretical approach used in this book —symbolic interaction—led us to ask: How do persons give meaning to, adapt to, and make intelligible their lives as city dwellers? We tried to illustrate the power of this and associated questions in directing our attention to: (1) possible gaps, omissions, or deficiencies in traditional theoretical explanations of city life, and (2) substantive features of city life that have been relatively neglected in the literature on urbanism.

One outcome of the thinking demanded by our questions has been a somewhat more positive view of city life than is found in most available literature. Persons can and do enjoy living in cities; persons identify with cities; persons appreciate the freedom that they experience in cities. At the same time, one might ask whether we have, in our concern with showing how city persons adapt and respond creatively to the city, simply substituted one partially correct image for another partially correct image. In trying to modify traditionally negative city images, have we ourselves ended up with an overly romantic view of cities and city life? Have we neglected to consider the larger social processes occurring in cities that may render them obsolete? In this chapter we must ask questions about the future of cities. As we speculate about their future and so about future forms of human association, we shall want to consider how the perspective adopted in this book ought to influence urban planning.

The consensus of intellectuals writing about cities today is that they face nearly overwhelming problems. The sociologist Scott Greer (1964: 208) has commented that "the older city appears to be dying—functionally, structurally, politically and eventually ideologically." Some argue (see, for example, Sternlieb, 1972: 263) that the crisis of cities is essentially one of function. In their view, the central city has become a victim of technological change. Cities, they say, are no longer necessary. They no longer offer the economic, social, and political advantages that they once did. Businesses, for example, no longer need to locate in central cities. Communication and transportation advances have made possible the movement of industry to the suburbs without any loss in efficiency or economic advantage. It follows that there has been a continuous outmigration of middle-class persons who seek the greater space, amenities, and job opportunities offered in suburban areas.

The result of these changes has been a progressive decay of central city areas. Increasingly, central cities are populated by poor whites and minority groups with little opportunity for mobility; single persons; the elderly; and some wealthy persons who are able to insulate themselves from the reality of substandard and often abandoned housing, deteriorating services, and the apparently irreversible growth of slums. Others are alarmed by the general trends precipitated by the decline of the central city: suburban sprawl and the disappearance of the countryside. Any distinctions between city and noncity life become blurred with the increasing "conurbation" of society. Such an image implies the disappearance of isolated cities and the spread of urban mass society over large areas of the country. One such megalopolis would, for example, extend from Boston to Washington. The scale of such settlements has been described thus:

> We can no longer use the word "city" without thinking twice because we all have an image of the city as a built-up area, and we forget that the ordinary man and his family no longer live within a city but within a system of life processes which extends well beyond the city, which it only touches at certain points. This system is growing continuously in space. . . . In consequence we have to recognize that our notion of villages and cities belongs to the past: in a few generations there will be no isolated villages left on earth. Instead we will have to think of systems that organize our

life, primarily the daily urban systems that encompass our daily movements and which can extend from twenty to thirty miles (Europe) to eighty or ninety miles (U.S.A.). (Delos Seven, 1972: 241)

DEMOGRAPHIC TRENDS AND THE URBAN CRISIS

In order to assess fully the problems and prospects for future urban life, we must examine some of the available data on urban demographic trends. As we noted in the last chapter, persons' images of the future are critical influences on their present behaviors. Such images and the aspirations or fears that they symbolize are of great significance in understanding the following questions: Which social groups are remaining in central cities? Which groups are leaving? How do the socioeconomic characteristics of suburbanites vary from those remaining in cities? Consistent with the theoretical perspective developed throughout this book, we want to analyze how these trends may alert us to the likely future meanings of being urban.

An important phenomenon of contemporary urban life is the increasing concentration of nonwhites in the central city area. As Table 7–1

Table 7–1. Nonwhite Proportion of United States and
Metropolitan Population, 1900–1970

	Nonwhite Population as a Percentage of:			
Year[a]	Total U.S. Population	Total SMSA[b] Population	Total Central City Population	Total Population Outside Central City
1900	12.1	7.8	6.8	9.4
1910	11.1	7.3	6.9	8.1
1920	10.3	7.2	7.3	7.0
1930	10.2	8.1	9.0	6.4
1940	10.2	8.6	10.1	6.0
1950	10.7	10.0	13.1	5.7
1960	11.4	11.7	17.8	5.2
1970	12.3	13.7	21.9	5.5

Source: National Academy of Sciences, *Toward an Understanding of Metropolitan America* (Washington, D.C.: Canfield Press Division of Harper and Row, 1975), p. 19, Table 3. Reprinted by permission of Harper and Row and of the National Academy of Sciences.

[a] Data for 1900–1960 refer to the coterminous United States, whereas data for 1970 include Hawaii and Alaska.

[b] Standard Metropolitan Statistical Area.

indicates, the percentage of nonwhites in the central city doubled between 1940 and 1970—going from 10.1 percent to 21.9 percent.

The changes described in Table 7–1 did not, however, occur at an equal rate throughout the entire country. A recent government-funded study (National Academy of Sciences, 1975: 20) showed, for example, that in the Northeast the black population increased by 35.5 percent, while the white central city population declined by 9.3 percent. With reference to the 1960–1970 decade, this same study noted:

> For all metropolitan areas of one million or more, nearly 80 percent of the black population live in central cities, as compared to 36 percent of the whites. In metropolitan areas with a population below one million, nearly 75 percent of the blacks and about 40 percent of the whites live in central cities. Washington, D.C., where seven out of ten residents are black, is an extreme example of increasing segregation of the central cities, but in 16 other central cities, blacks outnumber whites. (NAS, 1975: 20)

During the 1960s there was a trend of increasing black migration to the suburbs, although only 820,000 blacks were involved in the process compared to 15.3 million whites (NAS, 1975: 20). How have such migration patterns as noted in Table 7–1 affected the socioeconomic characteristics of residents in metropolitan areas? Table 7–2 presents data

Table 7–2. Distribution of Socioeconomic Characteristics in Metropolitan Areas, 1970

	Central City	Outside Central City
Percentage of persons below poverty level [a]	13.4	6.3
Percentage aged 25–29 with less than high school education	25.3	19.2
Female-headed families as a percentage of all families[b]	17.0	8.8
Percentage of population over 65	11.1	7.4
AFDC[c] families as a percentage of all families[b]	9.8	2.4

Source: National Academy of Sciences, *Toward an Understanding of Metropolitan America* (Washington, D.C.: Canfield Press Division of Harper and Row, 1975), p. 37. Table 8. Reprinted by permission of Harper and Row and of the National Academy of Sciences.

[a] 1969 data.

[b] 1971 data.

[c] AFDC—Aid to Families with Dependent Children.

comparing those living in central city areas with those living outside the central city (in suburbs).

Of critical importance here is the fact that residents of central city areas tend to be considerably poorer, less educated, more elderly, and more likely to be members of female-centered families than do their counterparts outside the central city.

Recent data also indicate that the socioeconomic gap between the central cities and the suburbs has been increasing. For example, the median income for central city families nearly doubled in the fourteen-year period from 1960 to 1974, rising from $5950 to $11,379. During that same time period the median income of suburban families more than doubled, going from $6707 to $14,056. The difference in suburban versus central city median family income, then, went from $767 in 1967 to $2677 in 1974 (Holsendorf, 1975: 46).

Such a gap reflects the fact that poor, rural migrants are most likely to settle in central cities, and that the more well-off segments of the central city (both whites and nonwhites) are the most likely to transfer their residences from the central city to the suburbs (Holsendorf, 1975: 46). In addition, as the more affluent blacks move to suburbs, the character of central cities, as we saw in Table 7–2, becomes increasingly made up of low income nonwhites.

Also of significance is the fact that the black population in every metropolitan area, as Taeuber (1965) has demonstrated, is restricted to largely black neighborhoods:

> This segregation is found in the cities of the North and West as well as the South; in large cities as well as small; in non-industrial cities as well as industrial; in cities with hundreds of thousands of Negro residents as well as those with only a few thousand, and in cities that are progressive in their employment practices and civil rights policies as well as those that are not. (Taeuber, 1965: 14)

Taueber's work clearly demonstrates that these residential patterns are not simply a function of low income but result rather from discriminatory housing policies restricting the range of possible housing sites for nonwhite urbanites.

From an interactionist perspective, it is important to stress that the processes just described are not the result of "natural," "inevitable" happenings, but rather derive from the ongoing activities of concrete acting persons who are seeking to construct "reality" in accordance with their values and aspirations. Of course, we have noted in earlier chapters, some persons are in a much more strategic social position than are others to have their aspirations translated into actualities. In reference to the issue before us, namely, the character of central cities and their relationship to the suburbs, we should note what Hartman (1972) has called "The Politics of Housing." Authors such as Hartman (1972), M. E. Stone (1972), and Mollenkopf and Pynoos (1972) call our attention to the role played by agencies such as mortgage bankers, the Federal Housing Administration, and large private property owners in defining urban residential patterns. Stone notes:

> The incredible inflation in urban land values can be traced in a very direct way to the changes in mortgage-lending practices caused by federal intervention in the housing sector. By inducing the creation of long-term low down payment mortgage loans which resulted in the post-war boom in single-family home construction, state intervention encouraged land speculation, created the present scarcity and high price of land in metropolitan areas and yielded immense profits to speculators and lenders. (1972: 34)

Other federal-private business ventures like urban renewal projects have also exacerbated the problems of the central city. According to Herbert Gans (1965: 29), from the time of its inception in 1949 to March 1961, urban renewal projects had torn down 126,000 dwelling units and had built only 28,000 new ones to replace them! In addition, *"only one-half of one percent* of all federal expenditures for urban renewal between 1949 and 1964 was spent on relocation of families and individuals" (Gans, 1965: 30). In effect, then, those low-income minority group members—Kimball (1972) has called them the "disconnected"—are largely at the mercy of the definitions of reality made by members of more powerful groups.

As we write this chapter, the headlines of our daily newspapers constantly inform us that New York City is on the brink of bankruptcy and that should such a situation occur, the financial stability of the entire country would be undermined. Further, the papers warn us, New York City's crisis is merely the harbinger of future municipal upheavals throughout the country. Indeed, as sociologists, we note that the nature of the present urban crisis should alert us to the possibility that we are entering a new historical epoch in which the previously dominant form of the industrial city may be undergoing a radical transformation.

In the previous section we presented some data on the major demographic trends affecting metropolitan areas in the United States. The nature of the services provided by the city and those used by commuters to the city is at the root of the city's present fiscal crisis. In an important article, whose implications urban sociologists have been slow in recognizing, Amos Hawley (1957) empirically examined this issue. Using data from seventy-six cities of 100,000 or more population and their metropolitan districts (as of 1940), he examined the relationship between municipal government expenditures and the use of municipal services by those living in suburban areas. According to Hawley:

> The outlying population uses the city streets and public buildings; it multiplies police problems, thus affecting the costs of that service; it creates additional fire risks which must be included in the allocation of funds for fire protection; its congregation in and traffic through the city is a factor in the budget of the health department. (1957: 773)

Hawley's data provide firm support for the argument that "the larger the proportion of the total population living outside the central city, the heavier (will be) the tax burden on the population living within the city" (1957: 77). Especially important is the fact that Hawley's data (1957: 775) indicate that the extent of municipal expenditures are more closely related to the population living *outside the city* than to the population *occupying the city*. Because expenses for city services are largely a function of the needs and demands of suburban residents, Hawley concluded his article by arguing that the entire metropolitan area, rather than just the central city, ought to be considered the appropriate unit for planning.

In one of the few follow-up studies to Hawley's, Kasarda (1972) investigated the influence that suburban population growth exerted on central city service functions. He examined all the metropolitan communities in the United States that were defined as Standard Metropolitan Statistical Areas (SMSAs) by the census as of 1950. There were 168 such areas. Kasarda's findings support those of Hawley by demonstrating that "the rapid growth of suburban population has contributed greatly to the increased demand, and, hence, increased expenditures for common central city public services" (1972: 1122). In view of the present fiscal crisis, we should especially note Kasarda's observation:

Through zoning restrictions and discriminatory practices, the suburban populations have been able to insure that most of the low-income, poorly educated, and chronically unemployed people in the metropolitan area are confined in the central cities. *Suburban residents are therefore able to avoid the costs of public housing, public health, and other welfare services, which often impose a heavy burden on the operating budget of central cities.* (1972: 1123) (Italics are ours.)

One central aspect, then, of the contemporary urban situation is the increasing demands made by suburban residents for city services, coupled with the increasing inability of the cities to pay for the provision of these services, given the socioeconomic characteristics of the city's remaining residents.

An equally salient issue in understanding the contemporary city concerns the changing political situation within the city itself. In "The Urban Crisis: Who Got What, and Why?" Frances Fox Piven (1974) presents a very penetrating analysis of the way in which the demographic changes described earlier have led to changing definitions of reality on the part of urban residents. These demographic changes and consequent redefinitions of urban life have drastically altered the previous political arrangements in the central city. Piven argues that the "needs" of inner-city blacks for city services, commonly put forth as an explanation for the urban fiscal crisis is, in fact, an inadequate one. If we look at the groups who have benefited from increased municipal expenditures, she notes (1974: 315) that, with the exception of public welfare recipients, "the expansion of services to the poor, as such, does not account for a very large proportion of increased expenditures. It was other groups, mainly organized provider groups who reaped the lion's share of the swollen budgets."

Piven argues that the service agencies existing in municipal settings are fundamentally *political* agencies administered to deal with political problems, not service problems. This is in keeping with our position in the previous chapter; there we noted the various agencies commonly existing in municipal settings that are likely arenas within which pluralist or pyramidical power relations develop. Here we agree with Piven that:

While we may refer to the schools or the sanitation department as if they are politically neutral, these agencies yield up a whole variety of benefits, and it is by distributing, redistributing and adapting these payoffs of the city agencies that urban political leaders manage to keep peace and build allegiances among the diverse groups in the city. In other words, the jobs, contracts, perquisites, as well as the actual services of the municipal house-keeping agencies, are just as much the substance of urban politics as they ever were. (1974: 315–16)

The present urban crisis, then, has a distinct political locus in that the demand for increased city services is the context within which urban group conflict has taken place during the 1960s and 1970s. Piven's position is that the "urban crisis is not a crisis of rising *needs* but a crisis of rising *demands*" (1974: 317, italics added).

The influx of new populations and the departure of previous residents introduces new elements into the urban scene. The previous political arrangements that existed between political leaders and their supporting bases now have to be realigned in the face of the differing characteristics of the newcomers. To employ an analogy from a more microsociological level, we are talking about a situation like that described by Simmel (1950) when a two-person group adds an additional member and becomes a three-person group. New kinds of social relations are possible in three-person groups—coalitions, for example—that are not possible for two-person groups. The immigration of new groups to the city may, given other certain conditions, lead to fundamental social and political changes.

The realignments in urban politics during the 1960s resulted from a number of factors. First, as we noted earlier, the period from 1940 to 1970 saw a major influx of blacks into the metropolitan areas, with the heaviest effects in the Northeast. Second, the low-income character of the migrants aroused the fears of the white ethnics. The former political arrangements, based on ethnicity, made it unlikely that urban politicians would be sensitive to the needs of these "disconnected" newcomers. Third, the intrusion of federal politics on the municipal level made it increasingly difficult for urban politicians to engage in patronage activities in the traditionally private ways. Meeting the needs of constituents now became a very public matter. Unable to satisfy the needs of the black migrants and unwilling to risk the ire of their traditional supporters, urban politicians chose either to curtail federal policies at the local level or to redefine them with the aim of subverting their intended goals. Thus, during the 1940s and 1950s:

In many places public housing was brought to a halt, urban renewal generally became the instrument of black removal; and half the major southern cities (which also received large numbers of black migrants from rural areas) actually managed to reduce their welfare rolls, often by as much as half. (Piven, 1974: 319.)

Finally, well-organized municipal employee groups—teachers, policemen, firemen, and so on—created additional obstacles to the adjustment of the black newcomers. These municipal employee unions managed to achieve a great deal of control over such issues as job entrance requirements, and tenure and retirement benefits. This constituted a major transformation in the nature of urban politics. Whereas the ward-based politicians formerly had some leverage over the job appointment process, it was now increasingly centered in the hands of the municipal unions themselves.

> As a result, a large population that had been set loose from southern feudal institutions was not absorbed into the regulating political institutions (or economic institutions, for they were also resisted there) of the city. Eventually that dislocated population became volatile, both in the streets and at the polls. By 1960 the volatility forced the federal government to take an unprecedented role in urban politics. (Piven, 1974: 320)

During the 1960s federal involvement in urban affairs took the form of medicaid programs for the poor and educational programs for low-income children. The federal involvement also led to a series of activist ventures in which "lawyers on the federal payroll took municipal agencies to court on behalf of ghetto clients. Later the new programs helped organize the ghetto poor to picket the welfare department or to boycott the school system" (Piven, 1974: 322). While low-income blacks received increased public welfare benefits during the 1960s, they got little else.

In sum, given the urban demographic changes noted earlier, urban political leaders could no longer count on their former sources of support, who were actively trying to leave the city for the suburbs. The instability of the situation made it possible for the more highly organized groups within the city—particularly the municipal unions—to escalate their demands to a higher level since "each job offered, each wage increase conceded, each job prerogative granted was now ensconced in civil-service regulations or union contracts and, thus firmly secured, could not be withdrawn" (Piven, 1974: 324).

The "vicious circle" nature of the present urban crisis results from most municipalities being forced by state political regulations to depend mainly on forms of taxation such as property and sales taxes, which, if raised, may have the consequence of "driving out the business and industry on which their tax rolls eventually depend, and also raising the political ire of their constituents" (Piven, 1974: 329).

PLANNING AND THE URBAN PROCESS

The implication of these dramatic changes in the form and structure of urban life are indeed far-reaching and raise serious questions for those whose professional interest is with the planning of cities. Sociologists, psychologists, architects, and city planners are at something of a crossroad as they try to plan for the future. Among the set of related questions that many have been asking are these: Can the city center be saved? Should additional monies be used in rebuilding central city areas? Is it possible to make changes that will stimulate a recentralization of cities? Can central city areas be made appealing to those middle-class whites and business persons who are, as mentioned earlier, leaving the central city areas? Has the trend toward decentralization reached the point of no return in a number of big cities? Can a reversal of migration trends be accomplished only in certain selected cities? And so on.

We would comment that there is an obvious assumption underlying the questions noted above. It is that the existence of a viable city center and the existence of a viable urban way of life are one and the same. The bias of professional planners and many sociologists has frequently been to see the reconstruction of the central city as their unquestioned goal. This has certainly been the supposition of many city programs funded by the federal government. The purpose of urban renewal, for example, started in 1949, is to rebuild and revitalize the city center. The attention paid to the center city is not surprising, as it has always been seen as the "organizational hub and symbolic hearth of the metropolis as a whole" (Greer, 1972: 325).

The equation of the central city with urbanism itself is not an unnatural one because this is the form of the industrial city—the city form that has been the basis for virtually all theorizing about and planning for cities. As we shall see, however, historical evidence indicates that this has not always been the form of cities and need not be in the future. If we are, in fact, undergoing an urban revolution or urban transformation, if we are entering a new urban epoch, proper planning may be dependent on our willingness to examine, and possibly to replace, the assumptions about the city and urbanism that have for so long seemed so obviously true. In the following section of this chapter, therefore, we want to examine some of the assumptions that have traditionally guided urban planning but that may not equip us to deal with the urban future already upon us. It seems best to begin by briefly describing the utopian city constructions of those whose ideas gave birth to modern city planning.

At the turn of the century Ebenezer Howard (1946), a self-styled intellectual, described his image of what cities and city life ought to look like in his book *Garden Cities of Tomorrow*. Like many at the time, Howard held a highly negative image of the industrial city. He shared in common with many of the social scientists discussed in this book an image of the industrial city as embodying all of the evils of modern civilization. The city, as he saw it, simply did not satisfy and, in important respects, militated against human needs.

> These crowded cities have done their work; they were the best a society largely based on selfishness and rapacity could construct, but they are in the nature of things entirely unadapted for a society in which the social side of our nature is demanding a larger share of recognition. (Howard, 1942: 146)

Decrying the high density of cities and what he saw to be the inhumane, selfish behaviors that they generated, Howard constructed his blueprint for the utopian city. In fact, it was not a city at all. His idyllic image was a combination of what he believed were the best elements of both town (city) and country. Garden city, a kind of town-country, would provide all the occupational, economic, and recreational advantages of the city with country-life amenities such as sunshine, low rents, and plenty of open space. Garden city would have all of the advantages and none of the disadvantages of each. More specifically, his vision was of settlements not exceeding 30,000 persons. This settlement would be well bounded by a wall of agriculture and green land that would simultaneously halt the spread of the settlement from within and defend the settlement from population increase from without. His idea was to build a self-sufficient economic unit in which strict limits would be placed on the spacing of buildings; the width of streets; and the placement of public parks, hospitals, and public facilities. Howard actually managed to build two garden cities, Letchworth and Welwyn, both of which never fulfilled his dream, suffering as they did from severe economic mismanagement and public apathy.

It is worth noting that Howard's complaint against the industrial city is based on a rigid conception of human needs. The supposition underlying his utopian views, as is likely the case whenever persons talk in utopian terms, is that human nature is constant and knowable; that persons universally have the same needs. One consequence of the same assumption held among recent planners has frequently been a discrepancy between their own visionary dreams and the reality of the quite diverse needs of those living in cities. As we shall see, the failure of many well-intentioned city projects stems from the assumption that a single pattern of city structure and life would satisfy all urbanites. Instead, "we must understand that the consumers of urban life are highly differentiated and that the . . . metropolis must be as variegated as its patrons" (Fiser, 1962: 11).

While the specific plans for other utopian cities have varied substantially from Howard's Garden City, many of the underlying planning premises have remained the same. Virtually all such plans for cities called for their "decitification"; called for "small townizing" cities. Sir Patrick Geddes introduced the idea of regional planning in which gardenlike cities would be distributed over large territorial areas. The American architect Frank Lloyd Wright's plan for "Broadacre City" called for radical city decentralization. In the 1920s the French architect Le Corbusier offered a somewhat different plan. His "Radiant City" would consist of a series of skyscrapers placed in the midst of a large park. True, this would necessitate a high-population density in the buildings; but, because they would be built so high, most land (95 percent) would be available for the city park. Le Corbusier's ideas eventually gave birth to Daniel Burnham's "City Beautiful" movement, which emphasized the construction of long, highly ornamented city boulevards and elegantly spacial city plazas.

It is fair to say that while their specific ideas may have varied, each of the utopian planners mentioned wanted to do away with the industrial city as it existed. Their architectural ideas mirrored the nostalgia for the small town that so often guided the urban theories constructed by social scientists discussed earlier in this book.

Like the work of their intellectual predecessors, modern city planning is often based on unverified assumptions about the needs of urban persons and the nature of their associations with one another. From the viewpoint of this book, a major problem of much urban sociology and planning stems from the failure adequately to understand or account for the diversity of urbanites' needs, motivations, and definitions of the city place. Ideas for the reorganization, rebuilding, and restructuring of cities proceeds without adequate enough knowledge of the social psychology of city life; that is, of what it means to be urban.

As mentioned in earlier chapters, the primary orientation and frequently the basic training of planners has been in architecture. We call your attention once more to the fact that some of the most influential of the visionary utopians—for example, Frank Lloyd Wright and Le Corbusier—were professional architects. Social scientists have long been critical of the errors committed by planners, who, in their zeal to create cities conforming to their private sense of architectural elegance, have neglected the architecture of social relationships. In Chapter 3 we described the community studies of persons like Herbert Gans (1962) and William F. Whyte (1943); these studies revealed the error of judging the viability of a community's social life by its external physical appearance.

The presumption of much planning is based on the apparently commonsense idea that persons necessarily want to live in, and be surrounded by, new, highly ordered, technologically convenient, quiet, and efficient buildings. In this presumption we find shades of Le Corbusier's Radiant City: a city of high-rise apartment buildings. Increasingly in recent years, however, it has become apparent that there is often a discrepancy between the aesthetic and practical ideas of planners and the needs of persons who eventually must live in the buildings that they have created. It is revealing that relatively little attention has been given in the past to the rehabilitation of city housing. The preference of those with a background in architecture has been to destroy existing "slum" housing and to create housing that often turns out to be negatively sterile for those who *must* inhabit it. Nowhere is the failure of this "obvious" assumption more apparent than in the fate of much public housing for the poor.

In an article titled "Deviant Behavior as an Unanticipated Consequence of Public Housing," Gerald Suttles (1970) cogently argues that there may be a disjunction between architects' conceptions of the way that a building ought to look and the symbolic meanings that persons attach to their homes. Conscientious efforts, made in good faith, to beautify public housing may not have the ameliorative consequences hoped for by those who plan such change if the housing does not reflect the tastes of their residents. Among other things, ecologically segregated, high-rise housing projects dramatize persons' poverty (why else would they be living in them?), rob inhabitants of their individuality, present a variety of impression-management problems for persons, and restrict channels of communication between them. Suttles puts it this way:

> It is fairly obvious that any large multiple family housing unit places a number of constraints upon what, in single family residence areas, is a much used channel of communication. . . . Perhaps a reasonable analogy would be if all business firms in an area were forced to locate in identical buildings and advertising were entirely prohibited. In corporate housing, uniformity of design simply rules out most of those subtle hints that a family can convey by a new paint job, a front lawn, an odd ball door knocker, or an old floor mat. In order to keep a large building looking the way architects and agents think it should, the occupants must forego many embellishments according to their own inclinations. As a result the external trappings of a project building cannot and do not say anything on behalf of the individual residents, but, instead, commemorate the skills, and tastes of architects, engineers and city planners. (1970: 164)

Probably the most dramatic instance of the failure of public housing is found in the history of the Pruitt-Igo housing project in St. Louis. Built in 1954, the Pruitt-Igo project had to be completely demolished twelve years later, as it had become an island of fear and criminality. Such dramatic failure illustrates the danger of accepting unquestioningly the assumption that the physical reconstruction of cities will have clearly anticipated consequences for the behavior of different persons and groups and for the meanings that they will attribute to their respective urban realities.

In addition to the objections already raised concerning some of the assumptions held by those concerned about city life, we must mention the following: We agree with Jane Jacobs (1961), who claims that many planners fundamentally misunderstand what a city is because they fail to see the city as constantly in a state of *process*. To view the city merely as a concrete, static object that can be manipulated the way that a natural scientist manipulates chemical substances to create new compounds does not account for the changing meanings of the city over time. Such a view misses the point we have maintained throughout this book. It is that the city is a symbolic entity.

> Why think about processes? Objects in cities—whether they are buildings, streets, parks, districts, landmarks, or anything else— can have radically differing effects, depending upon the circumstances and contexts in which they exist. Thus, for instance, almost nothing useful can be understood or can be done about improving city dwellings if these are considered in the abstract as "housing." City dwellings—either existing or potential—are specified and particularized buildings always involved in differing, specific processes such as unslumming, slumming, generation of diversity, self destruction of diversity. (Jacobs, 1961: 440)

There is an important transition to make here. In this and previous chapters we have emphasized process within the urban structure. The notion that all social phenomena are in a continual state of process is a basic tenet of the symbolic interactionist position. In Chapter 3 we focused on the processes through which urban persons transform the urban place to meet their needs for identity-sustaining relationships. On a more general level we tried to show the ways in which urban communities have changed and taken on new forms. In Chapter 4 we described the processes governing the anonymous interpersonal relationships of urban persons. And in Chapters 5 and 6 we tried to catch at the processes that make intelligible the relationships between different city groups—groups varying in their life styles, in their values and ideologies, and in their respective positions of power and influence. There are, however, even broader social processes that must be understood before we can clearly formulate the planning policies that will govern future urban life. Here we refer to processes transcending the life spans of individuals and indeed of cities themselves. We must consider likely future city forms in broad historical context. We particularly want to show, as mentioned briefly earlier, that it may be a serious error to model blueprints for future city life based on the industrial city form that we know best. We must recognize that what we call "social structures" are, in the final analysis, the forms given social processes at a particular time.

THE CITY IN HISTORY AND
THE CITY OF THE FUTURE

With a few notable exceptions (Weber, 1958; Mumford, 1961; Martindale, 1958; Meadows, 1969), urban sociologists have failed to view the city in historical perspective. The classic statements on city life with which we earlier took issue were based entirely on images of the industrial city. The visionary utopias recently described also stand in juxtaposition to the industrial city. Once we take a broader historical view, we may see that city forms have varied considerably from the industrial model. Most significantly, a historical analysis alerts us to the idea that the process of city change and development has not been a linear one. While it is generally appropriate to think about the history of human collective associations in terms of a folk/urban continuum (as did such writers as Durkheim, Weber, and Robert Redfield), we must not confuse that analytical conceptualization with the idea that there has been a continuous, absolutely serial historical progression of urban development. We prefer to speak in terms of urban historical epochs that produce quite distinctive and discrete city forms. Our reading of the historical record suggests that we have passed through two central historical epochs—the preindustrial and the industrial—and that we are presently entering into a new historical epoch best described as centering on mass consumption. We can clarify the differences between the three broad historical situations just named.

We argue that there is a relationship between a society's level or stage of economic development and the kind of city that one finds. What defines and distinguishes one historical epoch from another is the centrality or predominance of particular institutional behaviors. In each historical epoch persons are preoccupied with different institutional problems, and in each epoch, therefore, persons construct particular city types. In the preindustrial city the central institution is *religion;* in the industrial city the central, preoccupying institution is *work and the production of goods;* and in the mass consumption city the major institutional problem is the *distribution of goods and services.* These differences are represented on the chart.

SOCIO-ECONOMIC EPOCHS			
	Preindustrial	Industrial	Mass Consumption
Typical Cities	Jerusalem	Pittsburgh	Los Angeles
Major Organizational Form	Fortress and temple	Factory and center city	Freeway and urban sprawl
Central Institution	Religion	Work and productivity	Consumption and the problem of distribution

Since the focus of this chapter is on likely future city forms and the problems of planning that they will generate, we shall pay greatest attention here to the mass consumption epoch into which we are presently entering. To appreciate fully, however, how the mass consumption city will differ from the past city forms, we must describe in some greater detail preindustrial and industrial city types.

Preindustrial and Industrial Cities

Following Gideon Sjoberg's (1960) description, the preindustrial city appears to have been rationally planned, as it was built up around the fortress or the walled temple. The symbolic significance of religion and religious activity is signaled by the fact that the temple did occupy the center space of the city and that residential segments moved outward from these religious centers. Such early cities had to be relatively small, since limited agricultural technology made city dwellers dependent for their sustenance on the areas at the periphery of the city. Again, because of limited technology, there were considerable problems of storage and distribution of food.

Ancient or preindustrial cities probably included at most 10 percent of the total population of the large political units in which they existed. At least 90 percent of the total "national" population remained peasants involved in agricultural pursuits to sustain the preindustrial cities, which on occasion contained populations of up to 100,000 persons. In many ways the preindustrial city was thoroughly different from the kinds of cities that we know. Religion did permeate the lives of their inhabitants. Clearly, also, the market was not the center of the city (as the writings of Park, Simmel, Wirth, and others described earlier in this book would have us believe that it must be). Another interesting difference we may note is that lower-class persons and social outcasts lived toward the periphery of the preindustrial city, whereas in our own cities lower-class persons are primarily restricted to living toward the city center. In the preindustrial city, in other words, those who were socially mobile lived in the center city rather than the reverse, as is the case today.

In industrial cities, by contrast, the central institutional activity is work, and it follows that the form of the city mirrors that fact. To repeat, this is the city type that serves as the basis for virtually all contemporary thinking and theorizing about cities and city life. The industrial city depended upon the marketplace's being at its center. In industrial cities the factory and the slum become symbolic of the central organizational form of the city itself. In the industrial city, persons are preoccupied with production, that is, persons are certainly consumers as well as producers, but the central social fact of the worker's life in the industrial city is subsistence. It is in the industrial city that we find the highest expression of what the theorist Max Weber (1958) termed "the Protestant Ethic": persons do not work primarily to improve the quality of their lives; work is an end in itself.

We shall not describe the elements of the industrial city in any greater detail here, as virtually all our writing about city images, problems, and forms in earlier chapters had as their backdrop the industrial city form. We have already discussed in some depth how and why the images of the city flowing from classical theories and from the empirical observations of Chicago sociologists were incomplete. We only add here, in terms of our discussion of historical epochs, that there is a significant danger in generalizing from studies of American cities in the 1920s and 1930s, as did Wirth, to all cities.

Once we see that there can be exceptions to the industrial city, we must recognize the inappropriateness of universal generalizations based on studies of that city form. Remember that all of Wirth's generalizations about the social organization of cities, their ecological structure, and the social psychology of their inhabitants were based on the presumption that cities are cities only if they are large, dense, and heterogeneous. This may be true of industrial cities, but we make a mistake in assuming that the generalizations about the city given us by urban sociologists and based on these central variables will apply to cities around the world, as the latter may be caught up in a different historical epoch. It would, for example, be a mistake for planners interested in the problems of modernizing societies simply to transfer their baggage of ideological assumptions based on industrial city capitalism to these societies. The plans that they create must be responsive to the historical situation of the society itself. The same line of reasoning can be applied to those who must plan for the nonindustrial city type presently appearing in the United States. The emerging "mass consumption" city is as different from the industrial city as the latter is different from the preindustrial city.

The Mass Consumption City

The central organizational problem of our time has become less the production of goods than their distribution. In the 1930s Lewis Mum-

ford made a film titled "The City," which portrayed the plight of urbanites who were barely getting enough goods to subsist. Here was
pictured the central problem for the industrial urbanite. While we certainly would not deny the considerable poverty suffered by many today,
the picture presented by Mumford simply does not capture the life
style of the large number of city persons today. Relatively few in the
United States are preoccupied with subsistence today. The shift in the
structure and psychology of modern life has been to an overwhelming
concern with the consumption of goods. Indeed, we might argue that
the existence of what Harrington (1963) calls *The Other America* and
the poverty therein is largely a result of the fact that the technological
productivity of this society is increasingly constrained by a set of social
relationships dictating that goods are produced in accordance with a
person's ability to pay rather than with their genuine needs. Genuine
needs, then, are not met for many persons. In a society where the work
of large numbers of people is increasingly peripheral to the satisfaction
of basic needs (food, shelter, clothing), the consumption process becomes the source for what Kenneth Burke (1936) has called society's
"vocabulary of motives."

The rhetoric of consumption is fostered and sustained by an advertising industry that not only seeks to meet demands for certain products
but is also itself instrumental in *creating* a seemingly insatiable quest
for fulfillment through the ownership of particular commodities. The
"built-in obsolescence" and wastefulness of the economy can easily be
noted in our everyday experience. Consider, as an example, that in
order to buy a single washer persons are likely to find that they must
buy a plastic bag full of washers for which they do not have any use.
To buy a toy for their children, many parents buy a variety of cereals
that they may not eat. As an indication of the pervasiveness of the contemporary rhetoric of consumption, we might point to the changing
meanings associated with the observance of social customs such as
Halloween.

In an observational study bearing upon this issue, entitled "Halloween
and the Mass Child," Gregory P. Stone (1959) noted a significant transformation in the rituals associated with this holiday. When children
knocked on his door, crying, "Trick or treat," he responded by asking
them what in fact they would do if no treats were to be offered. Much
to his surprise, few, if any, of the children who appeared at his door
were prepared for—or, even more importantly, had anticipated—the
possible performance of a trick. These children, he argues, were well
along the road toward being socialized as consumers. They were there

at his doorstep in store-bought costumes eagerly awaiting the outpouring of an affluent society's goodies. At first glance the issue of Halloween customs may appear to be of little sociological significance; on a deeper level of analysis, however, it symbolizes some of the major institutional transformations that we have been describing.

Earlier generations of children, according to Stone, were reared on an ethic of work and production, which made the preparation for, and performance of, tricks on Halloween an emotionally laden activity. In other words, society's expectation that life and work were synonymous was clearly reflected in the activities engaged in by children. The fact that the work of everyone was needed in order for the industrial city to produce the goods and services required by its residents intensified the "anticipatory socialization" of children as future producers rather than consumers.

The stage of technological development associated with the industrial city made it imperative that industry be concentrated in specific spacial settings. Also critical here is the level of development of the communications technology. A significant factor in the ability of present-day industrial organizations to move out of the central city is the ready availability of a communications and transportation technology that enables a firm located in a small town to be plugged into an internationally linked economic system. The proliferation of these technologies, then, makes it possible for persons to be "of" the city but not "in" the city. Increasingly, as Scott Greer suggests, such processes may transform society to such an extent that there is no longer any need for urban centers.

> Such a society may be larger in scale than any we can conceive today, and its ways of life might well be described as "urbane" if not urban, but settlement would be freed from spacial limitations, and the city would be no more. (1962: 206)

Our treatment of the mass consumption city as the representative of future urban trends calls our attention, once again, to the fact that urban processes are no longer strictly contained within isolated geographical settings called "cities." We touched on this issue earlier in the chapter when, in our discussion of the fiscal crisis of the city, we noted that a large part of the crisis was a result of the costs incurred by municipalities in providing services to those who did not live within the city, yet commuted to it for work or recreation. In view of the previous discussions, then, we are led to the realization that the central problem of the mass consumption city is the *distribution* of goods and services. Given that fundamental character of the contemporary urban situation, it becomes imperative for urban planners to have as accurate an image as possible of the needs for goods and services of those for whom they plan.

In terms of the perspective maintained throughout this book, we may well ask what kinds of social processes enhance the abilities of planners to forecast accurately the needs of their client publics? Central here is the issue of what is called "role-taking" ability. As symbolic interactionists we argue that role-taking ability—the ability to look at the world from the perspective of others—is best established through open and unfettered dialogue among all the participants in the planning situation. Such a dialogue maximizes the ability of planners to develop sensitivities to the needs of their audiences, while it simultaneously increases the sensitivity of their audiences to the constraints within which planners must operate. Unrestricted communication lessens the likelihood of stereotypical responses on the part of all participants; that is to say, each side will now have to compare their "images" of each other with the actualities of behavior in a concrete setting. We saw earlier in this chapter how the imputation of "meanings" by planners to low-income urbanites led to the physical design for buildings (such as high-rise housing projects) that were responded to by the residents in ways totally unanticipated by the planners. Had the intended residents of such projects been engaged in a prior dialogue with planners about the nature of the facilities being designed for them, the likelihood of such problems might have been reduced. In effect, then, we are arguing here that accurate (that is, successful) and humane planning is a *collaborative* process.

A recent study by Godschalk and Mills (1969) nicely exemplifies the fruitfulness of the collaborative approach to urban planning. These authors see the role of the planner as similar to that of a counselor to the community, rather than, as is often the case, as an "outside expert" seeking to impose the conceptions of a bureaucratic planning agency on the community. In this situation "the planner's job is to assist the community in discovering and achieving its objectives. This does not mean attempting to sell a prepared plan, nor simply seeking the blessing of key people" (1969: 514).

With a strong commitment to the above definition of the planner, these authors conducted a planning program in a northern Florida city —Gainesville—with a population of about 55,000 people. Their sensitivity to the "mosaic of urban life" alerted them to the fact, which we have discussed in detail throughout this book, that the urban setting is composed of a number of different groups and subcommunities. In order to tap the different definitions of reality subscribed to members of these diverse subcommunities, the authors first conducted an "activities survey," which provided them with detailed information about issues such as attitudes held by the residents about their communities, their values, the composition of various neighborhoods, and life styles of residents. The data were collected through "open-ended tape recorded household interviews as well as neighborhood field observations" (1969: 518). Through the use of open-ended interview questions, the authors were able to get at the meanings of events as conceived by the residents themselves. This is different from the standard survey research approach that supplies respondents with a set of prepackaged answers from among which they must choose. A reliance on such a procedure maximizes the likelihood of the researcher's imposing his or her own meanings on the respondent without even being aware of doing so.

The results of the intensive interviews and field observations were then used by the Plan Board in formulating policy for the various areas of the city. Most importantly, as a result of these findings, members of various subcommunities were invited to engage in open dialogue with the Plan Board about possible changes in their locales. The collaborative approach to planning increases the possibility for relatively powerless groups—such as low-income people and transient students—to exert some influence on decisions affecting their living conditions. As Godschalk and Mills note:

> in the collaborative approach the activities analysis is not simply another project whose results are observations at one point in time, but an ongoing basis for community involvement at all levels— from the individual to the institution. (1959: 523)

The notion of collaborative planning means that planners must avail themselves of research strategies that allow for the exploration of urban social worlds as experienced by the participants themselves. Thus, in the Godschalk and Mills (1969) study, the authors relied upon the use of loosely structured open-ended interview questions coupled with fieldwork observational procedures that allowed for the observation of people's behaviors in their natural setting. We are not arguing here that other research strategies such as laboratory experiments, checklist questionnaire surveys, and analysis of census materials should be abandoned. Rather, our point is that a total reliance on such procedures produces an incomplete and potentially misleading understanding of human behavior.

Our concern as social psychologists of urban life is to establish the relationships in a person's environment, the meanings that one attributes to that environment, and the consequences of such "definitions of the situation" for the person's behavior. To do that, we believe, social scientists must become personally familiar with the ongoing worlds of those whom they seek to understand. We must encourage people to talk about their lives in their own terms, and we must observe their behaviors in the daily settings within which their lives occur.

Such a research strategy is clearly consonant with the theoretical position which we have maintained throughout this volume. As Herbert Blumer (1969: 2) has continually stressed throughout his distinguished career:

1. Human beings act toward things or situations on the basis of the meaning that the things or situations have for them.
2. The meanings of things is derived from or arises out of the social interaction that one has with his fellows.
3. These meanings are handled or modified through an interpretive process used by persons in dealing with the objects or situations which they encounter.

Our commitment to these assumptions about social life has been the basis for focusing upon the particular issues dealt with in this book.

REFERENCES

Blumer, Herbert. *Symbolic Interactionism: Perspective and Method.* Englewood Cliffs, N.J.: Prentice-Hall, 1969.

Burke, Kenneth. *Permanence and Change.* New York: New Republic Press, 1936.

Delos, Seven. "The Scale of Settlements and the Quality of Life." Pp. 240–44 in Gwenn Bell and Jacqueline Tyrwhitt (eds.), *Human Identity in the Urban Environment.* Baltimore: Penguin Books, 1972.

Fiser, Webb S. *Mastery of the Metropolis.* Englewood Cliffs, N.J.: Prentice-Hall, 1962.

Gans, Herbert. "The Failure of Urban Renewal; A Critique and Some Proposals." *Commentary,* 39 (April 1965): 29–37.

Gans, Herbert. *The Urban Villagers.* New York: The Free Press, 1962.

Godschalk, D. R., and W. E. Mills. "A Collaborative Approach to Planning Through Urban Activities." Pp. 513–25 in P. Meadows and E. Mizruchi (eds.), *Urbanism, Urbanization and Change: Comparative Perspectives.* Reading, Mass.: Addison-Wesley, 1969.

Greer, Scott. *The Emerging City: Myth and Reality.* New York: The Free Press, 1964.

Greer, Scott. *The Urbane View.* New York: Oxford University Press, 1972.

Harrington, Michael. *The Other America.* Baltimore: Penguin Books, 1963.

Hartman, Chester. "The Politics of Housing: An Introduction." *Transaction,* 9 (July/August 1972): 30–41.

Hawley, Amos. "Metropolitan Government and Municipal Government Expenditures in Central Cities." Pp. 773–82 in P. Hatt and A. Reiss (eds.), *Cities and Society.* Glencoe, Ill.: The Free Press, 1957.

Holsendorf, E. "Urban Crisis of the 1960's Is Over, Ford Aides Say." *New York Times,* March 23, 1975: 1, 46.

Howard, Ebenezer. *Garden Cities of Tomorrow.* London: Faber and Faber, 1946.

Jacobs, Jane. *The Death and Life of Great American Cities.* New York: Random House, 1961.

Kasarda, John D. "The Impact of Suburban Population Growth on Central City Service Functions." *American Journal of Sociology,* 77 (May 1972): 1111–24.

Kimball, P. *The Disconnected.* New York: Columbia University Press, 1972.

Martindale, Don. "Prefatory Remarks: The Theory of the City." Pp. 9–62 in Max Weber's *The City.* New York: The Free Press, 1958.

Meadows, Paul. "The City, Technology, and History." Pp. 10–19 in P. Meadows and E. Mizruchi (eds.), *Urbanism, Urbanization, and Change: Comparative Perspectives.* Reading, Mass.: Addison-Wesley, 1969.

Mollenkopf, John, and Jon Pynoos. "Property Owners." *Transaction,* 9 (July/August 1972): 38–45.

Mumford, Lewis. *The City in History.* New York: Harcourt, Brace and World, 1961.

National Academy of Sciences. *Toward an Understanding of Metropolitan America.* Washington, D.C.: Canfield Press, 1975.

Piven, Frances Fox. "The Urban Crisis: Who Got What and Why?" Pp. 314–51 in R. A. Cloward and F. F. Piven, *The Politics of Turmoil: Poverty, Race and the Urban Crisis.* New York: Vintage Books, 1974.

Sjoberg, Gideon. The Pre-Industrial City. New York: The Free Press, 1960.

Simmel, Georg. "Quantitative Aspects of the Group." Pp. 87–177 in K. Wolff (ed.), *The Sociology of Georg Simmel.* New York: The Free Press, 1950.

Sternlieb, George. "Are Big Cities Worth Saving?" Pp. 263–72 in *The City in the Seventies,* ed. Robert K. Yin. Itaska, Ill.: F. E. Peacock Publishers, 1972.

Stone, Gregory P. "Halloween and the Mass Child." *American Quarterly*, 11 (Fall 1959): 372–79.

Stone, Michael E. "Mortgage Bankers." *Transaction*, 9 (July/August 1972): 31–37.

Suttles, Gerald. "Deviant Behavior as an Unanticipated Consequence of Public Housing." Pp. 162–76 in D. Glaser (ed.), *Crime in the City*. New York: Harper and Row, 1970.

Taeuber, Karl E. "Residential Segregation." *Scientific American*, 213, No. 2 (1965): 12–19.

Weber, Max. *The City*. New York: The Free Press, 1958.

Weber, Max. *The Protestant Ethic and the Spirit of Capitalism*. New York: Charles Scribner's Sons, 1958.

Whyte, William F. *Street Corner Society*. Chicago: University of Chicago Press, 1943.

Index